G000140927

# STUDENT
## The Push guide to Money
# SURVIVAL

### by Johnny Rich and Mikki Goffin

**2002 Edition**

**Project Editor:** John Barratt
**Special thanks to:** Kieron McCaffrey, Ed Suthon, Kevin White, Zog, Sophie Dennis, Rachael Reeves, Andy Robinson, Nicole Linhardt, Ian Carter

**Design by:** Colleen Crim

**Published by:** The Stationery Office

**Push™ Online:** www.push.co.uk

The Push™ Guide to Money: Student Survival
by Johnny Rich & Mikki Goffin
Copyright © The Push™ Partneship 2001.

ISBN  0 11702 833 9

**Editorial:**
Push
The Stationery Office
Nine Elms Lane
London, SE1

**Ordering:**
The Stationery Office
PO Box 29,
St Crispins House
Duke Street
Norwich NR3 1GN
Telephone: 0870 600 5522
Fax: 0870 6005533

**E-mail: editor@push.co.uk**
**Push™ Online: www.push.co.uk**

**E-mail: esupport@tso.co.uk**
**Website: www.clicktso.co.uk**

All our facts and figures were correct when we went to press (or to the
best of our knowledge after a lot of checking), so if anything's changed in
the meantime or it's just wrong, we're really cut up about it and very
sorry, but we take absolutely no responsibility for it. Blame someone else,
but let us know, okay? Cheers.

A few of the tips are illegal and are intended for amusement value only.
Of course, Push would never seriously suggest doing anything against
the law. If you want to get in trouble, that's your look-out, but don't go
blaming us.

# Contents

# Part 1
# So, you think you can afford to be a student?

Part 1: So, you think you can afford to be a student?
Chapter 1

# Introduction

## What's this book about?

This book is about eight quid.

£7.99 to be precise, unless you've managed to get it discounted – in which case, good luck to you. That's the student spirit. Shave whatever you can off the price, whenever you can.

The irony of asking you to cough up for a book about how poor you're going to be as a student isn't lost on us, but the idea is that your eight quid investment now will pay you back hundreds of times, over your student career and beyond.

**This guide will help you choose a university you can afford (they're not all the same), will help you maximise your income as a student and minimise your outgoings and then, when you end up in debt – and you will – it'll help you manage it.**

All that for about half the price of a chart CD. Can't say fairer than that, guvnor.

**This Guide is divided into seven parts...**

## Part 1: So you think you can afford to be a student?

This section is a general introduction to all things dosh-related.

The chapter you're reading now sums up the rest of the book. So, if you're already trying to save money by not buying a copy for yourself, you can read this chapter in the shop and decide if it's worth it.

The following chapter will talk about how the whole nightmare issue of money could, and indeed should, influence students' choice of university in the first place. From university to university, costs are more wide and varied than the effects of a hot curry on the digestive system – from average rents three times higher in some places than others to beer at half the price. See **Chapter 2**.

# Part 2: How much will you have?

The next part of the book is about students' income and is quite disproportionately large considering how little money there is to talk about.

We break down the income into every likely source – not to mention some that are either less likely or best avoided.

There are so many exceptions to the rules that you could write a book about it (which is why we have), but basically the income sources are as follows:

### AWARDS AND GRANTS
**Local Education Authorities** (LEAs – local government, basically) give most students at least some money in the form of 'awards' which pay towards the cost of their course only (except in Scotland where they might get some to live on too).

**The amount students receive depends on all sorts of factors, the most important of which is how much money their parents have (unless they're already all grown up).**

Before you get too excited, students don't see the money. It goes straight to the university. See **Chapter 3**.

### STUDENT LOANS
There's a Government-financed system, run by the **Student Loans Company**, under which students can borrow money cheaply to live on while they're studying and pay it back once they've got a job.

**The amount students can borrow, like the awards, is down to how much their folks earn. See Chapter 4.**

## PARENTS

**If the LEAs decide students' parents can afford it, then the parents are expected to shell out to their offspring, not only to make up any shortfall in the course costs because they didn't get a maximum award, but also to help out with the students' living costs.**

Not every parent, however, is able (or occasionally even willing) to afford it. But no one can force them and, although the system is designed to help students whose parents can't, some end up with even less money than they're supposed to.

On the other hand, some parents are more generous and are so proud of their kids going off to study, they either give or lend them more money. It's alright for some. See **Chapter 5**.

## BANKS

Most students rely pretty heavily on the black hole known as their bank account, not just as a place to keep the money they don't have, but as a potential source of more.

Whether they use it to tide over almost inevitable cash flow problems or to supplement their income, students usually make use of the free overdraft limits and favourable terms offered by most banks to students. Then when they graduate, they have to pay it back. See **Chapter 6**.

## PAID WORK

Most students either have a part-time job while they're studying or look for temporary work during the vacations. Either way, working for a living while trying to study for a degree has its pros and cons.

Quite a few students – those on 'sandwich' courses – do a job as part of their studies, killing two birds with one sandwich. It's not as crazy as it sounds – they're usually on a work placement as part their training for a career. See **Chapter 7**.

## BURSARIES, SCHOLARSHIPS, SPONSORSHIPS AND GRANTS

The next best thing to money for nothing is money for very little. There are all sorts of bursaries, scholarships and grants available to students, offered by charities, organisations and even by universities themselves for students who're hard up, especially talented or in some other way exceptional or deserving.

Meanwhile, some students are sponsored to study, usually by businesses or organisations that want to employ them either during their studies or on completion. Often the student has to make some sort of commitment to the company or organisation to get the dough. See **Chapter 8**.

**OTHER SOURCES**

We also run down the other potential money pots – pretty much everything short of selling a kidney (not advisable) – and tell you the hows, whys and why nots.

For example there are access funds, hardship funds, you could sell or pawn stuff, become a landlord or borrow from friends, relatives, on credit cards and from loan sharks.

See **Chapter 9**.

# Part 3: Tuition Fees

There's been so much fuss and so much fear about tuition fees, since they were introduced in 1998, that they get a section all to themselves.

Students usually only ever pay a small proportion of what it actually costs to run their degree course, to employ staff to teach it and to put books in the library and sherry in the fridge in the vice-chancellor's office.

**The student's contribution is just over a thousand quid, but they don't all have to pay all of it.**

**For about a third of students, their contribution is met by the local education authorities after they've looked at the student's parents' income and totted up how much to contribute (as an award, see above).**

**Another third pay the full whack.** Currently just over a thousand smackers.

**Almost all the rest pay something in between, again depending on their parents' ability to add to the pot.**

Part 3 lays out the rules and regulations, whys and wherefores of who pays for what, when and how. See **Chapter 10**.

8

## Part 4: Where does it all go?

One way or another, at the end of the day, after they've paid any tuition fees they may owe, most students can reckon on having each year between £3,500 and £5,000 that they've begged, borrowed or earned.

**So where does that money go?**

Part 4 provides a breakdown of the wallet leaks, how they vary from place to place and how to keep them down without living like a nun.

**Chapter 11** looks at the main expenses – the roof over your head, the food in your belly, the bills, the clothes, travel costs, books, biros, computers, insurance, night club admissions and the beer.

Then there are the hidden extras – the costs that bugger up the budget – such as the cost of getting settled in, of Christmas and birthdays and trips backpacking in Borneo or tanning in Tenerife. See **Chapter 12**.

> When you've been out on the razz, you always buy food from the chip-shop on the way home. If you find you're too full of beer to eat them or pass out first, just put the cold chips under the grill the next day until they're hot. They'll taste even better than when you bought them.
>
> Jenny Blyth, University of St Andrews

## Part 5: Finance for real people

Not everyone's an average case and because students are real people – or they look quite like them anyhow – we look at all the special cases out there.

**Chapter 13** does money for the masses – including postgrads, mature students, overseas students, part-timers, student parents and students with disabilities

# Part 6: The Push Guide to Penny Pinching

**Chapter 14** lays it on the line, then it picks up the line and shows you how to make both end meet with *Push*'s own guide to living on a budget.

**When it comes to students, finance is a four-lettered word and that word is 'debt'.**

That's how they fund themselves – by borrowing.

And when you borrow money, somebody usually wants it back. And when they want it back, they want interest. What's so interesting about it? Good question.

**Chapter 15** is a guide to handling debt, living off someone else's money and how to pay it back.

# Part 7: In the back

So you can choose the right university for your pocket – and exclusive to **The Push Guides** – **Chapter 16** dishes the dirt on the real costs of being a student at every university in the UK.

And finally, there's a list of useful contacts and sources of further information in print, on the web and on the blower.

# So is it worth it?

Given that volunteering to be a student is equivalent to volunteering to be poor for at least three years while mates from school are out there earning a wage, is it worth it?

**Some might say poverty is what student life is all about – getting by cheaply, putting up with squalor and somehow learning to make the most of it.**

There's some truth to that. Learning how to live on less money than you'd like is something most people have to do sometime – although getting by as a student is pretty extreme way of learning it. Nevertheless, along with the sex, the drugs and the rock'n'roll, it's part of the wider education that you get along with a university degree (fortunately at no extra cost).

But the sad fact is that many students end up quitting their courses for no other reason than simply not being able to manage on their limited means.

**In fact, nearly 16% of students flunk university. That's one in six. Most people think it won't be them. One in six are wrong.**

Of course, not all of them flunk because of money. Far from it. But for almost all of them, poverty's another nail in the coffin and many of them wouldn't give up if it weren't costing them so much money.

Yet there *are* effective ways of minimising debts while maximising your enjoyment of the whole university experience.

It is just a matter of striking the right balance through careful budgeting and cost-cutting (which doesn't have to be as boring or as puritanical as it sounds).

And in the long term, there is a huge gain to be had.

Apart from anything else, what else would you do with the money anyway?

You get intellectual stimulation, access to cheap but kicking night clubs, inexpensive bars, some of the country's best leisure and sporting facilities, memories you'll never forget and, finally, letters after your name if you last the distance.

Being a student for three or four years is worth tens of thousands in anyone's money – if only to put off for another few years the rat race, the mortgage, the 2.4 kids and the slow march to retirement and death.

**Not convinced?**
Okay, let's get hard-nosed and financial about this now.
Your degree will cost you the following:
- The debt you end up with when you graduate – currently running at around £10,000, but let's say £13,000 by the time you get through the system.
- The money you could have earned during your years as a student minus any money you do earn as a student. School-leavers' starting salaries are around the £10,000 mark rising to £13,000 after three years if they're good at their job.

Take off the money students earn on average – probably only a couple of grand (there aren't any stats available) – and that's about £35,000.

Therefore, the total cost – using the harshest measure – is £48,000 (although it's not as if you actually have to pay that money or would have had it if you hadn't gone to uni).

Nevertheless, financially, what do you get for your investment?

- You will have greater earning power. Most employers prefer to hire graduates. Ten years after graduating, men earn 30% more and women 46% more on average than non-graduates.
- A few years after graduation, most people who've got a degree are earning more than people of the same age without one.
- Your income will rise by more and it will rise sooner and faster. Most starting salaries advertised for graduates are at least £12,000 – more in the London area, usually averaging something like £18,000. Promotional prospects are far greater.
- A quarter of graduates receive starting salaries of £21,000 or above.
- Graduates' salaries are rising faster than non-graduates' across the board.
- Your chances of ever being unemployed will be cut by half.
- You'll have a wider range of career options open to you, whatever your subject.
- Over a working life, even in today's money, graduates can expect to earn an extra £250,000.

**In other words, apart from a 500% index-linked return on your investment, you have added security.**

Financial case closed, I think. (We're not saying the system's right, just that, financially speaking, it's usually worth it.)

Part 1: So, you think you can afford to be a student?
Chapter 2

# Choosing a university

## Not all universities are the same

So many applicants are told, 'It doesn't matter where you choose. You'll have a good time wherever you go.'

Along with feeding pigs' brains to cattle, playing a five-a-side primary school team against Lazio and standing anywhere near a paddling pool whilst being videotaped, this is one of the world's stupidest ideas.

Not all universities are the same and evidence suggests that students who choose their university using the dart-in-a-map method (aka the Clearing system) are more likely to be among the one in six students who drops out or fails.

That goes ditto for choosing a course.

**There's no such thing as the country's best university, nor even the cheapest and there's no such thing as the best course.**

It depends on you, on what you want from student life, what you want to study, how you want to study it and, since you're unlikely to work for more than eight hours a day, what you want to do the other two-thirds of your time.

After you've chosen your course, there are still thousands of factors you could consider when choosing a university. Location, atmosphere, accommodation, welfare arrangements and the facilities and opportunities for entertainments, social life and sports to name but a few.

There are so many that we at *Push* just felt we had to provide a couple of books on the subject: **The Push Guide to**

**Choosing a University**, to give the low-down on how to make the choice and **The Push Guide to Which University**, to give you the information about every UK university to help you decide.

But one of the most important factors when choosing a university or a degree is money.

Not only will your costs vary depending on where you are, but so too will your opportunities for finding extra income. In this chapter we run the gamut, showing the choices you face and saying why, frankly, my dear, we think you *should* give a damn.

In Part 7, we also break down some of these variations university by university, so when you're choosing your university in the first place, you can stack the odds in your favour when it comes to stashing the cash and diverting the debts.

# Maximising income
**Maximise your income and you're in a better position to minimise your debt.**

We'll go into more detail about all the possible sources of income in Part 2, but in the meantime, here are a few tips on how to squeeze out a few extra pennies by picking the right course for you at the right place.

### AWARDS AND GRANTS
**As a rule, the level of your award doesn't depend on where you go but on what your parents earn. But student finance is a world where there are exceptions to every rule – except the rule that there are exceptions to every rule.**

For Scottish students studying at Scottish universities, there's a different and more generous system of funding. It doesn't mean they're loaded or anything, just that none of them has to contribute anything to their tuition fees while they're students (although they may have to pay £2,000 when they graduate). For more details, see **Chapter 3**.

The effect is that for Scottish students, choosing an English university is like choosing a more expensive brand of toilet roll – either brand gets the job done, it's just that the more expensive option has to do something quite special to your rear end to be worth the extra cost.

## STUDENT LOANS

Similar rules apply to student loans as to awards – what matters is not your choice of university, but your parents' money-making. But, of course, there are exceptions. Two of them.

The first is that students in London qualify for bigger loans than everyone else, because London's so damned expensive. At the moment they get nearly £900 more, but whether that makes up for the extra expense is doubtful.

If, however, you've boiled your choice down to, say, Oxford Brookes University, Brighton University and Goldsmiths College London, the little bit extra may make all the difference because it's not actually that much cheaper to live in Oxford or Brighton than in London (especially not South East London, where Goldsmiths is located).

The second exception applies to students who live with their parents. They're entitled to less generous loans than everyone else because, it's assumed, parents aren't going to charge their kids rent while they're students, so their costs will be lower.

As it happens, living at home can work out a lot cheaper – not only is rent usually free, but bills are thrown in, the fridge is stocked, there's a washing machine and you don't have to shell out if you want access to things like TVs or VCRs. You might even be able to borrow the car. Of course, not every home has all these freebies thrown in, but the standard of facilities in most parents' houses is better than in most students'.

The bad news is, of course, that although it may work out cheaper to live at home, it cramps your choice. You can only pick a university within commuting distance.

Go to off licences like Oddbins and
Majestic Wines that run free tastings.
Sniffily decide not to purchase anything.
(May not work more than once.)

For some people – an increasing proportion – the saving is worth it. For most, however, not only would it cramp their choice, but living at home would cramp their style, too. Unless your parents are more understanding than multilingual Samaritans, it's hardly part of the full monty traditional student experience.

For more details, see **Chapter 4**.

**PARENTS**

If your parents are contributing to your costs, they may expect a say in where and what you study.

In an ideal world, they'd be more than willing and able to indulge your every whim, whatever it may be. Sad to say, in case you hadn't noticed, student finance is not an ideal world and if you can butter them up by choosing a course and/or a university that might make them especially happy, well, then you might want to factor it into your decision.

I'm not saying that if they pay, they get to say. On the contrary, it's your call and it has to be right for you.

It's just that, all else being equal, there are times to dis parents – the time when you expect them to fork out for something is not one of them. If only to keep them sweet, ask them if they've got any thoughts (then ignore them if you want).

For more details, see **Chapter 5**.

**BANKS**

If you treat it right, a student's bank can be a like a little pot of gold at the end of the rainbow. A very little pot of gold, admittedly and they'll want the money back eventually, but in the meantime they're very handy.

**Banks, however, have more patience with some students than with others and it's not all down to how nice you are.**

They cut medical students quite a bit of slack, for instance, letting them run up debts like mice run up clocks. It makes economic sense to them, because those students are more likely to be safe bets financially.

Similarly, it can make economic sense to you to choose a course that's going to hit pay dirt one day.

You should bear this in mind not only when choosing your course, but even when choosing your university.

Some universities are more successful than others at getting students into jobs. (Their employment stats are in **Chapter 16**.) Almost every university has a careers service, but in some places it consists of little more than a cleaner who occasionally reads the job ads, while at other universities there's a busy team of highly trained careers experts with excellent links to industry and a nice line in skills training.

It's students with that kind of back-up that banks like to lend money to.

For more details, see **Chapter 6**.

Buy fresh food from greengrocers. Not only are fruit and veg cheap and nutritious, but they're also cheaper from greengrocers than supermarkets, often by as much as half.

## WORK

Not every university offers the same opportunities for part-time work and if you're likely to need it to make ends meet, it's worth thinking about this as you choose your university.

**In big cities it's not too hard to find an endless stream of student-friendly jobs, but the more remote you get, the tougher the job hunt gets.**

Certain places have a particular blossoming of casual work ideal for strapped-for-cash students, particularly the coastal resorts like Brighton and Bournemouth. Meanwhile, tourist punters flock to St Andrews for the golf – and whilst caddying is a lot tougher than it looks, there's always the possibility of serving whiskies at the nineteenth hole.

In order to help students track down suitable jobs and to make sure they're not whipped like slaves when they find them, many universities (more usually the students' unions, in fact) run 'jobshops' – employment agencies, basically.

**Invariably, one of the biggest local employers of students is the university itself or the students' union, who take students on to do everything from being nightclub bouncers and working behind bars to looking after conference guests**

**and phoning ex-students and asking them for money. But, again, different universities have different needs for cheap labour.**

A lot of students look for work during their vacations as well as, or instead of, taking part-time jobs during term. Again, the choice of university makes a difference.

Not every university has the same length breaks, for instance. An extra week or two – at, say, £150 a week – might make be the difference between a week in Ibiza in the summer or spending it stacking shelves in Tesco. But don't be fooled into thinking that the eight-week terms at Oxbridge leave more than half the year for earning. Like many universities, they set enough work over the vacations to keep you busier than during term-time.

Then there are certain courses which, if you choose them, can scupper your earning potential faster than poisoning your boss.

Medicine, for instance, might be a sure-fire money magnet in the long term but, whilst studying, students not only have less time off over the summer, they don't even have the same time off during the day or at weekends.

Students on sandwich courses, on the other hand, have just about the easiest time of it. They have work placements that not only count towards their course, but which almost always pay them decent money too. Don't get me wrong, they still end up in debt – just not up to their necks in it.

For more details on paid work, see **Chapter 7**.

### SPONSORSHIP

Short subject, as there's not a whole lot of sponsorship money out there — not any more. Mostly, it comes with strings attached and among those strings is what course you choose and where you choose to do it.

Virtually the only courses that attract sponsorship are the ones where employers have real trouble recruiting talent. They tend to be hard-line sciences, technical subjects (such as engineering) or vocational courses. Don't even bother looking for sponsorship to do philosophy, English literature or sociology.

If you're likely to be in the running course-wise, check out which universities have good reputations with big employers and with industry.

**Again, it's sandwich courses that are the best way to earn while you learn and many of them are similar to the old sponsorships in many ways, but involve more guaranteed rewards for the employer.**

Many 'thick' sandwich courses involve a deal with an employer where you work for them for, say, a year before you start your course, every summer vacation during your course and then you carry on working for them when you graduate.

For more details, see **Chapter 8**.

## BURSARIES AND SCHOLARSHIPS

Most bursaries and the like are only available at one university and some universities have a lot more than others. Since most of them are endowments from charities and ex-students, the longer an institution has been around, the more likely it is to have stocked up on the goodies. This may be something to think about when making your choice.

For more details, see **Chapter 8**.

## HARDSHIP AND ACCESS FUNDS

If you find yourself in deep financial doo-doo as a student, there may be help available.

Every university has an 'access fund' which is supposed to support students so they can afford to study. But each university decides its own rules about how it's going to hand it out – in general the idea is that it should go to students from backgrounds with little tradition of higher education. If that's likely to be you, you might want to make enquiries before applying, although be warned that access hand-outs are rarely more than £500 a year.

Most universities also have a hardship fund to help out in a cash crisis. The available amounts vary, as do policies on how and when they hand them out – often they lend money only to tide you over, rather than give out wads of notes. But, again, if you're likely to find yourself in the muck brass-wise, it might be reassuring to have chosen a university with a safety net big enough to help you out.

For more details, see **Chapter 9**.

# Minimising costs

It's not just the income that varies from university to university.

In fact, bumping up your student income by choosing the right university and the right course is peanuts compared to the coconuts you can save by choosing a university where the costs are lower. The differences can run into thousands of quid without even trying.

### TUITION FEES

Unless you're Scottish and want to go to a Scottish university (see above), there's not much you can do to reduce your contribution to tuition fees (apart from persuading your parents to earn less, which, ultimately, would be self-defeating).

However, there is a risk that your choice of university might make your fees even higher.

Universities are responsible for collecting the fees and how and when they do it is up to them. Some charge fees if you pay late – sometimes as much as £50 regardless of whether it's your fault – which may not be much to them, but it may be a week's rent and food to you.

Some universities let you set up direct debits (which, while they're not cheaper, can be simpler) and they even offer small discounts if you do.

Then there's Buckingham University, which is a special case. It's a private university where the students pay all their own tuition costs and so their fees are usually several times what you'd pay at most institutions.

If, however, there's any reason why you'd have to pay in full anyway (you're not an EU citizen, for instance), then it can work out cheaper because Buckingham crams what would normally be a three-year course into just two years. And guess what: three-quarters of Buckingham's students are, indeed, overseas students.

For more details on tuition fees, see **Chapter 10**.

### RENT

Most of your income – or quite often all of it – goes on rent.

Of course, not everywhere costs the same. In London it's not uncommon for students to pay rents as high as £80 a week

– or £4,160 a year. Students in London get about £900 more than everybody else, but that still means that before they've so much as sat down to their first lecture, their budget's already in the red to the tune of about £250.

At the other end of the scale, in Hull, Teesside and Northern Ireland, it's perfectly possible to find somewhere decent to live for under £35 a week. That means you've got an extra £780 to spend.

This is one of the reasons why choosing the right location is such a big deal – but it also makes a difference what you get for your money and how likely you are to be able to live in university housing (which usually works out cheaper). At some universities, more than two-thirds of the students live in. At others it's only a handful of overseas students and students with special needs.

The gaping hole that rent takes out of student finance is the reason why so many students now decide to stay with their parents (see above).

For more details, see **Chapter 11**.

## LIVING EXPENSES

You wouldn't have thought that the cost of things like food, clothes and bills would vary that much from place to place, would you? And, sure, if you buy your clothes in chain stores and your food in supermarkets, the differences aren't that great.

**If you're wise, however, your shopping habits will be different. Markets are often cheaper (and for clothes, way cooler), but not every university is in a town that has markets – or, at least, not anything decent.**

In London, for instance, Camden market offers very fine gear at perfectly reasonable prices. Similarly, there's so much competition between food shops that you can almost always find better prices if you know where to look.

The problem is that places like Camden market are just too damn cool. You go to save a few quid on threads and end up splashing out a couple of hundred on a half a dozen tops, some DMs and a lava lamp.

As for bills, they're not the same all over. In Exeter, for instance, you can expect mild winters and hot summers –

compared to Aberdeen, at any rate. And if for six months of the
year you need to have the heating on full blast before you can
poke a toe out from under the duvet, your bills are going to
rocket.

For more details, see **Chapter 11**.

## TRAVEL

Obviously, the further you go from home, the more it's likely to
cost – although it depends how you get there.

Buses and coaches are the cheapest way to travel, but not
everywhere's on a route and if it's a ten-hour trip, then you may
want to think about the train – or even a plane.

The last bit of the journey is often the killer. Lampeter is
about twenty miles from the nearest train station, so a taxi will
add twenty smackers to the cost of any trip. (There is a bus,
which costs £3.50, if you fancy lugging your bags on to it.)
Fortunately, National Express now stops at the University, but it
takes a while to get there.

London, for once, is on average the cheapest place to get
to – but, once you're there, getting around town is as absurdly
expensive as a diamond encrusted nasal hair trimmer. Travel
in the capital often drains another £15 a week from a
student's budget.

But at least London has night buses. After a night out in
Newcastle, Sunderland University students have to dig deep for
a ten-mile taxi-trip.

In Manchester, on the other hand, the city is compact
enough that you can get from campus to the nightclubs and back
to the student ghettos, all on foot. (Or, failing that, by
tram or bike.

God had students in mind when she created bikes. Around
many universities pedestrians walk in fear of being hit by
oncoming two-wheelers. But at others it's just too bumpy, too
spread out or just too expensive to keep replacing bikes every
time they cycle off on their own.

It's very rare that cars are the answer – they're dirty things
that cost a packet to buy, a packet to maintain and a packet to
fill with fuel. Not to mention parking (oops, mentioned it.) But at

some universities – particularly the more remote – they're the most practical way to get about.

For more details, see **Chapter 11**.

## ACADEMIC COSTS

**You'll wear out more than a few pencils during the course of a degree. Apart from pens, paper and Winnie the Pooh pencil-cases, students have to find the money for books, floppy disks and specialist materials like paints for art students, flash calculators for mathematicians and lab coats for chemists.**

Your choice of course affects these academic costs as much as your choice of location, but both factors make costs swing like pants in the breeze.

In this respect, art is just about the most expensive course you can do – all those oil paints and canvasses don't come cheap – but it's far from the only one with costs attached. Archaeology, for instance, means getting down and dirty with the digging once in a while. And no one's going to be falling over themselves to pay for your field trip costs.

All courses have some costs – think ahead to work out what they might be. If in doubt, ask the university department before you apply.

Meanwhile, different courses have different demands for books. On an English course, for example, you need loads of books, but most of them are quite cheap and you might find quite a few of them second-hand (if your university has a second-hand bookshop, that is). For biology, it may only be a few books a year, but they all cost a limb. For law, you not only need *lots* of books, but they're all expensive.

At least when you've finished with your biology books you can flog them to next year's students. English students may not want to give up their Austens and Amises. As for computer studies students, their books will be out of date by the time they've finished with them anyhow.

**But, I hear you cry, why buy books? Isn't that what the library's for?**

**It should be, but some university libraries are less well stocked than a fish farm in a drought. Oxford and Cambridge,**

on the other hand, both have copyright libraries, which means they get a free copy of every single book published in the UK (including this one).

Even if they do have the book, your university's library may have annoyingly short opening hours and you may find that the book you want can't be borrowed – that's when students spend hours and pounds, standing by the photocopier. Libraries vary big-time and a bad one not only costs you money, but can stunt your study too.

As for computers, the good news is that students get free internet access from university computers. If they can get access to the computers, that is. Most universities have too few (I mean, how many would ever be enough?) and sometimes they're slower than a Virgin Train, but the level of availability – how many and when – varies more than the weather at Wimbledon.

Of course, all students would like to have their own computer, but don't count on being able to save up for one. If the university's provisions are good enough, you can sidestep the issue and save money.

For more details, see **Chapter 11**.

Get your parents to call you back when you phone them. But call them regularly. You don't want the only time you speak to them to be when either they call you or you're asking them for money. Not only is it tacky, but, far worse, it looks tacky too.

## ENTERTAINMENTS AND LEISURE

The standard and style of entertainments will vary hugely depending on where you go, not to mention the cost.

For example, some university bars are no cheaper than the pub next door. In the case of Imperial College, however, the pub next door is in one of London's classiest areas (South

Kensington) and a pint there won't leave you with much change from £2.50. In the college bar, however, it's half the price.

That shouldn't be a temptation to drink twice as much (students get pretty practised at nursing the same pint all night), but at least it means that if you do you'll have one less reason to regret it in the morning.

**It's important to pick a university with the right spread of distractions for you (see 11 below). If name DJs and dance music are your scene, your social life may cost you more if you end up somewhere like the Courtauld Institute, which has little more than the occasional school disco. You'll end up going to non-student venues and paying non-student prices.**

If, on the other hand, you're a junkie for indie bands who can't let a gig go by, you may want to avoid Leeds Metropolitan, where the calendar of events will empty your pocket faster than a hole.

Most universities have student balls (I'm talking about the ones with fancy frocks and penguin suits, okay?), but at some of the posh universities they're a big deal and you feel a bit left out if you don't go to at least one or two. But they can set you back the best part of the cost of a dirty weekend in Paris. Tickets alone can cost upward of £70 and on top of that there's the outfit, drinks and the cost of a hangover cure.

**It's not just the cost of entertainments that vary – whatever you're into, if your university caters for it, you could save major-league money. (Well, a bit anyway.)**

For example, sailing's not exactly a sport for anyone short of a bob. You need a boat for starters. If your university has a sailing club, chances are it's because they've got something to sail, so you could be saving yourself the cost of a yacht. Okay, so maybe you wouldn't have bought one, but at least it allows you to carry on sailing.

The same is true of photography, another expensive hobby, where a university darkroom could save you a fair whack.

For more details, see **Chapter 11**.

**INSURANCE**
Insurance looks simple enough. Endsleigh, for instance, has a
flat rate premium for student rooms in halls of residence,
whatever university they choose.

That's all very well, so long as you're in halls. If you're not
living in university housing, all insurance companies charge
premiums for high crime areas that are so huge it's almost as
bad as being robbed (but only almost – so don't try to
penny-pinch by not being insured).

# Where can you afford to go?

**Money is a big bubble of worry in the gut for most students
most of the time.**

**By choosing a university carefully, they can at least deflate
that bubble to the size of a small football.**

**Different universities cost different amounts, even if the
fees are the same.**

Living in college usually works out cheaper than renting your
own place, but not every university gives you the chance (and
only a very few let you live in for your whole degree).

Local costs like travel, entertainments and shopping vary, as
do different lifestyles that affect what you spend your money on
and therefore how much of it you have.

**On average a student needs around £5,000 a year to live
on after they've paid their fees. That leaves a shortfall of about
£1,500 a year on what they get in student loans and standard
parental contributions.**

**It's no surprise then that the average student debt –
excluding the student loan – for each year of study is about
£1,480.**

**But that figure varies.** At some places it's well over two
grand (particularly medical schools where the opportunities to do
paid work are slimmer). At other places, it's under a thousand.

London students tend to have the highest debts on average,
but the strange thing is that it's not just costs that affect the
level of student debt. A whole bunch of factors drag it around
like a rat on a string. Apart from simple costs, here are some of
them (but bear in mind they often cancel each other out):

**KEEPING IT LOWER:**

- A high proportion of students living in
- Good general level of facilities
- Campus universities
- Being in a town or city
- Being in a cheap part of the country
- Collegiate universities
- Smaller universities and colleges
- Availability of paid work locally.

**SENDING IT UP:**

- A high proportion of students renting privately
- A truly kicking nightlife
- Middle-class universities (where students don't panic about debt so much) – except collegiate universities
- Poor choice of shops
- Being in an expensive town – especially London.

When choosing a university, you could do a lot worse than eliminate anywhere that you decide you simply can't afford.

**What you can't afford to do is make the wrong decision. If you drop out, you quite probably won't be able to afford to go back. Unless you drop out quickly, you will almost certainly lose a year's funding – that's a year's student loan, a year's award and possibly even the Government's contribution to your tuition costs for a year. In other words, there's funding for you to do a degree, but if you screw up somehow along the way, you may well be paying privately for any extra years it takes.**

Yet another good reason to choose the right university in the first place.

## Taking a Year Out

Most universities are quite chuffed if you decide to take a year out (aka 'a gap year'). As far as they're concerned, you'll probably arrive at university a bit more mature and rounded and ready to be a responsible student. They may or may not be right.

But they don't want you to take a year *off*. That's why people call it 'a year *out*'.

1

A year spent with the cast of assorted Aussie soaps and miscellaneous sofa cushions is not what anyone has in mind.

The universities hope you'll broaden yourself somehow (mentally, that is – becoming physically wider is only good for goalkeepers). They imagine you'll go travelling or do voluntary work or get work experience – you know, something horribly worthwhile.

However, these worthwhile things are, strangely enough, the most worthwhile things you can do. They're fun and mind-expanding and, if in your first week at uni you can talk about camping under the stars in the Kalahari or squatting in trees scheduled for destruction for a new bypass, it'll make you a damn site more interesting than the geeks comparing A Level results and bizarre coincidences involving UCAS codes.

Sainsbury's, Tesco and some of the other supermarkets offer loyalty cards with money-off vouchers if you spend enough. Apart from making sure you collect your own, ask your parents if you can have theirs too. (But don't buy stuff you don't need, just because you've got a money-off voucher.)

### What's this got to do with money and student survival?

There's another worthwhile activity to add to the list: earning money.

Work experience is all very well, but the problem is that it usually falls into one of three categories.

Firstly, the genuinely helpful experience that pays nothing – sometimes even less than nothing because you get charged for it or at least have to pay your own expenses.

Secondly, the completely useless experience that pays nothing. I mean, how much experience do you need to make tea and lick stamps?

And finally, the completely useless experience that at least pays decent bucks. This is more commonly known not as 'work experience', but simply 'work'.

**Getting a job may allow you to put a bit aside for the lean years ahead as a student and, if you've got all year to save, you may even notch up a few grand if you really try.**

If you live at home whilst working your way through your gap year, your parents may well not expect any rent or contribution to the family finances – especially if you point out that you're saving up so that you won't always have to turn to them for help once you're a student. (Don't push that argument too hard, though – in the end it may not be true.)

**You may decide, on the other hand, that you've got all your life to spend working. Your gap year is your one chance to do some serious budget travelling. The problem is that even *budget* travelling may not fit *your* budget. Which is another good reason to work for at least part of the year and save up enough for a few classic year-out adventures.**

**At the very least, you can make sure you don't turn up at university with a big hole in the bank before you've even started to rack up your student debts.**

## LONG-TERM BENEFITS

Any work experience at all, anything from shelf-stacking to fruit-packing, is useful in improving your employability.

The fact that you've turned up every day, done what you're told and basically put up with it proves that you understand the crappier side of working for a living. Employers like to know that you can hold down a job and so any experience is better than none.

So, while your eyes may be on the money at the end of the week, you may also do yourself some financial good in the longer term. If you're more likely to get a job and more likely to keep it, you're also more likely to get a higher wage and have a more secure future.

Whilst that fact may not help directly with cash in the medium term, it should give you some comfort as the debts double and the bank balance bottoms out.

# Part 2
# How much will you have?

# Awards, grants & assessments

## Briefly, what's an 'award'?

You've probably heard of student grants in the same way people talk about four-star petrol, space hoppers and bands getting to the top of the charts because they're good and not because they're hyped. All these things, however, are long-distant memories, fading like red knickers in a whites wash.

If someone who went to university five years ago starts trying to explain to you how the whole funding system works, just tune out for a while. It's all changed. Forget mandatory grants, discretionary grants – all that stuff. Grants are as extinct as dead parrots.

Except grants aren't quite extinct. The good news is that about two-thirds of UK students still qualify for what is now called an 'award' for their first degree.

The bad news is, they never see a penny of it. The cheque goes straight to the university to pay part of their tuition costs. The rest is paid mostly by the Government and most students have to pay something themselves in the form of tuition fees (up to a maximum of £1,075 a year). More on fees in Chapter 10.

Even if you get the maximum award available, that's all it covers: part of the tuition fees. The two issues – awards and tuition fees – are basically two sides of the same coin (or, in this case, cheque).

**Whether you get an award and how much, depends on what your parents earn (or your guardian or sugar daddy – whatever). They consider things like whether your folks have**

**to fork out for a brother or sister at uni too. But when it comes down to it, the more they earn, the less you get.**

If you're over a certain age and earning for yourself, they'll do the sums based on your own money.

Basically, they look at whatever might be available to you.

**Grants also still live on in Scotland.** Scottish students studying in Scotland (but not Scottish students in England or English students in Scotland) still get their fees paid plus a grant to live on. In fact it's not quite such a good deal, because on graduation they have to pay a two grand 'endowment' for the privilege.

Wherever you're studying, once you've been accepted by a university, to sort out your award you'll need to get in touch with your local education authority (LEA) in England or Wales, the Student Awards Agency for Scotland or the Department of Education for Northern Ireland. This is so they can assess your parents' income and so they know who to pay, when and for what. If you're in doubt about who to call, try asking your school, college, local library or local council. **And don't forget to do it or else you'll be paying for it all yourself.**

# Explain that again, but in more detail

### LEAS

**Local Education Authorities** – or **LEAs** as we'll call them – are the guys responsible for handling the whole awards deal for undergraduate degrees.

In Scotland, that's not actually true. Instead of an LEA it's a body called the Student Awards Agency for Scotland (SAAS). And in Northern Ireland, it's the Education and Library Boards (ELBs). But to make matters simpler (and, let's face it, that's no bad thing), we'll just call them all LEAs, okay?

Whatever, LEAs (or things very much like them) do an **Income Assessment** for each student to tot up who gets what and then they pay it out.

The relevant LEA for you is the one that's in charge of education for the area where you normally live before you start your course.

# Will I be getting anything?

That depends on whether you meet certain conditions:

### Where you live

You've got to be a **home student**, which means you must have been 'ordinarily resident' in the British Isles for three years immediately before the start of your course.

You don't have to worry about going travelling in a gap year or long holidays or even your parents working abroad. It's the 'ordinarily resident' thing that counts.

On top of that, your home should be in England, Wales, Scotland or Northern Ireland on the first day of the academic year in which your course starts.

You must also have 'settled status' – for example, if you were born in the UK (and are therefore considered a British citizen) but have lived abroad for a number of years, they might not count you as a 'home' student.

If there's any doubt, give your LEA a bell and they'll advise you.

### Whether you've studied before

The Government only pays for you to do the whole higher education thing once. So, if you've taken a higher education course before, at university or college, either in the UK or even outside the UK, but with financial help from UK or EU public funds, then you may not be entitled to a second bite at the academic cherry.

The various rules and regulations on this are more convoluted than a Brookside storyline and, since the decisions come down to individual judgements by the LEAs, the best thing is to give them a call if you think there might be a problem.

This does, however, highlight an important aspect of going to university: it's vital to pick the right university and course for you as an individual. If it doesn't work out – you don't settle in, you can't afford to carry on or maybe you just don't enjoy it – then you could end up paying heavily for a second chance.

For more on making the right choices, see Chapter 2 and take a look at **The Push Guide to Choosing a University**.

### What you study

LEAs only have to fund students to do certain types of course. That includes all first degrees and quite a lot else, but part-time students and certain art and drama students ought to read the small print in particular and, if in doubt, give the LEA a call.

Anyway, the courses the LEA will cough up for are:

- Full-time first degrees (eg. BA, BSc or BEd), including sandwich courses
- In particular cases, part-time courses of initial teacher training
- A Diploma of Higher Education (DipHE)
- A Higher National Diploma (HND)
- A Higher National Certificate (HNC)
- A Postgraduate Certificate of Education (PGCE) or other postgrad course of initial teacher training which qualifies you as a teacher. Also, specified equivalent qualifications or an NVQ at level 4 where this is awarded along with a first degree, DipHE or HND. Some teacher training courses also get extra money, not necessarily from the LEA – but more about that later.
- A course which prepares for a professional examination higher than GCE level, Scottish Higher, National Certificate or National Diploma.

There are also certain courses where students don't have to contribute anything to their tuition costs anyway, so there's no need for LEAs to make awards, but we'll look more at these later (see Chapter 10 on tuition fees).

### Where you study

It's not just what course you study, but where you study it.

It has to be a publicly funded UK university or college (ie. not the University of Buckingham). Or it has to be a specified private institution. Or a group of schools that's taking part in the School Centred Initial Teacher Training (SCITT) scheme.

If it doesn't fall into any of these categories, you'll almost certainly have to dig deep.

**Your age**

Actually, so long as you pass all the other conditions, it doesn't matter how old you are.

The only difference age makes is how likely you are to still be depending on your folks for your up-keep. Once you're not, the LEA checks out your own income (or even your husband's or wife's) instead of theirs, but if that's likely to be lower then it might work out in your favour and qualify you for an award.

For more on being classified as an **independent student**, see below.

## HOW MUCH MIGHT THEY GIVE ME?

The LEA won't actually give you anything. Not personally.

**However, they will assess your family's income to work out how much they're willing to give your university or college to contribute towards the costs of your tuition.**

**At most, they'll pay all your tuition fees – that's £1,075 per year** (at this year's levels, but it'll keep going up approximately in line with inflation, as should the awards). **About a third of students get that much.** They're students from poorer families where, after a few allowances, the income is under about £20,000 a year.

**Another third of students get the smallest possible amount from the LEA – ie. no contribution at all.** They're the ones whose folks earn more than £30,000 a year and, in theory at least, the parents end up paying the £1,075.

**The students in between get something in between.**

This Government-funded amount that the LEA stumps up is known as a **mandatory award** (because, if you meet the conditions, by law your LEA has to pay up).

Occasionally, LEAs will shell out a bit extra – a **supplementary grant**. But to qualify for that you generally have to have either a disability or kids or be a mature student or in care. (There's more on that in Chapter 13.)

The same assessment that the LEAs perform is used by the Student Loans Company to work out how much they'll be willing to lend you. (More on loans in Chapter 4.)

## HOW MUCH SHOULD I EXPECT?

LEAs all work to the same rules when deciding who to help and by how much.

There's a standard application form which asks you, among other things, all about your parents' salaries. Even if you're earning, unless you're an 'independent student' (see below), they're not generally worried about your own income.

From what you tell them on the form, the LEA works out your parents' **residual income** – in other words, what they have left after various allowances. But if you want to work out for yourself roughly what you'll get, it's best to play it safe and estimate on the low side. So forget about the allowances for now and just add up your parents' incomes for last year and check out how you stand using the table:

| Your parents' residual income | LEA Award |
| --- | --- |
| Below £20,000 | Full fee of £1,075 |
| £20,000 | £1,030 |
| For every £9.50 over £20,000 | Subtract £1 |
| £21,000 | £925 |
| £25,000 | £504 |
| £29,000 | £83 |
| £29,784 and above | Zilch |

As usual, the calculations only really work if you happen to be a bog standard case, which almost no one is. However, the LEAs do look at each case individually.

So, over the page, there are just a few factors that fudge those figures.

### Brothers and sisters

If your parents have other offspring to support, the award goes up by £79 for each one. If, however, they also happen to be in higher education at the same time as you, then it gets even more complicated. You'll be glad to hear the LEAs do make further allowances, though.

### Changes in circumstances

If the situation changes for whatever reason – your dad loses his job, your mum gets a whacking great pay rise, they get divorced, your sister goes to university and so on – then your LEA needs to take another look at the sums.

You only have to apply once to get on the books, as it were, but once you're there the LEA will review the situation every year.

### Parents without the blood tie

Step-parents' and guardians' incomes don't count when in the LEA is doing its assessment, but adoptive parents do.

### Divorce

Try to persuade your parents to get divorced or at least to separate – that way the LEA only counts the salary of whichever is more appropriate (usually whoever earns more). It also puts you in a great position to use emotional blackmail to sting both parents for money.

### Independent students

Independent students are students who the LEA reckons aren't supported by their parents, so they don't bother with what the parents earn but instead assess the student's own stack.

If that's less than the parents', the student might find themselves more likely to get a bigger award. But to see yourself classified as an **independent student**, it's not good enough just to say your parents can't or won't help out.

You have to prove that, by the date your course is due to start, you'll match at least one of the criteria:

- You'll be over 25
- You'll have been married for at least two years
- You'll have been supporting yourself for the last three years or more – including being unemployed or doing a training scheme
- You're permanently 'estranged' from your parents
- Or they're dead (murder is rarely worthwhile – *Push* would advise against it).

It's not automatic, but you also stand a good chance of being treated as independent if you're in care (or were until you were

18), your parents can't be traced or if they're abroad and contacting them might put them in jeopardy (such as refugees).

If you're classed as independent, then the LEA looks at your own income, which, while you're studying, is not likely to be all that big anyway. What's more they won't bother themselves about certain bits of income like scholarships and sponsorships (up to £4,000), NHS bursaries, access funds, hardship loans and casual or part-time work during term-time or in vacations.

**Married students**

If you're thinking of getting married, do the sums first. If your financé – oops, sorry – fiancé(e) is less well-off than your parents, go ahead as soon as possible.

But if they're quite rich, hold off till at least two years from the end of your course. Apart from the fact that university is a great place to meet people, if your husband or wife has enough residual income, the LEA will look at that instead of your parents.

Of course, if they're really rich, marry them and get them to support you through your studies.

If the LEA does decide to assess your spouse, they'll use basically the same assessment method and rules as when they're assessing parents.

Get condoms for free from the doctor or family planning clinic in advance. Your sex life is at its most expensive if you rely on slot machines in pubs and clubs.

# How do I apply?

**IF I'M NOT GOING TO GET ANY MONEY, DO I NEED TO APPLY?**
However rich you or your parents are, however lazy you may be, however much you hate filling in forms, you still have to apply to your LEA for an award – even if you know you won't get one.

If you don't, you may end up having to pay your entire course costs – around £4,000 a year – instead of the regular full contribution of £1,075.

## ALRIGHT, SO HOW DO I APPLY THEN?

On the next couple of pages, there's *Push*'s handy guide to what to do and when, but the general rule is annoyingly trite: 'Don't delay, do it today'. (You can hate the slogan, but the sentiment's sound.)

### Step one - Getting started

**What to do:**

Contact your LEA for an application form (HE1) if they haven't already sent you one.

**When to do it:**

If you haven't got a form by January of the year when you want to start you course (ie. Year 13), get one. In fact, you might as well do it sooner or, at least, as soon as possible after applying for your course. You shouldn't wait till you've had your place confirmed or even until you get an offer.

**Why do it?**

You need to fill in the form so they can assess your financial situation. This form isn't so they can do the assessment itself, just so they know whether they need to.

**Anything else?**

*Your* LEA is the one for where you live, not where you'll be studying. Your school, college, local library or local council can help you find the contact details if necessary or they may even be able to give you the form themselves.
Depending on your LEA, you might be able to download the form from the internet

## Step two - The LEA checks your eligibility

**2**

**What to do:**

Complete and return the form.

**When to do it:**

The form itself will tell you the deadline (around 17th March). Don't only meet it. Get the form in as long before as you can. Don't just leave it in a drawer and forget about it till the last minute. The sooner you do, the sooner you'll know what your financial situation's going to be and the sooner you'll get your money (including your student loan). What's more, if there are any problems, you'll have time to sort them out. (The absolute deadline is the end of the first term – after that you've missed your chance. But don't even dream of leaving it that late. Get it in before you even start. Now. I think we've made our point.)

**Why do it?**

Your responses will help your LEA to determine whether you are eligible to receive help with tuition fees and living costs.

**Anything else?**

Make sure you fill everything in carefully. If you're eligible for an award, the LEA will send an 'Eligibility Notification' and a 'Financial Form' (HE2), usually within a month or two of receiving your application. Chase them if it doesn't turn up. **NB.** You can choose not to have your parents' income assessed, in which case you'll skip the next stage (Step 3) and you won't get any award and only the minimum loan. Only choose not be assessed if you absolutely know your parents earn way too much for you to get anything and you really can't be arsed filling in any more forms.

## Step three - The LEA checks your eligibility

**What to do:**

Complete the Financial Form (HE2). It's like the scissors bit on Blue Peter – you'll need your parents (or spouse) to help, but only because they need to sign the details about what they earn. When it's completed, return it to your LEA by the specified date.

**When to do it:**

Pronto. As soon as the form arrives (usually at any time from the April before the start if yourcourse), turn it around as fast as poss. The LEAs recommend that you return it around the middle of March if you want your award by the start of term, but in any case get it back before 18th June or there could be problems.

**Why do it?**

This gives the LEA the details about your parents' income and blah-de-blah so they can work out whether you deserve an award (and how big a loan) and, if so, how much. If you don't do it, they'll assume it's no problem for you and your family to shell out the full £1,075 contribution to your fees plus the maximum amount twoards your living expenses.

**Anything else?**

When you've sent it back and the LEA has had a chance to check it through, they'll send you a 'Financial Notification' that will officially confirm how much assistance you're entitled to.

## Step four- Applying for a student loan

**What to do:**

When you get your 'Financial Notification', you get one copy
that has the Loan Request Form on the back. You use this
to apply for your student loan (more on this in Chapter 4) by
filling it in and sending it off the Student Loans Company,
letting them know how much you want to borrow up to the
maximum you're allowed. (Don't faff about trying to keep
your debts low, take the maximum – you'll need it.)

**When to do it:**

The earlier you do it, the more likely you are to have money
in the bank by the start of term. You're really going to need
every penny then (see Chapter 13), so pull your finger out
and do the necessary as soon as the Financial Notification
turns up. Definitely don't leave it later than mid-August. (You
can still get a student loan any time up to one month before
the end of the relevant academic year.)

**Why do it?**

You're probably sick of all these damn forms by now, but the
student loan will probably provide the bulk of your funds
during your student life so it's pretty important.

**Anything else?**

When you send off for your student loan, you'll have a
pretty good idea of your basic income and you can start
picking at bones or, as it's also called, planning your
budget (see chapter 14)

Give blood. You get free tea and biscuits
afterwards.

## WHAT IF I AM NOT SATISFIED?

Good question. What if the LEA takes forever, turns you down for an award unfairly or palms you off with less than you reckon you deserve?

LEAs do cock up from time to time. It's only natural. Forms fall down the back of the radiator or they read one too many noughts in somebody's salary. There's no need to panic or give them a hard time about it though – start off with a simple polite phone call. That's usually enough to sort it out.

But if it isn't, get the name of someone at the LEA to whom you can complain and put it in writing, stating clearly why you think you've had a bum rap and tell them you're giving them, say, 21 days to respond. Wait 21 days and then phone again if you haven't heard. Be polite, but be firm.

Once you're at university or have even been offered a place, if you're having problems with your LEA you can get help from the university's students' union. (Phone the university and just ask to be put through to the students' union welfare department.)

Alternatively, most universities and colleges have student funding and/or welfare departments too. Either that department or the students' union will usually take up your case with the LEA and answer any questions you've got about what might have gone wrong and how to fix it.

Don't jump straight to conclusions about it all having gone pear-shaped. It's a pear-shaped system and confusion is pretty much par for the course. Rather than rushing in to complain, always feel free to phone the LEA to ask questions or just to check on progress.

In fact, call the LEA about anything you like – how to fill in the forms, whether you're likely to be eligible or how to remove egg stains from a silk blouse – okay, maybe not about the stains, but they're there to help and they should treat everyone as an individual case.

# Frequently asked questions

**If I have my own savings, will I have to declare them?**
If you're still dependent on your parents, then almost certainly not. It's only their income that the LEA counts when they do the Income Assessment.

Generally you don't have to worry about any of the following:
- Your savings
- A trust income
- The first £4,000 from any scholarship or similar award
- Any income from casual, part-time or temp jobs during or just before your course.

There are other sources they won't worry about either – the forms make it pretty clear and, if you're still not sure, ask.

If you have savings and investments and don't expect to earn over your personal allowance in the tax year (currently £4,535, which doesn't include any loans), arrange for your interest to be paid without tax being deducted (see Chapter 7 for more on tax). Then you won't have to claim it back.

**Which courses _don't_ get any financial help?**
Basically everyone gets one chance to take a degree or equivalent qualification, but _only_ one. That means that students don't normally get Government funding for any of the following, although there's often another source you can try (for more info, see Chapter 13):

- **Postgraduate courses, including NVQ Level 5:** Unless they're training to be teachers (PGCEs or similar), postgrads either have to pay for themselves or get funding from the British Council, one of the research councils, their employer or some other organisation.
- **Any nursing or midwifery course:** Instead, students gets a non-income-assessed NHS bursary or a special award for health services.
- **Access or conversion courses** which prepare students to take a higher education course.

- **Further education courses** like A Levels, AS Levels, Scottish Highers, NVQs, GNVQs, most BTEC courses, City and Guilds and so on. Funding for these is a whole different system – talk to the LEA.

### What if I don't live in the UK?

Then it depends on where you do live. If you normally live in any EU country other than the UK, you should be able to get assessed for help with your tuition fees (but you won't qualify for a student loan). It's down to individual circumstances, though.

For starters, contact the LEA that covers the university or college where you want to study.

### And what if I don't live in the EU?

In this case, you're an overseas student and you're going to have to fund your course costs all by yourself or apply in your own country for whatever educational funding may be available. What's more, you're going to have to pay the full cost of your course (starting at around £3,500 a year), not just the £1,075 contribution.

See Chapter 13 for more on overseas students.

### What if I drop out and want to get back in?

Sometimes students avoiding flunking altogether by repeating a year or dropping out of one university and starting again somewhere else.

Most LEAs won't support you financially for a repeated year, especially not if they reckon it's your fault. Reasons for it being considered 'your fault' might include not liking the university you chose, hitting the financial rocks or getting drunk and missing all your lectures. They might be more lenient if you're sick.

The policy on all this varies from one LEA to another, however, so if it looks like you may have to flunk, first check out how they'll react and, if it's likely to be a no-no, try to hang in there.

If you do want to repeat a year, you'll probably have to pay tuition fees for the time you're repeating and it may be not just the £1,075 contribution but the whole whack (the same as an overseas student).

You might well get an extra year's student loan though – for all the good that'll do you.

The message is: choose your university carefully in the first place (see Chapter 2) and don't screw up when you get there by either not budgeting your money or by being a complete dosser. So long as you do that, no one can blame you and you'll avoid the worst of the financial rough justice for flunking.

## Still confused?

Fair enough.

Read the DfES booklet *Financial Support for Higher Education Students*. Call their information line on 0800 731 9133 for a copy. It's free.

Unfortunately, it'll make even less sense than this chapter.

So try completing as much of the application forms as you can, phoning up as you go along whenever you need to. If necessary, slip a letter in with your form giving the low down on your personal situation – but remember that it's all more straightforward than it seems.

So long as you get the money, no one complains and you don't lie on the forms, it doesn't matter if the detail is clear as vomit in a toilet bowl.

There's a veritable library of suggested reading and recommended websites near the back of the book.

At the end of each academic year, sell the books you no longer need to someone in the year below. They'll pay less than the full price and you'll get some of your money back — everyone's a winner.

Part 2: How much will you have?
Chapter 4

# loans Student

## Briefly, what's a 'student loan'?

**Awards take care of part of a student's tuition costs, but they're only a paddle in the pool of payments compared to the full-on skinny dip of living expenses.**

**And, just as awards cover part of the cost of tuition, student loans cover part of a student's cost of living – 'maintenance costs', as the jargon has it.**

The student loan is split into two parts. Everyone who qualifies for anything gets three-quarters of the full loan – that's between about £2,000 and £3,000 a year depending on where they're living and studying.

They can only borrow the second part – the other quarter – if their LEA decides that they need it after they've assessed the students' parents' income. Again, it's like the awards (see Chapter 3) – the more the parents are getting, the less the students get and the more the parents are expected to cough up.

Depending on how much their folks earn, students can borrow up to a further £1,645 a year.

**Most students – all UK undergraduates on full-time courses – qualify for at least the first three-quarters (75%) which they receive from the Student Loans Company (SLC),** a name so imaginative and obscure it's a shock anyone ever works out what they do.

Student loans have to be repaid, of course. That's in the nature of a loan. But students don't have to even start settling up until they've got a job earning more than £10,000 (although, if they've got other debts to settle – as they usually do – ten grand doesn't leave much room to live the high life). If they never earn that much, they're off the hook.

In addition to the pretty soft repayment terms, the interest is fairly cushy too. Contrary to popular belief, there is interest on student loans – in other words, they do want more back than they lent you – but it's pegged to inflation and, relatively speaking, it doesn't really get much lower than that.

Even the maximum loan (which assumes your folks won't be able to spare a penny) is rarely enough, so students almost invariably rely on hand-outs from parents, paid work or borrowing from banks on top of what they're lent by the SLC.

## Explain that again, but in more detail

For students, debt is not something to avoid. It's something to accept as a fact of life and which you simply try to keep to a minimum.

**In the long term, students are likely to land better jobs, with better pay and their student debts will be paid off eventually. That's only the *average* scenario, however, and there are some for whom the legacy of debt is harder to shift than an elephant with no legs.**

For anyone at all, starting a career with a debt hanging over you like a concrete cloud isn't ideal and some students feel that the burden of borrowing just isn't fair given what they ultimately contribute to the economy. But most just feel that, by their age, they don't want to have to rely on their parents for money or to try to use the cash machine with their fingers crossed.

It's certainly debatable whether it's a good idea to fund our higher education system by forcing millions of young people so far into the red that wearing green becomes painful. And, indeed, it is much debated.

But that's not what this book's for. If you think it's unfair, you can campaign all you like, blow up Parliament and moon the Queen – but, like it or lump it, that's the score for the time being. Deal with it. *Push* tells you how.

A large part of a student's debt will usually be owed to the Government, who skulk around behind the **Student Loans Company (SLC)**, funding the whole operation but keeping it out of smelling distance. It's the SLC that does the lending.

**WHAT ARE STUDENT LOANS FOR?**
The Government-funded student loans available from the SLC are most students' main source of income to cover the costs of living – somewhere to live, something to eat, something to wear, books, travel, beer money and maybe the odd Ferrari from any left-overs.

It's only 'income' in the sense of being money available to them, not in the sense of it being their money, because, of course, they have to pay it back eventually. Along with any awards from the LEAs, student loans come under the umbrella term 'student support'.

**Students don't *have* to apply for student loans (not even in the way that they should for LEA awards) – but don't try to be a hero, the one student in the country who makes it through university without borrowing. Unless you start off rich, it's not possible.**

Even if you do have more money than a director of Railtrack, you should still try to get a loan. If you don't need it, dump it into a high yield account and earn more interest than you have to pay. Should be worth a few hundred quid over eight years.

Unfortunately, that's not an option for most students. Student loans are an inevitable necessity rather than a fall-back option. They're what you've got to live on.

If you're having second thoughts about the whole idea of student life, check back at the reasons why it's worth it at the end of Chapter 1.

### DEBT IS INEVITABLE – SO WHAT'S THE GOOD NEWS?

The good news is the terms. They're better than almost any personal loan (unless you happen to be an MP borrowing money from a mate for a home in Notting Hill). Students get pretty good deals from banks (see Chapter 6), but even they are rarely as good as this.

See 'Paying it back' later in this chapter for details.

### WILL I BE ABLE TO GET A STUDENT LOAN?

Most students can. In fact, all students under 50 are entitled to apply, if they normally live in the UK and are doing a full-time course lasting a least a year to a first degree, a higher diploma or one of the other eligible qualifications (basically, any course that might qualify for an award – see Chapter 3 for more details).

Even if you're over 50 and under 54, you can still receive an award so long as you intend (or say that you intend) to go back to work after studying.

Some part-time students without much money can also get a loan, but not through the same route (see below).

You won't be able to get a loan, however, if you're not a UK student. Not even our Euro-cousins.

### HOW MUCH *MIGHT* THEY GIVE ME?

Every year, the Government bumps up the maximum available loan – good news as far as having access to cash is concerned, but not so good given that it means students' debts are snowballing every year, if not avalanching.

Currently, the most anyone can borrow in a year is £4,700, but most students can't get anything like that much. It all depends on the following factors...

Never, ever use your debit (or credit) card for a 'tab' behind the bar. You'll invariably end up feeling sick, skint and sorry.

## Where you live and study

Students living at home (with their parents) aren't allowed to borrow so much, because it's reckoned that they either don't pay rent or that it's a darn sight cheaper and comes with a tray-full and a laundry-load of extras.

On the other hand, living in London is more expensive than most places and so students whose courses are based in the capital are entitled to borrow more (although for most students, it's not enough extra to cover the additional costs and they end up even further in debt).

## What you study

The course has to be eligible – which means it has to be on the list of courses for which LEAs pay awards (see Chapter 3). It doesn't matter if you don't actually get an award because you don't qualify for some reason, so long as the course does.

If you're doing some weird qualification and you're worried about not getting a loan, give the SLC a call. As they used to say on the ads, it's good to talk.

## Which year of your course you're in

In your final year, you're not entitled to quite as much. The same goes for courses that last only one year.

The theory is that in most years you'll need the loan to see you through the summer, but in your final year you're free to start work the day after you leave university.

This cuts both ways because, while you're a student, you're not able to get any unemployment benefit – oops, 'job-seekers' allowance' – but the day after you leave university, if you're not marching into your new job you can get down to the dole office and sign on.

Do your supermarket shopping on a Sunday or at the end of the day when things that could go off get marked down. Then don't forget to eat them before they do.

**How much you and your family are expected to contribute**

If you're eligible for any loan, you're eligible for at least 75% of the full amount that anyone in the same situation could get (as far as the factors above are concerned).

The other 25% is based on the assessment of your family's income that the LEA does when deciding whether to give you an award (see Chapter 3).

**The length of your academic year**

If your course is longer than average – such as most medical degrees – then they'll lend you a bit more.

If the course itself lasts longer than 30 weeks and three days in any year, then you get into the zone. Once you're in, then you're eligible for an extra loan allowance for each additional week up to 45 weeks. After 45, the SLC says 'what the hell' and just calls it a whole year, basing the amount on 52 weeks.

Whatever you get for the extra weeks is worked out on essentially the same terms as what you'd get if you and your course hadn't made it into the zone.

**SO, HOW MUCH SHOULD I EXPECT?**

It starts with your LEA (see Chapter 3). They decide whether you should get an award and send you a 'Financial Notification' telling you how much help (if anything) they will give you towards your tuition fees.

The LEA's Financial Notification will also tell you how much you can apply to borrow from the SLC and, on the back of one of the copies there'll be an application form to send off.

**Even if the LEA decides that you're not going to get anything towards your tuition, it doesn't mean you won't get a student loan. It just means you'll only be able to borrow the first part of the loan – ie. 75% of what someone else in the same situation but with poorer parents could get.**

On the next page are the amounts you might be able to borrow in the academic year 2001/2002. It'll be going up each year (probably) in line with inflation.

The columns labelled as the 'first part' are the 75% than almost everyone gets.

The second part is means-tested, in other words, it depends on your family's fortune (well, their income anyway) and so the columns labelled 'maximum' are only available to those whose parents earn under around £20,000 a year. If they earn between £20,000 and £30,000, you should be able to borrow something between the two amounts.

| Students living & studying | Full Year | | Final year | | For each extra week (over 30 in one year) £ |
| | First part (75%) £ | Maximum £ | First part (75%) £ | Maximum £ | |
| --- | --- | --- | --- | --- | --- |
| In London | 3,525 | 4,700 | 3,055 | 4,075 | 86 |
| Elsewhere | 2,860 | 3,815 | 2,485 | 3,310 | 65 |
| At parental home | 2,265 | 3,020 | 1,975 | 2,635 | 45 |

## HOW AND WHEN DO I GET THE MONEY?

Usually you get it in three instalments – one at around the beginning of each term, but occasionally the money comes in two payments or even just one (but only, as a rule, if you've applied after than the beginning of the year). The SLC will send you a schedule to let you know when they'll cough up and how much.

The SLC also usually transfers the money directly into your bank or building society account. That robs you, unfortunately, of the elation of holding a stonking great cheque in your sweaty paw.

It's not that the SLC doesn't trust you with your money, but direct payments in instalments does help avoid the feelings of recklessness that might overcome even the most normal student when confronted with the ability to pump nearly three grand into their bank account.

Even when it's only a thousand, don't be tempted to splurge on a cruise in the Bahamas, a half-tonne bar of chocolate or a dead cert in the 2:30 at Newmarket. The money has to last. That's why you should have a budget – to scare yourself into appreciating the truly tiny amount you really have.

# How do I apply?

Applying for a student loan is part of a paperchase – first you pick up form HE1, then HE2, then your Financial Notification which doubles as a Loan Request Form, then visit Guatemala on a Thursday with a herring in your pocket, etc, etc, etc.

But seriously, it's part of the process that starts when you apply to your LEA for an award (contributing to your tuition fees). We covered that process in the last chapter, but just as reminder, here's Step 4 again– the bit that relates to getting a loan.

## Step four- Applying for a student loan

**What to do:**

When you get your 'Financial Notification' from your LEA, you get one copy that has the Loan Request Form on the back. Fill it in and send it off the Student Loans Company, letting them know how much you want to borrow up to the maximum you're allowed. (Don't faff about trying to keep your debts low, take the maximum – you'll need it.)

**When to do it:**

The earlier you do it, the more likely you are to have money in the bank by the start of term. You're really going to need every penny then (see Chapter 12), so pull your finger out and do the necessary as soon as the Financial Notification turns up. Definitely don't leave it later than mid-August. (You can still get a student loan any time up to one month before the end of the relevant academic year.)

**Why do it?**

You're probably sick of all these damn forms by now, but the student loan will probably provide the bulk of your funds during your student life so it's pretty important.

**Anything else?**

When you send off for your student loan, you'll have a pretty good idea of your basic income and you can start picking at bones or, as it's also called, planning your budget (see chapter 14)

There's nothing to stop you applying for your loan as soon as the Final Notification drops on the doormat, so you might as well do it to save time or hassle later. The only thing is that the SLC won't pay anything out till your university confirms that you're going to be studying there.

Even if you've applied in plenty of time, until you get the wonga in your hands, it's best to be sceptical about it turning up promptly.

The same is true even if you don't apply till after you've started your course (which you're allowed to do if you enjoy the financial equivalent of walking on hot coals). Leaving it till you're really skint is like waiting till your clothes have all rotted before buying new ones – you're going to have to go out there naked. It's the same with money – you don't want to end up unable to buy food because you're waiting for the SLC's bureaucracy machine to clunk its way through to issuing your loan. Better to apply early, before you're truly broke, and leave yourself enough of the folding stuff to cover you till the loan arrives.

Nonetheless, you can still apply for your student loan anytime up to one month before the end of the academic year. Each year you need to apply again and should you not apply in any year for some reason, you can still apply again in the next year.

> If you're going out with mates, meet at home first, do most of your drinking there and then go out. The off licence is way cheaper than pubs and clubs.

## THE PAPERWORK

Applying for a student loan seems to involve digging out every document other than your primary school reports (and they'll probably start asking for them too, now we've suggested it).

Actually, it's only four documents, but it seems like such a pain in the posterior to get them together. Anyway, this is what you'll need:

- Your **birth certificate** – if you were born in the UK. Or your adoption certificate if appropriate. If you can't find the original, you can contact the Registrar General (see the back of the book for addresses, phone numbers and so on) for a 'certified copy' or 'extract'. Photocopies won't do.

  If your birth or adoption wasn't registered in the UK and you are not a refugee, you'll have to provide your passport (if you have one) along with a letter giving your full name and where and when you were born. This letter needs to be signed by someone reliable like a minister of religion, doctor, lawyer, teacher, civil servant, police officer or consular official.

- **The letter from your LEA** to confirm your award status (if you have one).

- Proof of **your bank or building society account number** and sort code. Something like a cheque book, a statement or an official letter from your bank manager (and you'll have no shortage of those over the next few years). You must have a UK account to get a student loan, otherwise it's no dice (see Chapter 6 for more info on student accounts).

  Before giving your bank details, however, give them a call just to check that they accept direct credits and debits through the Banker's Automated Clearing Services (BACS). Almost all banks do, but they don't always work with certain accounts. It's pretty important since this is how the SLC is most likely to send your money and it'd be a shame not to get it. It's also the method they'll use to get the money back off you when the time comes.

- Proof of **your National Insurance number**. Your NI card is best, but a letter from the Benefit Office or a payslip (so long as it's got the number on it) will do.

If you send them the right paperwork, the first instalment should be sorted within three or four weeks, although the SLC will wait till your university has confirmed that you really are a student there (or about to become one) before paying out.

If you need to send your papers to the SLC, use recorded delivery. In the first place you don't want to lose important documents, plus you don't want the hassle of trying to get them all together again because Postman Pat has torn them up for cat litter.

In the winter, work on a clapped-out PC at home rather than the more expensive networked ones on campus. Not only do you do more work than chat, but you also save on heating 'cos of the amount of heat that they produce.

## Paying it back

A loan wouldn't be a loan if they didn't want it back and although you don't need to worry about it while you're still a student, it's just as well to know the score so you know what to expect later and they don't have to send the boys round.

### WHEN YOU HAVE TO REPAY

You don't have to pay back a penny until after you've finished your course (or dropped out). In fact, not until the following April – usually a whole nine months later.

You also don't have to pay until you've got a job that pays £10,000 a year.

Whatever your situation, the SLC will write to you in February to let you know how much they think you'll owe them on 31st March of that year. They also tell you the monthly amount you'll need to start paying.

By April they'll write to you again with a schedule of the actual monthly repayments that will be taken out of your salary (or out of your bank account) between April and August unless you let them know otherwise.

## HOW YOU REPAY

How can they just take money from your salary, you may ask.
Because the SLC works with the taxman, that's how.

Using your National Insurance number, the Inland Revenue
will charge your employer the repayments and, come the April
after graduating, they'll just take it out of your pay along with
your income tax and your national insurance contributions. Your
pay statement each month will show how much they've lifted.

If you're self-employed, of course, you have no 'salary' as
such and no employer for them to deal with. But then, you have
to let the Inland Revenue know what you've earned each year
anyway (on a tax self-assessment form) and you pay your tax
later. They'll just ask for the loan repayments then as well.

Every year in September, until you've paid off your debts, the
SLC will send you a schedule to show you how you're doing.
They'll also let you know if you need to pay more or less per
month over the next year, depending on how much interest
they're charging you.

This whole conspiratorial alliance with the Inland Revenue is a
new scheme and only applies to loans issued after 1998 –
so-called 'income contingent loans'. So if someone tries to tell
you how it works based on their personal experience, bear in
mind they're probably talking out of the wrong orifice, because
their experience isn't relevant.

Current students may find themselves repaying through the
old system where the SLC takes the money direct from their
bank accounts.

When the SLC sends you the letter in February, they'll also
enclose a direct debit instruction form, that you need to sign and
send back, letting them know whether your bank details have
changed since the days when they were paying in rather than
taking out. That gives them permission to take your money.

Direct debits are a convenient way to pay because they don't
involve remembering to send off cheques and, as a system, it
has anti-fraud guarantees. Because the money is simply taken
from your account, however, you have to watch your balance
(your bank balance, that is – debt repayment only rarely induces
dizzy spells).

Come April, the money starts to disappear out of your account automatically. You can choose to pay on a particular date in the month – on or near payday, for instance.

## HOW MUCH WILL I HAVE TO REPAY?

It depends on what you're earning, but it's worked out as 9% of anything you earn over ten grand. Basically it's a pretty small slice of your pay packet. The table shows how it works out.

| Income each year £ | Repayment as a percentage of income % | Monthly repayments £ |
|---|---|---|
| Up to 10,000 | 0 | 0 |
| 11,000 | 0.8 | 7 |
| 12,000 | 1.5 | 15 |
| 15,000 | 3.0 | 37 |
| 17,000 | 3.7 | 52 |
| 20,000 | 4.5 | 75 |

If your salary goes up, your repayments go up and, obviously, you keep making your monthly repayments until you've given back everything you borrowed, but then there's a bit extra too – the interest. (So called because interest is what makes banks interested in giving anyone money.)

## WHAT INTEREST WILL THEY CHARGE?

**The interest rate on student loans is linked to inflation, so in 'real' terms the amount you ultimately pay back may be more than the amount you borrowed, but it's an equivalent amount nonetheless.**

In other words, if you borrowed enough for 2,000 pints of Stella, 2,000 packets of peanuts and 500 cheese and bacon toasties, by the time you come to repay it, you'll only have to give back the cost of the same again, please, barman.

At the moment the rate is hovering at around 2.6% a year.

They start adding the interest from the day you get your first loan payment and annual statements each September after graduation show you the interest charged.

## HOW LONG WILL IT TAKE TO REPAY?

That depends on how much you borrowed in the first place and on how quickly you're able to pay it back which, in turn, depends on your income once you've graduated.

**If everything goes well – you get a job, it pays something around the average for graduates and you don't suffer any major illnesses or accidents – then most student loans can be paid off within five or ten years of leaving university.**

In the meantime, the monthly repayments are such a small percentage of your income that, unless you stretch your bank balance to the point where cheques become rubber, you'll hardly notice the effect on your income. Compared to some of the other monthly salary-guzzlers once you've graduated – income tax, council tax, rent or mortgage, bills, other direct debits and so on – student loan repayments are just another fly on the windscreen.

If you do want to pay more each month or shell out one big lump sum to get yourself out of debt sooner, no one's going to stop you. Just contact the SLC. Plenty of graduates do it, especially if they begin to earn a tidy package, but if you're in a position to pay off debts, pay off any others first because, if you're paying interest at all, you won't be borrowing more cheaply than this.

## WHAT IF I CAN'T PAY?

Some graduates don't find a job immediately after they leave university. Some go on to do more studying – postgraduate courses and the like. Some pack their bags and go travelling. And some are unemployed – it's not common and it usually doesn't last, but it happens.

If it happens to you, you can 'defer' your repayments.

Likewise, if your income is under the specified threshold (currently £10,000) or if it was higher but drops below, repayments can be postponed until you're making a bit more.

Whatever the reason, if you need to defer, you'll have to fill in yet another form. This time it's a 'deferment application form'. If your case is sound, your deferment will be authorised and you'll be off the hook for a year in the first instance. After a year, you'll have the option of deferring for another 12 months.

However, all the time you're not paying back, the amount you owe will carry on growing because of the interest.

## CAN YOU GET AWAY WITHOUT REPAYING IT?

There are only four ways to get out of paying back your student loan or any part of it that you still owe:

- If you get to retirement age (60) first
- If you never earn more than the minimum salary threshold (currently £10,000)
- If you become permanently disabled
- If you die.

It's still better than most loans, though – most lenders wouldn't let a little thing like death stand in the way of getting their money back.

Nonetheless, that doesn't mean that you can avoid starting to repay when they ask you to on the basis of some flimsy excuse. If your salary's still more modest than a bashful nun or you don't get a salary at all, then fair enough – but otherwise forget about dodging the system.

It may not sound like the most foolproof scheme in the world, but trying to cheat the taxman is like giving yourself an enema with battery acid – it's something you don't even want to try.

Not only will tax evasion land you in jail, it's also a pretty despicable way to behave towards other students who need your taxes to pay for the chances you've had.

If you change your address, your name or anything else relevant, you need to let the SLC know. Ultimately, there's no point running from them. There's nowhere to hide.

They may not be into horses' heads in beds, but they'll be willing enough to use the legal thumbscrews if you get shifty and, unless you have a completely fair case, they'll wipe the floor with your sorry ass.

Get a real crappy second-hand bicycle. Get replace-as-new insurance. Wait two weeks.

# Frequently asked questions

**I live in the UK but I'm doing part of my course abroad – will I get a loan?**

Yes, if your study abroad is a necessary part of your course. Most language degrees involve some time abroad and that's covered.

The amount that the SLC will be willing to lend you will depend on the country you're going to. Japan, for example, has a higher cost of living than the UK, so you'd probably be able to borrow more.

However, if your course is studied abroad entirely, the SLC probably won't pay out anything. If in doubt, ask your LEA.

**I've finished my degree. I'm off travelling. Do I still have to repay my loan?**

You need to let the SLC know what you're doing and they'll tell you where you stand.

It's in your interests to tell them as soon as possible because it's your responsibility to have them allow you to defer your repayments. If you just scoot off without getting your deferment authorised, you'll have some serious explaining to do and some big payments to make when you come back.

If you're going travelling and won't be working, deferment shouldn't be too big a problem because you'll be under the ten grand income threshold for repayments anyway.

If, however, you'll be living outside the UK tax system and will be earning above the threshold, you'll need to make repayments direct to the SLC and not the Inland Revenue. You will need to provide evidence of your (expected) income for the financial year so they can calculate how much you should give them each month.

**If I'm away, can anyone else talk to the SLC about my loan on my behalf?**

Afraid not.

It's a legal thing. The Data Protection Act means the SLC can't discuss it with anyone – not parents, not partners, not even your employer (they tell them no more than how much to give them out of your salary each month).

The only way round it is to write a Power of Attorney letter to the SLC authorising them to release information to a named individual. Giving somebody Power of Attorney means they have the legal right to act on your behalf, so don't go giving it to anyone unless you trust them completely.

By the way, you can give someone Power of Attorney over your bank account, for example, but that doesn't mean they have the same power over anything else – that includes your student loan.

**I only wanted to borrow part of my loan allowance at first. Can I get the rest now?**
Yes, but you only get one chance to go back.

In other words, if you're entitled to £3,815 a year and you only apply for £1,000 at first, then you can go back for more later (up to the remaining £2,815), but you can't go back for another £1,000 and then another and then the final £815. Whatever you do, though, it won't affect how much you can get the next year.

To get a second amount in one year, you will need to get, believe it or not, another form – a Loan Adjustment form. Call the SLC on 0800 405010 and ask them to send you one.

If in any doubt about how much you need, it's pointless to try and keep your debts down to a minimum by applying for anything less than the full allowance.

If you think you might not need the money and you're frightened that just by having it in the bank, you'll spend it, just shove it in a separate savings account until you graduate and then pay it back to the SLC in a lump sum. At least you'll have earned some interest on it in the meantime.

Frankly, the chances are that you'll be more desperate for cash than you ever thought possible. The best way to keep your debts down is to minimise what you spend, not to minimise what you have available to spend.

### What happens if I drop out or need to take some time out from my course?

If you drop out during the academic year, then that's it – you're cut off. You won't get any more loan instalments and you'll need to start paying your loan back the April following the end of the academic year.

If you're away from your course for more than 60 days because you're sick or have personal problems, then you should let your university's Student Loans Administrator know as soon as possible. Usually, they'll make sure you to continue to get your loan instalments so long as you don't actually drop out.

### Can part-time students get student loans?

Not the regular version.

Instead of their LEA or the SLC, part-time students should talk to their university or college about financial help with their tuition fees. Depending on their status, they might get £500 a year, paid in a single instalment.

As for money for living costs... er, no. If you're studying part-time, it's assumed you can spend the rest of your time earning a wage.

To find out more, first read Chapter 13, but if that's not the answer to all your dreams, try calling the DfES information line on 0800 731 9133.

Part-time teacher training is treated differently and usually more generously, because the Government desperately wants more teachers.

### I am utterly skint. Can my future instalment(s) be brought forward?

No way, José.

The rules are the rules as far as the SLC concerned.

If your pocket is really hurting, read what Chapter 9 says about hardship loans and access funds and then go ask your university's or students' union's Student Loans Officer if you can get one.

**I have received the full loan allowance. What if I still don't have enough money to get by?**

Again, no dice.

Try hardship loans, access funds (see Chapter 9) or singing in the street till people pay you money to stop.

## Still confused?

The SLC are quite happy to answer questions and their helpline is mostly staffed by people with lovely Scottish accents, so trying giving them a call (contact details at the back of the book). Or you can visit their website at www.slc.co.uk which is helpful, but doesn't have the accents.

Also your LEA should send you a booklet called *Student Loans: Guidance on Terms and Conditions* when they send you the copy of your Financial Notification which has the Loan Request Form on the back.

Help out at the soup run dispensing food to the homeless. There's always spare food and often it's M&S sandwiches. Plus you get to feel good about yourself.

Part 2: How much will you have?
Chapter 5

**2**

# Paren£s

## What should you expect from your parents?

For most students, their parents are an essential part of the financial equation.

It's not just that most students hope they might bung them the odd few quid here and there. The whole student funding system actually relies on the expectation that parents who can afford to help will actually do so.

**Rather than the parents or even the students, however, it's the Government (through the LEAs) that, in effect, makes the official decision about what parents can or can't afford.**

Well… the Government can decide whatever it likes, but ultimately, it's the parents who make the choice about whether to put their hands in their pockets at all. It's also up to them to decide, when they pull their hand out, how much they're clutching.

According to how the funding system is set up, parents should be the main source of income for about a third of students but, in reality, it's nearer 40% that depend on their folks for most of their dough.

Many parents are so proud that any son or daughter of theirs is going off to university that they're only too pleased to fork out whatever they can.

Others want to know if there's some particular amount they're expected to provide – they don't want to give too much and make you into the big spender at the student bar, but nor do they want you to be so hard up you can't be a brilliant scholar.

Some parents, however, don't place the same importance

on university as others (or as you). Or they think that by the time you get to 18, they shouldn't have to support you anymore. They might even think that not being supported after a certain age is an important part of your education.

And some parents – many, in fact – may want to help and the Government may expect them to, but they have too many other financial commitments and simply can't afford it. (This is particularly likely if the family income drops for some reason.)

As far as the students are concerned, let's face it: most look at university as a chance to be independent and they find it more than a little frustrating and demeaning to have to rely on mummy and daddy for pocket money.

## IS THERE A SPECIFIC AMOUNT I SHOULD EXPECT?

There is an amount that, as far as the Government is concerned, you should expect from your parents, but it's not as simple as that. Is it ever?

Before we can open the envelope to reveal that amount known as 'the **parental contribution**', we need to explain the thinking behind it.

In theory, all students should end up with approximately the same amount of money at the end of the day. The idea is that students with rich parents shouldn't have a significantly better opportunity to study than student from poorer backgrounds. So the exact amount depends on what other money you're getting from awards and student loans and where you're living and studying.

Parents make up the difference between what you get from the LEAs and the SLC and the amount the Government thinks you need to live on for a year. In reality, unless you're some kind of economy freak, you can't actually live on what the Government thinks you need – but never mind, crap happens. For what it's worth, this is what they reckon you should have to

| Students living and studying | Full year £ | Final year £ |
|---|---|---|
| In London | 4,700 | 4,075 |
| Elsewhere | 3,815 | 3,310 |
| At parental home | 3,020 | 2,635 |

live on after you've paid your tuition fees (see Chapter 11):

If these figures look familiar, it's because they're the same as the maximum student loan allowances.

The idea is that if you receive a smaller loan allowance, it's because your parents can afford to make up the difference. Also, if you're getting a smaller loan, it means you won't be getting an award from your LEA either and so there'll be £1,075 in tuition fees to pay as well.

So, the parental contribution is whatever amount is necessary first to top up your LEA award to £1,075, so you can pay any tuition fees, and then, if you didn't receive the full loan allowance, to top that up too.

Whether your parents actually give (or lend) you that amount is up to you and them.

Part of the reason for student loans in the first place was that 42% of parents were choosing not to make up the difference between the grant (as it was in those days) and what the student was supposed to have to live on.

Whether the current system is better or not isn't for us to say, but it certainly works better in making sure that parents give their kids the money they're supposed to. Perhaps the fact that students themselves have to make a personal investment by borrowing a student loan makes parents want to back them up.

Whatever, more than 80% of parents now contribute the amount needed to bring their kids up to par in the finance stakes and many go further.

Only share accommodation with other poor students or they'll want to do unreasonable and expensive things like heat the house.

## HOW MUCH SHOULD I EXPECT?

Once your LEA has completed its assessment of your parents' income, they'll not only let you know how much they're going to give you, how much loan you'll get, but what they think your parental contribution should be.

At around the £30,000 mark, their income will start to affect your loan allowance and the more they earn the less you'll be able to borrow till it hits 75% of the maximum loan available.

At the moment, the figures look like this:

| Your parents' residual income £ | Parental contribution to fees £ | Parental contribution to living expenses £ | Total parental contribution £ |
|---|---|---|---|
| Below 20,000 | 0 | 0 | 0 |
| 20,000 | 45 | 0 | 45 |
| For every additional 9.50 | add 1 | 0 | add 1 |
| 21,000 | 150 | 0 | 150 |
| 25,000 | 571 | 0 | 571 |
| 29,000 | 992 | 0 | 992 |
| 29,784 | 1,075 | 0 | Full tuition fees of 1,075 |
| For every additional 9.50 | no more | add 1 | add 1 |
| 33,000 | 1,075 | 338 | 1,413 |
| 40,000 | 1,075 | 1,075 | 2,150 |

The parental contribution maxes out when the part for living expenses hits 25% of your maximum loan allowance (given where your studying, living, what course you're doing, how many weeks in the year it runs and so on – see Chapter 4).

The absolute total any parents are ever expected to contribute is £6,591 for which not only would they have to be earning over £82,000 a year, but you'd also have to fall into all the most expensive categories of course, location and the rest of it.

There are various factors that affect the sums a bit, in particular, if you've got brothers or sisters.

If they're still at school or, at any rate dependent on your folks, then for each child, the LEA knocks £79 off the parental contribution.

If, however, they're at university of college too, then the LEA usually takes the total contribution from the table above and splits it between all the students in the family.

# Case Study Quiz

Because this whole thing is just so much fun, here's a little quiz just for a laugh – a few examples with multiple choice answers.

Have a go. It'll either help you get your head round awards (see Chapter 3), student loans (see Chapter 4) and parental contributions or bore you senseless. Possibly both.

Send your answers on a postcard to someone who gives a damn.

**2**

## CASE 1: NADIA NEEDSALOT

Nadia, 18, is from Northampton where her dad works down the last cheese-mine in the country earning £12,000 a year. Her mum does a part-time job painting the feathers on parrots at a nearby pet shop, putting another £6,000 a year into the family purse.

Nadia has got a place at North London University to do a degree in Nursery Rhyme Technology. She's got no brothers or sisters and the course lasts a pretty standard 29 weeks in each year.

She applies to the LEA for an award contribution to her fees, then sends off to the SLC for a student loan.

**1** What should Nadia expect by way of an annual award?
**a** Nothing  **b** £45  **c** £1,075  **d** £4,000

**2** What should she expect by way of a student loan for her first year?
**a** £3,020  **b** £3,525  **c** £3,815  **d** £4,700

**3** What should her parents expect to contribute each year?
**a** Nothing  **b** £45  **c** £1,075  **d** £1,175

If you're small enough, buy clothes in the children's department. There's no VAT, so it's like January sales all year round.

## CASE 2: LAWRENCE LOOT-LOADED

Lawrence, 17, is from Eton where he attends a local school. 'Pater' does something awfully important in the city – a banker, indeed, a right banker – and takes home a six-figure sum (all before the decimal point). Mumsy does jolly lovely things for charity.

Lawrence is off to St Andrews to study Imperial History with Capitalism. His little sister Letitia is about to do her GCSEs.

**1**  What should Lawrence expect by way of an annual award?
**a** Nothing   **b** £45   **c** £1,075   **d** £4,000

**2**  What should he expect by way of a student loan in the first year?
**a** Nothing   **b** £2,860   **c** £2,939   **d** £3,815

**3**  What should his parents expect to contribute each year?
**a** £1,075   **b** £1,951   **c** £2,030 &   **d** £3,333 &
                                 a Convertible
                                 Golf GTi

## CASE 3: MAGGIE MIDEARNERS

Maggie, 19, took a year out and saved up about £6,800 selling stress-removal kits to the team of *Push* researchers.

Her mum earns £24,000 a year in an animal sanctuary shaving badgers to make brushes. Maggie's dad ran off to sea with a primary school teacher named Albert when she was three.

Loving only-daughter that she is, Maggie has decided to live at home with her mum in Bolton during her degree course in Doll's House Architecture with Engineering in Lego.

**1**  What should Maggie expect by way of an annual award?
**a** Nothing   **b** £466   **c** £609   **d** £1,075

**2**  What should she expect by way of a student loan for her first year?
**a** £2,265   **b** £2,599   **c** £3,020   **d** £3,815

**3** What should her mother expect to contribute each year?

**a** Nothing  **b** £466 &  **c** £609 &  **d** £1,308,
               free rent     free rent     free rent &
                                           a badger

### CASE 4: SIMON SIBLING

Simon, 18, lives in Liverpool and is one of eight offspring of Stella Sibling. The father is rumoured to be a Catholic Bishop, but only Stella knows for sure.

Stella has a private income of £35,000 a year from a mysterious Vatican-based trust fund.

All four of Simon's older brothers and sisters are already at university and Simon intends to join them doing Contraceptive Technology at Christ's College Cambridge.

**1** What should Simon expect by way of an annual award?

**a** Nothing  **b** £443  **c** £800  **d** £1,075

**2** What should he expect by way of a student loan for his first year?

**a** £2,860  **b** £3,265  **c** £3,344  **d** £3,815

**3** What should Stella expect to contribute to Simon each year?

**a** Nothing  **b** £275  **c** £549  **d** £1,387

Many male medical students make a small deposit in their banks by making a small deposit at a sperm bank, but there's no reason why trainee doctors should have all the fun. Besides, not every kid wants a medical student as their anonymous dad.

# Answers

### CASE 1: NADIA NEEDSALOT

**1** Her award should be the most you can get which is (c)
£1,075 because her parents earn less than £20,000 a year.

**2** She'll be entitled to borrow the maximum for a student doing
a full year, living away from home in London, ie. (d) £4,700.

**3** The answer's (a). Her parents won't have to contribute a
penny which is just as well because it's hard to imagine that
on £18,000 a year, they'd find it easy.

### CASE 2: LAWRENCE LOOT-LOADED

**1** He won't get an award and will have to pay his own tuition
fees of £1,075 (see Chapter 11). So the answer's (a).

**2** His loan would have been £2,860 – in other words, the first
bit only which isn't means-tested. However, the true answer is
(c) – he gets an extra £79 because little Letitia is taken into
consideration.

**3** His parents, therefore, are only expected to stump up (b)
£1,951, although we have our suspicions he may end up with
a bit more.

### CASE 3: MAGGIE MIDDEARNER

**1** Maggie's award should be around about (c) £609. That's
£1,075 minus £45 (for the first £20,000 of her mum's
income) minus £1 for each £9.50 over £20,000 (ie. £421).
So that's £1,075 – (£45 + £421) = £609. Maggie's own
savings are irrelevant.

**2** She'll be able to borrow (c) £3,020. Since her mother's
income is under £29,784, Maggie's entitled to the full loan
allowance for anyone living at home.

**3** Her mum will be expected to fork out (b) £466 towards
Maggie's tuition fees and, since she's living at home,
probably she won't charge for rent.

## CASE 4: SIMON SIBLING

**1** Simon's award should be around (c) £800. His situation is complicated by the hoards of brothers and sisters. Normally someone whose parents earn £35,000 wouldn't get any award, but when Simon goes to Cambridge, his mum will have five kids at university and she can't be expected to pay £1,075 for each of them.

**2** For the same reason, Simon will be eligible for a full loan allowance of (d) £3,815.

**3** In total Stella will be contributing about £1,387 to her various kids' costs as students, but that's not the right answer, because her contribution is not only reduced by £79 for each of her three children who aren't at university, but also it is split between all her student kids by being divided by five. Therefore her contribution to Simon's costs will be about (b) £275.

## SCORING

Give yourself a point for each correct answer. If you scored...

- **More than 12:** You cheated.
- **9 to 12:** Have you thought of a career in the civil service?
- **5 to 8:** Nice, nothing too showy.
- **2 to 4:** Perhaps another look at the last few chapters, eh?
- **1 or 2:** Debtsville, you have another visitor.

# Borrowing from parents

There is a saying that goes something like, 'to find your place in the sun you must first escape the shade of the family tree'.

But when you're a student, all those hopeful delusions of independence and financial freedom will probably be shattered as, recovering from freshers week, you realise that all you have left is £19.63, seven slices of bread and half a packet of Nurofen to last you the rest of the term.

Depending on what your LEA gleans from your Income Assessment form, parents who are expected to contribute to fees may well be expected to make further contributions towards your general living costs. But if they've already doled out said dosh and you've cheerfully frittered it away on copious ethanolic refreshment, post-pub kebabs and CDs, you could find yourself paying them a little cap-in-hand visit.

Of course, some students are fortunate enough to have wealthy/generous/understanding/indulgent (delete as applicable) parents who'll shower them with cash in times of financial embarrassment (let alone genuine monetary misery). Even if you fall into this fortunate category, you wouldn't want to take it for granted.

And for every student who can rely on their parents for hand-outs, there are dozens whose parents can't or (perhaps sensibly) won't.

Spend as little money as you can by buying supermarket's own economy brands. People may think you're cheap, but at least the cash will last longer.

James Williamson, Bishop's Stortford College

If your parents are willing and able to help, **borrowing** rather than taking money from them seems like a sensible compromise – and who better to borrow from than parents?

They're not likely to charge you any interest, they won't come round and kneecap you if you miss the odd repayment and sometimes – either deliberately or due to a touch of brain rot – they may actually forget about the loan altogether.

Just don't expect your parents to bale you out all the time. You don't want to be a scrounger all your life, do you?

**Money management means learning to make your budget stretch, to economise wisely and to provide for yourself whenever you need extra cash.**

**Failing that, it means at least facing up to the consequences for yourself.**

There's no question about the fact that university's a major financial challenge and seeing yourself through it is part of the education (and, luckily, there's no extra charge for that). A mission impossible, if you will. But, hey, you chose to accept it.

Parents, however, aren't completely ignorant of the fact that you'll be receiving less money than a fruit machine in a Methodist chapel. So it's comforting to know that they're only a (reverse charge) phone call away if you do make the odd cash-related cock-up.

If they have the money, most would probably much rather you borrowed from them than from anyone else.

And, if they do offer you a nice long-term interest-free loan, bear in mind that however much you would like to flex your self-reliant muscles, a churlish refusal during your spell as a cash-strapped student may be extremely poor timing. Especially if it means you'll only have to borrow the money elsewhere and borrow it more expensively. Just take it gratefully and gracefully and pay them back when you can.

Repaying this debt will probably be lowest on your list of priorities, but it's still a debt. Unless they have unequivocally reassured you that they don't want their money back (in which case, consider yourself a very fortunate person indeed), you should feel like a total heel if you go so far as to exploit your parents' generosity.

For their sake as much as yours, you may do better not to simply ask for money every time.

**Instead of hard cash, for instance, you might suggest they buy whatever you would have bought with the money – books, clothes, tinned food, coffee, bus or train tickets, travel cards, postage stamps (for all those summer job applications), phone cards or pre-pay mobile phone top-up credit (for calling them, natch). Quite apart from the fact that it may feel less embarrassing for all concerned if no actual money changes hands, it will reassure your folks that their money's going on stuff you actually need. (And to be fair, it does stop you spending it on stuff you don't.)**

There's also a kind of halfway house. They can give you book tokens, clothes vouchers, Sainsbury's reward vouchers (very useful) and the like. It's money really – it's just there's a limit on how you spend it.

Why not get your parents to visit every now and then? They'll feel loved and needed, which is all very nice, but more importantly you can often get them to take you out for a slap-up meal. After surviving on an uninterrupted diet of baked beans on toast, pasta and tinned tomatoes, beer and burgers, your stomach will be grateful for some proper nutrition.

Parents may also consider getting a strictly 'emergency use' credit card or opening an emergency instant access account as a safety net, just in case. Stranger things have happened.

Depending on the idea behind a gesture like that, you will presumably not want to abuse it. Just having something like that, however, can lift from your shoulders the ever-present panic at being completely without money or any means of getting any.

Ultimately, not all parents are that much wealthier than their student offspring. They probably already don't feel overchuffed at the prospect of not being able to help you out.

If they can't afford to help, there's nothing to be gained by making them feel bad about it.

**If, however, your parents genuinely can't help, the bursaries and access and hardship funds you can get from your university are there to provide the kind of just-in-case cushion other students get from their parents.**

Part 2: How much will you have?
Chapter 6

# B?a?n?k?s?

## Do I need a bank account?

As a student you will need to make your bank your friend. And it will feel like cuddling up to a rabid dog.

Not that banks are nasty to students. It's just that most students are scared of talking to their bank because they owe them so much money, and they know the bank has the power to cut off their cash supply.

In fact, most banks suck up to students like they were millionaires (because they hope one day that's exactly what they'll be – or, at any rate, they know they're likely to be richer than non-graduates). To entice students to open accounts, banks offer them freebies, good deals and, more importantly, free overdrafts.

**Student loans are really only enough for those weird people whose powers of budgeting defy imagination. So borrowing from the bank is almost a necessity for students. Even the weird people may at least have cash flow difficulties.**

Normally, if you want to borrow from a bank, they charge you for it, but for students (for as long as they remain students) the big banks offer interest-free overdrafts of between £750 and £1,500 per year.

The crunch comes, however, when you graduate. Unless you walk into a megabucks job, you'll have your student loan to pay off plus your bank overdraft, and that's when the interest can start to rack up (although some banks offer helpfully slow repayment packages).

It's best to get chummy with your bank from the start. (If you already have a good relationship with a bank, you might want to keep your account right where it is. By all means switch to a student account to get the freebies, but don't switch banks.)

Also, always let them know what your situation is, however bad it gets. They don't often cut students off if they're acting responsibly.

## Bank deals explained

Banks speak a language of their own, invented by customer service experts in a secret underground facility beneath Alton Towers. At great personal risk, however, *Push* has acquired a black book containing translations of common terminology. Here are some extracts...

### STUDENT ADVISERS

Most banks take apparently ordinary staff and specially train them to act as student advisers in their campus branches and/or those close to universities and colleges.

These advisers are under instructions to be sympathetic to the plight of students – many of them are recent graduates themselves so they will nod empathetically.

As the name 'advisers' suggests, not only do they nod, but they can also give advice about how to handle your cash flow situation, should you want it (or should they think you need it).

Although you'll probably never be swearing eternal love to one another, you should get to know your adviser pretty well, and you should contact them whenever you want to change or discuss any aspect of your bank account (such as getting overdraft extensions), or if you have any specific money worries.

This isn't so they can snatch your plastic and cut it up before your eyes, but so they can work with you to make sure you have enough to live on without going too far into the red.

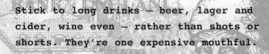

Stick to long drinks — beer, lager and cider, wine even — rather than shots or shorts. They're one expensive mouthful.

## OVERDRAFTS

**An overdraft is a minus amount of money in your account. So an 'overdraft limit' is the sum that your bank has decided you're allowed to take out of your account even though you haven't actually got any money in there.**

An overdraft is usually denoted by the letters 'OD' on your bank statement. So if the months go by and the amount in your account just seems to be growing, but there are these strange two letters after the totals, start to worry.

'£700 OD' means that's what you owe them, not the other way around, and so if you paid £150 into your account, you'd then be £550 OD. Or if you paid in £701, your balance would swell to the knee-buckling sum of £1 CR (CR standing for credit).

Most banks offer a free overdraft facility to students up to a certain limit. This means that, so long as you don't go over the limit, you won't get slapped with any unexpected charges.

Always get official confirmation from your bank of what your overdraft limit is, and make sure that it's going to be enough. Depending on your year of study, the overdraft limit is usually between £750 and £2000 (it grows as your student debts accumulate). If there's any danger that you're not going to be able to stick to the limit, you need to have a chat with your bank's student adviser to arrange an 'extension'.

A couple of don'ts... **Don't wait till you're nearly at you limit before trying to arrange an extension, 'cos then you're stuffed if they say no.** You should be able to do the maths and – on the basis of what's coming in (student loan payments and parental contributions) and what's going out (see Chapter 14) – work out whether your balance is going to drop below the limit. They'll be more likely to help you if you're being all responsible about it.

**And don't exceed your limit without getting authorisation to do so.** Your overdraft is then no longer free, and you get hit with charges and fines. There'll be fines for going over the limit and for bouncing cheques (ie. not honouring them), and they'll even charge you for sending you a letter to tell you that you're over your limit. Then they'll fine you because you can't pay the charges.

Worst of all, they'll charge interest. Interest rates on unauthorised overdrafts can be huge. In fact I'd say they were immoral if it weren't for the fact that an unauthorised overdraft is essentially taking their money without asking – so you started it.

**While you're a student, your bank overdraft is the cheapest and easiest way of borrowing – cheaper even than student loans, because there's literally no interest on most authorised student overdrafts while student loans rack up interest from day on.**

However, overdrafts do have to be paid back eventually, and the bank theoretically has the right to ask for the money at any time. After you've graduated, most start charging interest (although often not immediately) and it doesn't take long for overdrafts to become an expensive form of amusement.

So don't get complacent about your overdraft – it's certainly a lifeline for most students, but it's not an automatic right.

## CHEQUE BOOKS

Most banks will give you a cheque book as part of your basic welcome pack when you open an account. They'll give you a paying-in book too, which will probably see less use.

The cheque book will be essential for paying rent, bills etc, but these days you won't need it for much else because you'll usually be able to use plastic. Nevertheless students are famous for writing cheques for a packet of crisps or a pint of milk when the cash machine has turned them down with the fateful familiar phrase: 'Insufficient funds. Refer to bank'.

## CHEQUE, DEBIT, CASH AND CREDIT CARDS

Most accounts come with at least one slice of plastic, but the cards themselves do different things. (Incidentally, make sure you sign the strip on the back.)

There are four main types of card, and some cards can be more than one type at the same time.

### Cheque guarantee cards

Most places won't accept a cheque unless you have a matching cheque guarantee card. By writing the number of your card on the back, they have a guarantee from the bank that they'll get their money without worrying whether you've got anything it your account or not.

Students' cards usually only guarantee cheques up to £50. They come in higher denominations, too, but banks don't trust students with those.

If you write a cheque and offer the card, make sure your balance can stand it. Otherwise you'll find yourself with an unauthorised overdraft and all the deluge of poo that entails.

### Debit cards

If you need a card to write a cheque, why bother with writing the cheque?

Sure enough, that's a debit card. You offer it. You sign. The money comes out of your account.

The shop (or whatever) can phone up to check whether your account can handle whatever payment you're trying to make although, since debit cards are also usually cheque guarantee cards, they usually won't bother if it's under the cheque limit. (Often the phone call is made automatically by the till.)

### Cash cards

Slide it in a hole in the wall, punch in your PIN and get cash up to a daily limit or whatever your account can pay out.

PIN stands for 'personal identification number'. Please don't say PIN number. The word 'number' is redundant and it really bugs me. Thanks.

Be aware that you may be charged if you use another bank's cash machine, so find out what kind of penalties apply. You'll be told to look out for a particular symbol such as the Switch, Link, Visa or Cirrus logos.

Save all your coppers and 5p coins and put them in a jar. They always come in handy at the end of term when you're completely broke.

Jenny Blyth, University of St Andrews

### Credit cards

At first a credit card seems to work the same way as a debit card. You hand it over. You sign a slip. Everyone's happy.

In fact, they're not the same, because it doesn't matter how much money there is in your bank account if you're using a credit card. Instead the money is added to your credit account, and you get a bill at the end of the month for everything you spent on the card.

You can either settle up then, or pay a minimum payment and let the rest sit there. Bad idea. If you leave a balance unpaid on your credit card account, they'll charge interest on it, and we're talking interesting levels of interest here. It's an expensive way of borrowing, and not recommended for students without bottomless pockets.

More on credit cards in Chapter 9.

### CAREER DEVELOPMENT LOANS

Career Development Loans (CDLs) are a Government-funded scheme to help people who are doing vocational training courses. The loans are offered by just four banks (Barclays, Clydesdale, The Co-operative and The Royal Bank of Scotland) but most undergrads don't qualify anyway.

For more on CDLs, see Chapter 9.

### ONLINE AND TELEPHONE BANKING

Internet banking is becoming increasingly popular, and students can get in on the act as easily as anyone – not least because most universities provide free web access to all their students.

This means that rather than traipsing to your nearest branch and queuing up for hours behind someone with 4,317 pennies that need to be counted, instead you can sit at a terminal in the university library, picking your nose and avoiding the essay you're supposed to be writing.

Many students prefer to speak to someone, however, especially if they want to give excuses or get advice. But the internet banks have thought of that. Most offer a 24-hour telephone banking service (or at least a service beyond the usual nine to five).

Even so, the face-to-face contact of a student adviser who you recognise is still popular. It's up to you.

Also check the costs – there may be charges for banking down the wires.

## DEFERMENT PERIOD

Slim Jim the Fence owes Joey the Knife $10,000. Joey gives him three days to come up with the money – that's a 'deferment period'.

To put it another way, it's a period of time that a bank gives you either to raise the funds to repay an overdraft or loan or, more usually, to find work.

When banks offer a deferment period, it tends to be more by way of a practical approach to debt management rather than a threat (as it is with Joey the Knife).

Rather than immediately snatching every penny you earn and landing you in as much financial crap as you endured as a student, a deferment period helps you settle into a job and ease your way into repayments. Banks usually give students a year or two (or even three) after they've graduated before giving them a hard time about repaying their overdraft.

If a bank doesn't offer a deferment period to graduates, you may want to look elsewhere.

## REPAYMENT HOLIDAYS

A repayment holiday is similar to a deferment period, but usually shorter – a matter of a few months.

It's a period when they'll let you off repayments while you're having a hard time, so long as you start paying again when you're out of the woods. It can be either before or after you've started repaying.

## BANK LOANS

The difference between a loan and an overdraft is that an overdraft is simply what's not in your account, whereas a loan is an agreement to lend you a certain amount for a certain period on certain terms.

Most banks do offer loans to students, although some of them need to be paid back before graduation. That rules them out as a way of financing anything other than a particular expense that you know you'll be able to repay. Definitely not the right choice for students who foresee the financial swamp just getting deeper and swampier further down the line.

One of the best student loans on the market at the moment is the Barclays Educational Loan – you can borrow up to £10,000 and pay it back at a decent rate once you've finished your degree. It's still not as good as the Government-backed student loans, though (see Chapter 4).

All loans are subject to various terms and conditions, however, so do some thorough investigation before applying.

For more on loans from banks, loan sharks and anyone else, see Chapter 9.

If you're thinking of getting married to someone better off than your parents, hold off till at least two years from the end of your course. It may reduce your funding. If, however, they're really rich, go ahead.

## Which bank?

Of course, you've probably had a bank account since the tooth fairy gave you 10p for your first milky peg. But becoming a student give you a great opportunity to review the situation.

Look out for special offers and incentives. And that's 'look out' in both senses of the phrase.

On the one hand, there are some genuinely valuable bribes out there. Last year, for example, Clydesdale Bank said that if a student banked with them throughout their university course, they'd pay off the accumulated interest on their Government-funded student loan once they'd graduated.

That could work out at several hundred quid. It puts the traditional offers of music vouchers and novelty piggy banks into perspective.

On the other hand, it's not worth being duped by the offer of
a cuddly Barney the Banking Bear if that means you're stuck
with an account that makes loan sharks look like kippers. Keep
your eye on the long term.

The banks usually change their package every year, and full
details aren't usually available until mid-June.

Most of them have now shut down the loophole whereby you
could open five accounts, collect all the freebies, and then close
down the ones you don't need. They now require that you bank
with them *exclusively* as part of the agreement when you join up.

You may already have a bank account you are quite happy
with. In this case, let your bank manager know you are going to
university, and s/he will transfer your current account to a
special student one and give you all the info you'll need – and,
hopefully, shower you with perks.

Try to join up with a bank at least a few weeks before
starting university to take full advantage of any offers (some are
offered on a while-stocks-last basis). It'll also mean you avoid
long queues at the bank at the beginning of term, you should get
your plastic in plenty of time, and you'll have a chance to get to
know the bank's particular facilities and arrangements. Perhaps
most importantly, it'll mean you can tell the SLC where to put
your student loan.

## THE DEALS

Following is a summary of what the four big high street banks
are offering this year (2001/2002), but remember, they're not
only not the only banks, and they're not even necessarily the
best for students.

For example, check out student deals from Clydesdale,
Abbey National, Nationwide, The Co-operative, Alliance &
Leicester, Royal Bank of Scotland and Halifax (now also known
as HBOS  after its merger with Bank of Scotland). If you live or
study in Ireland, try Bank of Ireland (NI) or Ulster Bank (NI).

There's also a bundle of banks on the internet now,
including Smile (good interest rate when in credit), First Direct,
Cahoot, and Intelligent Finance, to name but a few.

| | NatWest | Lloyds TSB |
|---|---|---|
| **Website** | www.natwest.co.uk | www.lloydstsb.co.uk |
| **Phone** | **0800 881 771** (Textphone: 0800 917 0526) Lines: Mon-Fri 8am-8pm Sat 9am-6pm | **0845 3000 116** e.bank for students; or, if you're already an account holder, freephone 0500 222444 |
| **Freebies (liable to change every year)** | Has the most branches on campuses; £35 cash or Panasonic CD player worth £49.99. | £40 cash to children of existing Lloyds customers. |
| **What do you need to apply?** | UCAS or university letter, one form of official ID (eg. a passport), confirmation of home and term-time addresses and course | UCAS letter and one other official piece of ID showing name and address. |
| **Interest on current account when in credit** | 0.1% AER (paid monthly) | None |
| **The Full Deal (liable to change every year)** | Free online banking if required; 24-hour freephone help-desk; NatWest Service Card; monthly statements. | Interest-free overdraft; free internet banking; debit card (£100 cheque guarantee); cheque book; telephone banking; an Asset credit card on application; monthly statements; computerised phone-bank express service; can be used abroad. |
| **Overdraft facility/ Credit zone** | Interest-free prearranged overdrafts individually agreed with advisers. Graduate account: maximum £2,000 interest-free for the first year following graduation; £1,000 in 2nd year; £500 in 3rd year. Interest rate if over maximum authorised overdraft: 17.8% EAR | Limits: Years 1-3: £1500 Subsequent years: £2000 Interest rate if over maximum authorised overdraft: 29.8% EAR |
| **Student adviser** | All branches on or near campus have Student Advisers. | In branches and telephone contact from 9-7 daily. |

| Barclays | HSBC |
|---|---|
| www.barclays.co.uk | www.banking.hsbc.co.uk |
| **0800 400 100** | **0800 130 130**<br>Lines: Mon-Sat 8am-10pm<br>Sun 10am-4pm |
| Up to £30 worth of book, CD and video vouchers. Additional discounts on books and CDs throughout the year (from Waterstone's and HMV). | Free 4-year railcard or £50 cash; student insurance policy from £22 per year. |
| UCAS letter and one other official piece of ID showing name and address. | UCAS letter and confirmation of university place, plus additional proof of name and address. |
| 0.1% AER (paid quarterly) | 0.1% AER (paid monthly) |
| Easy online banking; Barclays Connect Card (debit); cheque book; offers and discounts throughout year; direct debit and standing order facilities; monthly statements. | 'Flexibility and Freedom' is their motto. £100 cheque guarantee and debit card (can withdraw up to £500 a day provided finances available); cheque book and paying in book; direct debit and standing order facilities; monthly statements, student service welcome pack. |
| Automatic interest-free buffer of £200 available on opening account Up to a further £1,050 interest-free on request. £1,251 to £3,000 at a preferential interest rate of 8.9% EAR for as long as you need it. Interest rate if over maximum authorised overdraft: 29.8% EAR | Interest-free overdraft limits:<br>• 1st Year: £750<br>• 2nd Year: £1000<br>• 3rd Year: £1250<br>• 4th Year onwards: £1500<br>Overdraft limit goes up each year only if you have proved that you can manage the facility responsibly. £27 fine applies if you exceed limit. Interest rate if over maximum authorised overdraft: 29.5% EAR |
| Available at nearest campus branch. | Student Counsellors in nearest student branches. |

2

|  | NatWest | Lloyds TSB |
|---|---|---|
| **Graduate loan & Overdraft schemes** | Up to £10,000 at preferential rate of 7.5% APR over maximum 5 years (7 years for loans of £5100 or more). Optional 4-month repayment holiday. | Up to £10,000 over 5 years at 7.8%. Optional 4-month repayment holiday. |
| **Cash machines** | NatWest plus HSBC, Clydesdale, Ulster, Isle of Man, Coutts, Northern and National Irish Banks | Lloyds TSB plus Barclays, Royal Bank of Scotland, Bank of Scotland |
| **Career development loan** | Professional Trainee Loans for those studying longer, specialist courses such as law and medicine – leaflet available at branches. | Professional Studies Loan – enquire at nearest branch. Enquire at local branch for deals. |
| **Insurance** | Student belongings insurance and student travel insurance | |
| **Credit card** | No annual fee. | Asset credit card on application; free for up to 4 years. |
| **Anything else?** | NatWest card protection scheme from £12 a year with the NatWest Student Mastercard. Combined student account and credit card application available from all branches (you don't have to apply for both). | Fully comprehensive internet service for students and graduates. Phone Bank Express and commission-free travel money. |

| **Barclays** | **HSBC** |
|---|---|
| Option to transfer student overdraft of up to £3,000 at 8.9% APR. 2 years' repayment holiday available. Up to £1,250 interest-free overdraft for up to 2 years after graduation. Additional graduate loan for larger purchases at 8.9% APR, with up to 3 months repayment holiday. | Up to £10,000 at preferential rate (currently fixed at 7.8%) over maximum 5 years. Graduate interest-free overdraft: <br>• 1st Year: £1,500 <br>• 2nd Year: £1,000 <br>• 3rd Year: £500 |
| Barclays plus Lloyds TSB, Royal Bank of Scotland, Bank of Scotland. All with VISA sign. Over 500,000 cash machines worldwide. | HSBC plus Nat West, Clydesdale, Isle of Man, Ulster. Over 400,000 cash machines worldwide, wherever you see the Cirrus sign. Small charge applies when debit card is used abroad. |
| From £300 to £8,000. Call 0800 60 900 60 for more details. Professional Studies Loan also available – up to £10,000 (£25,000 for full-time Law students). Enquire at local branch. | HSBC offer a postgraduate and professional studies loan. The loan amount and interest rate depends on the course, but loans of up to £15,000 can be paid over a period of up to 7 years and loans over £15,000 up to 11 years. Apply at local branch for more details. |
| Special deal negotiated for students. Cost depends on location and type of accommodation. | Special student package available. Pick up Student Insurance leaflet from nearest branch or call 0800 277 377. Application form included in Student Welcome pack. Travel Insurance available (for students aged 17 to 30), for details call 0800 299 399. |
| Student Barclaycard – no annual fees plus additional benefits. Money-off vouchers when you apply; Barclaycard Travel Accident Insurance and International Rescue. Preferential rate of 19.4% APR. | No annual fee. Automatic credit limit of £500. Up to 8 weeks' interest-free credit when balance is paid in full. |
| Commission-free travel money, holiday discounts from over 120 major tour operators. Automatic upgrade to Barclays Graduate Package for student when you complete your course. | Automatic transfer to 3-year graduate service. 24-hour telephone banking. |

# Graduate packages

**Postgrads have different needs of their banks.** They're often meeting the whole cost of their course, and their living expenses tend to be higher, but they also often stand to gain even more financially from their course than undergrad students.

Most banks have packages for postgrads, although not every student is able to get them. Here's what's on offer from the big four. Again, they're likely to change every year and they're not the only ones – HBOS, Clydesdale and the Co-op Bank all offer loans at lower than standard rates to postgrads too.

| Bank | Loans |
|------|-------|
| NatWest | **Professional Trainee Loan** – up to £15,000 (for barristers, solicitors, doctors, dentists, pharmacists, vets, chiropractors, optometrists, osteopaths etc). No repayments during study or for six months after completion. **MBA Loan** – various amounts. No repayments during study or for three months after completion. |
| Lloyds TSB | **Professional Study Loan** – of £15,000 or two-thirds of your salary. Repayments over five years, with an option to defer for the first six months. Graduate Loan Repayment Protection Insurance. |
| Barclays | **Professional Study Loan** – up to £20,000 max (for law, medicine, dentistry and veterinary science students). **Career Development Loan** – £300 up to £8,000 (vocational courses of between one week and two years, see Chapter 9) |
| HSBC | **Professional Study Loan** – up to £5,000 plus course fees for each year of study (medical, dental and veterinary students). |

# Learn to love your lender

### PICKING A BANK

A quick summary then.

Faced with the fountain of freebies and the glut of goodies on offer from every high street bank, it's almost as hard to choose a bank as it was to choose a university.

They nearly all provide online and telephone banking services, and most offer interest-fee prearranged overdrafts, preferential rates on loans, and probably staff who'll perform sexual favours.

Don't get suckered by the gimmicks. It's worth shopping around to get the best banking deal you can.

Before deciding, you should get answers to the following questions:

- How much interest will you get on money in your account for the short period that you happen to be in credit (usually that's only for a few weeks after getting your first student loan instalment)? The interest is often so small you can't even fold it.
- What's your maximum overdraft limit? And check it's interest-free.
- How quickly do they expect you to pay off your debts and when?
- How nasty are the charges levied for unauthorised overdrafts? They will be nasty, but some are the stuff of nightmares.
- What are the facilities like, such as the number and location of cash machines? Is there or will there be a cash machine near where you go every day as a student (either on campus or wherever you're living)?
- Is there a branch somewhere convenient?
- If you can't get to a branch when it's open, what other banking services do they offer – such as over the phone or on the internet? What can and can't you do by phone or online?

- Do they charge anything if you use another banks cash machine and if so how much?
- Do they offer specialist advice for students and graduates?
- How easy is it to set up and cancel standing orders and direct debits?
- If you care, how sound are they? For example, do they have shady connections in other countries propping up dictatorships that abuse human rights?
- What freebies do you get and what are they really worth to you?
- Do they offer student bank loans beyond overdrafts and on what terms?
- What support will they give you once you've graduated?

Other people – especially other students – may have useful tips. They want to plug a particular bank to you or warn you off another one. Don't necessarily take what they say at face value, but a tip's a tip.

Besides, you may be able to get extra-special 'family loyalty' treatment if your parents recommend their own bank to you – ask them.

The top tip of all is to think about the long term. The freebies are all very well for as long as they last, but a relationship with a bank is something you enter for the long haul. Who's going to be offering you good deals in three years when you need to extend your overdraft for the 93rd time?

Think about the practicalities, too – which banks are most convenient? That's when it gets down to individual choice. It's all very well being told by a friend about the great deals on offer from the Scilly Isles Bank, but it's no good if you're going to want a bit of face-to-face with someone miles off the Cornish coast.

10% of something you didn't want at full price isn't a saving, it's a waste of 90% of the cost.

Make a list of your priorities, and then find the bank that most closely matches your own individual criteria.

Ultimately, you'll be doing the bank a favour by opening an account with them. In a few years, you will no longer be a student with barely two coins to rub together, but an extravagantly wealthy graduate with years of fabulous earning power ahead of you. Or something.

**2**

## STAYING FRIENDS WITH YOUR BANK MANAGER

Staying on your bank's good side is in your interests. Not only will they send you fewer stroppy letters (with the added insult of charging you for them), but you'll also get more out of them.

One of the best ways to keep in with the guys in suits is to practise sensible banking.

**Safe sex is best until you're in a long-term relationship. Sensible banking is the same – don't try anything else till you've been sleeping with money for a while.**

Here then are *Push*'s top tips for sensible banking.

### When in credit

Sensible banking doesn't mean leaving all your money in your bank account. It means doing the best for your money, and your money will do its best for you. What's more, your bank will respect you for it.

For instance, take advantage of being in credit. It won't happen often or for long.

**When you're in credit – or should that be 'if' – don't keep all your student loan or other money in your student bank account. The rate of interest will probably pay out something like 10p a year for every hundred pounds.**

Instead, transfer some of it into a separate savings account that you should keep on one side for any windfalls such as money you earn over the summer, birthday paydirt, inheritances from your long lost Aunt Maud, whatever.

Your bank manager knows that your student bank account is there for your short-term cash needs. That's why it has the overdraft facility. But just because the account might spend most of its time in the red, it doesn't mean that when you've got money your bank manager will expect you to keep more in your current account than you have to.

In fact, s/he'll probably be only too glad to open another account for you that pays interest, but that you won't be able to overdraw.

That way, while you've got money, you won't be losing out on the opportunity to make your money earn you more money.

### Cash machines just give cash, they don't print it.

Limit your cash withdrawals to one a week and don't be tempted to draw out more than you need. That will stop you blowing your budget without noticing, because you'll only ever be able to spend what you've got.

Most banks allow up to about £250 cash out per day (funds permitting, of course) – but your budget should see you taking out way less. Fifty quid is nearer the mark. On the other hand if you prefer paying for things with the genuine folding stuff, and rarely use your debit card or cheques for purchases, then you may need a bit more.

### Keep your balance

Keep a watchful eye on your balance and print out a mini-statement at least every few days to keep a check on any splashing out you may have inadvertently done on the plastic.

You'll get an official statement from the bank every month. Don't throw it away – read it, check it, and look for mistakes. Even banks make them sometimes. (Point out the mistake, even if it's a bank error in your favour. Unfortunately this game doesn't work like Monopoly – when they realise, they'll want the money back which may be tough if you've already spent it. Strangely enough, however, the mistakes are more usually tilted the other way.)

### Pen pals

Keep a record of all correspondence from your bank and reply promptly to the letters – even the nasty ones. In fact, *especially* the nasty ones.

### Check your cheques

It's all too easy to use your debit card without realising you don't have enough overdraft left to cover it.

It's even easier with cheques, because you can forget about one you wrote some time ago, but then it gets cashed and the money disappears from your account when you least expect it.

So when you use a cheque to pay for something, bear in mind that it could take several days or even weeks to go through. Similarly, when you pay a cheque into your account, it will take a while to clear – three to four working days usually.

Don't be fooled into thinking you have more money than you actually do.

Ideally, you should keep a note of what you think your bank balance should be and compare it with your monthly statement when it arrives. In reality, that may be too much to expect from most people but, believe me, there are folks out there that do it. (And they're the ones in credit.)

### Know your limits

Because unauthorised overdraft charges are higher than an airliner on acid, never exceed the limit you've agreed with your bank, and make sure you've had written confirmation from your bank of what your limit is.

Going over the limit is like being caught sleeping with someone else. Your bank may say they forgive you, but you'll always have this uneasy feeling that they don't really trust you. (And you're probably right.)

If you are having real trouble coping with the limit at its current level, talk to your bank's student adviser before it's too late. They can usually work something out.

Libraries: large places with books, quiet, full of heaters. Good for winter snoozes.

## Protect your plastic

Be very careful with your debit card (and extra careful with your credit card).

If you lose it or it gets stolen, report it immediately. Even if you think it's probably hidden somewhere and you don't want to have to wait for a new one to arrive by post, report it anyway. If it's used fraudulently by someone else, if the loss hasn't been reported you may find yourself at best doing some embarrassing explaining – and at worst, shelling out yourself.

Don't even think about 'kiting' – see Chapter 9.

Don't keep your chequebook and your cheque guarantee card together. If they're both stolen, you could have your entire account cleaned out.

Don't write your PIN down. Keep it to yourself and be careful that nobody's checking it out over your shoulder when you use the machine.

**And never, ever, put your card behind the bar for a tab. You'll end up drinking more than you intended, and every pisshead in the bar will be putting their drinks on your slate. You'll wake up feeling sick, skint and sorry.**

Part 2: How much will you have?
Chapter 7

# Working
## for dough

PART TIME=£

Most students work at some point during their time at university
or college.

Some of them even work at their studies – but never mind
that, most do *paid* work for readies.

For some it's the only way they can afford to do any
travelling over the summer. For others, it's the only way they can
justify more than one pint in the student bar. For all too many,
however, it's the only way they can keep their finances from
going into free-fall.

At any one time, over a third of students have regular part-
time jobs to supplement their income during term-time. Then
there are the temp jobs in the vacations.

And the proportion is on the up. Three-quarters of all
students take on paid work at some time during their
university career.

**THE PROS**
**Working for money has its advantages.**

**For starters, there's the money. Don't underestimate the
importance of that.**

**Some jobs – however dull – offer a break from academic
work. Sometimes the more mindless they are, the better.**

And many have great little perks such as staff discounts (if
you work in a shop) or free food and drink (if you work in
catering).

There's also the fact that, quite apart from making money, most jobs – because they take up so much of your time – stop you doing anything that might involve spending money.

If you work behind a bar, for instance, you can't spend all your evenings on the other side of it handing over cash. What's more, you don't lose out entirely when it comes to socialising with the people who do spend all their time and money in there.

There's also the work experience. Most part-time or temporary student jobs may not quite be rungs on the career ladder, but there is the opportunity to work in a variety of different work environments, to meet new people and to learn new skills. It all adds horsepower to your CV.

Even if you're just pulling pints at your local bar or scanning barcodes at the supermarket, every little helps. It proves you can be relied on to show your face regularly and not hurl abuse at your boss or the customers. Both valuable assets in an employee and rarer than you might imagine.

Ultimately, having to work usually boosts a student's employability and therefore not only their present, but also their future, finances.

As more graduates turn out with work experience, employers get more choosy about what they expect from the top recruits. Whatever you can do to make yourself stand out as jobworthy is worthwhile.

Employers want all the buzzwords and phrases — highly developed communication and interpersonal skills, teamwork, ability to meeting deadlines, IT literacy, numeracy, the ability to stay calm in a crisis, initiative, managerial potential, quick and reasoned decision-making and a demonstrable analytical approach – all that waffle. Scary, but true.

Doing a job helps prove you've got at least some of them and, with luck, your degree does the rest.

Oh and did we mention the money?

**Set up an e-commerce website featuring voyeuristic webcams showing your housemates' bedrooms.**

Save coupons. No, really. We're serious.

## THE CONS

Ideally, of course, students should spend every waking moment with their minds bent on the high ideas involved in their studies.

Whilst it's not true that if you've got a job you can't possibly get a good degree, it is important to maintain your perspective.

**You're doing the job to support your studies and your studies should come first. However, if your boss is more pushy than your tutor – and, since s/he is paying you, s/he probably will be – when it comes to a choice, it's often your studies that are left behind while you go out to work.**

Universities usually recommend that students do no more than 15 hours work a week, but most students who work ignore the recommendations. The average is around 20 hours.

It sometimes hard to find a job that offers the right number of hours at the right times and which has the flexibility to let you rearrange your hours once in a while if you have a study commitment.

It's not just class work that's important. Students have to make time for individual study – in fact, quite a bit of it. If it means missing an essay deadline or skipping a lecture or seminar, you shouldn't be going to work.

To put in the hours both studying and working for money, something's gotta give. Just make sure it's the right thing. There's no point finishing your degree without debt if you don't pass.

Then again, stressing about your debts isn't exactly conducive to good study, so there's a whole swings and roundabouts scenario going on here.

The solution for some people is to work full-time and study on a part-time basis. That's your call, but unless you've got a good job that you want to hang on to and you're in no hurry to get qualified, you might find yourself higher on the stress scale and not an whole lot better off, because you aren't eligible for the same support.

**Oxbridge**

At Oxford and Cambridge, the terms are shorter than usual – just eight weeks – and the level of academic intensity during that time is turned up a bit. They – and other universities with short terms – are a bit firmer about what students should and shouldn't do to make ends meet.

Term-time jobs get a big frown and, although you might get away with it if you keep quiet, if there's any hint of conflict with your studies it'll be a them-or-us situation.

You'd have thought that longer vacations mean you could just make up the money doing full-time temp work. Afraid not. At Oxbridge, you tend to get almost as much work set between terms as during them – and if you don't, then you'll probably want to get ahead on next term's reading list while there's time.

Finding the time for more than a couple of hours of paid work a week is not easy and anyway it's hard to find jobs with such minimal commitment of time. But on the up-side, Oxbridge students tend to have fewer financial problems – partly because more than 40% went to private schools and partly because the collegiate system with most students living in college is quite cheap way of doing things.

# Finding a Job

**WHAT KIND OF WORK AM I MOST LIKELY TO FIND?**

Clearly not every job is suitable for students. After all most involve going to work during the day.

There are some obvious candidates, however – casual work in bars, restaurants and hotels (and catering in general), shops and supermarkets. Other that get a look in include childminding and care work, cleaning, warehouse jobs, market research and temporary office work.

**If you fancy something a bit more unusual, how about life modelling for artists, being a teaching assistant, a psychologist's guinea pig, telesales, DJing, taxi-driving, nightclub bouncing or exotic dancing.**

Depending on what you're willing and able to do, there's really no such thing as a typical job.

It's worth trying to think of the jobs that don't require you to do much more than sit there, occasionally move about a bit doing stuff and then sit there again – night security, for instance, or baby-sitting (once the kid's in bed). You can use the time for study – or at least reading – and, bonus, you get paid for it.

**When dropping in on friends, try to time it just as they're about to eat.**

### JOBSHOPS AND JOB OPPS

Although they'd rather their students didn't have to work for money, most universities came to terms with the reality of the situation a while ago.

And if you can't beat 'em, join 'em.

Most universities now have a **jobshop** based on campus – basically a job agency that finds employment for students and finds students for employers. These are different from the university careers offices which try to find jobs for students once they've graduated. Jobshops find work during the vacations and, sometimes, part-time jobs during term.

Jobshops, however, do more than your bog standard temp agency – apart from anything else, they don't usually take a slice off your wage packet (or if they do, it's a smaller one than usual).

Their difference to employers is that they specialise in students, which, to many of them, is a good thing. Students tend to be intelligent, keen, polite and, on average, no less reliable than anyone else. Most importantly, however, students are cheap.

**Their difference to students is that jobshops specialise in jobs for students. The vacancies they've got tend to be the ones that have some flexibility over hours and where the boss understands some of the commitments students have to juggle.**

Jobshops are in a good position to do a nice bit of matching. But their responsibilities usually go further. Often they'll exercise a cut-off point on wages.

For most people the minimum wage (as of October 2001) is £4.10 an hour, but for 18 to 21 year-olds, it's only £3.20 an hour. Many jobshops impose their own minimum of around £3.50 – sometimes higher – and they'll tell employers looking for slave labour to shove it.

Jobshops will also sometimes lay down the law on other things, such as better-than-minimum working conditions, holiday pay and so on. (Even part-time workers are entitled to paid leave.) How successful they are depends on how needy the local job market is.

One of the biggest local employers of students tends to be the university itself, which smacks just a tad of hypocrisy – but who's complaining?

Universities often need people to work in bars, shops, cafés and cafeterias or cleaning rooms, doing admin work, looking after conference guests, serving drinks at functions, looking after new and prospective students, even phoning former students and asking them to donate generously to the vice-chancellor's retirement fund. All ideal work for students.

There are often still more jobs going at the students' union, which is the student-run organisation that usually manages most of the bars, shops, nightclubs and other non-academic services for students within the university. As often as not, it's the students' union that runs the jobshop and it employs students to do it.

Some universities are in areas so devoid of job opportunities that the jobshop doesn't even bother to try to find jobs for students off-campus and lists only vacancies on offer from the uni itself or the students' union.

Tempting as it sounds to go and drink yourself to death each night, I suggest you only take a small amount of cash with you so you can't spend too much. (Also, stick to drink soft drinks only – they're cheaper. Yeah, right – as if.)

James Williamson, Bishop's Stortford College

Every jobshop operates slightly differently and some might just as well try to find Ann Widdecombe a date for Saturday night as try to find you a job. Either they're not very good at it or there just aren't the openings out there. (By 'openings' we mean job opportunities – we not talking about Ann Widdecombe any more, okay? Ugh, nasty thought.)

Flexible evening and weekend work is easier to come by in a large city than in a small town and it's often possible to get longer shifts during holidays or even go full-time if you're jammy.

If, however, you're at university is Smallsville, you'll probably want to head home for the holidays to find work. (Unless, of course, you come from Tinytown.)

Obviously, if it's not local work you're looking for, your university jobshop will be less use than a cricket bat in a snow storm. So, a few weeks before the end of term, get in touch with a few agencies or businesses near your home. That way you avoid the post-term flood of students.

**Christmas is an especially good time to find shop work and summer is, of course, tourist season. Lots of big companies have summer vacation schemes, sometimes called internships (see below), of usually between four and eight weeks.**

## OTHER PLACES TO LOOK

Most student jobshops worth their salt come up with something within a few weeks if there's anything to come up with.

But what do you do if they draw a blank? Or there is no jobshop? Not even a vacancies noticeboard?

The local job centre may be able to help, but their main priority will be getting jobs for the unemployed, not (as they may see it) feathering the nest of students who're already sitting on a cosy little egg of a future.

Local newspapers, employment agencies and even postcards in newsagents' windows may be a better bet. Some temping agencies specialise in finding short-term assignments for young people – the work tends to be menial, but if it's really crap you can turn it down. Sign up with more than one if the work is a bit thin on the ground.

Also, try the university's own bulletin – not the student newspaper, but whatever newsletter the authorities produce for staff. Or why not just barge into the uni's conference office and see what they've got.

Don't be afraid to go into a pub, a restaurant or a shop on spec and ask. What's the worst they can say?

> **Never buy your own drinks. Invest in a Wonderbra and practise smiling alluringly. I covered the cost of my holiday in Spain exclusively by being treated to drinks.**
>
> **Francoise, University of Edinburgh**

Even if the jobshop can't find you anything, they should be able to give you advice. And if there's no jobshop, the careers office might be turned on to a few ideas and opportunities.

Ultimately, if the regular avenues turn into dead-ends, it's important to try the alleys that other people haven't. Chances are there's a job going somewhere that someone's desperate to fill, it's just that they're not trying the right channels. If you can tune in to same channels, you may find you're the only person chasing the job.

Lateral thinking is called for.

If, for instance, it's coming up to Easter, think about who does a lot of business then. A quick phone call to Thornton's the chocolate egg-makers and you may find yourself helping them meet the extra demand (not to mention acquiring a revulsion to chocolate). Or, since the horse-racing and big sporting seasons are just getting under way around then, maybe the bookies will need someone numerate.

You can even advertise your own services – childminding, house cleaning, dog walking, gardening, DIY, underpants scouring, etc. And how about teaming up with a friend or two and offering yourselves as a multi-skilled 'student workforce'?

Back to the windows of the newsagents and corner shops. But this time, you could be putting up a postcard for about 50p a week.

If you're offering services, however, a couple of things to bear in mind. You may find you need to provide references, to prove you can do what you're advertising and that you're reliable. It's also best if you can find someone to check out anyone you're working for.

With certain jobs, such as childminding, there may be legal dimensions that you're not aware of. A bit of babysitting's not a problem, but pretending to offer a full-scale crèche could land you in more than a pile of smelly nappies.

Get advice from the jobshops, careers service or the local Citizen's Advice Bureau if you're worried.

There are also some useful web addresses in the back of the book that are worth a surf.

### HOW MUCH CAN I EARN?

Obviously it depends what you do. Students usually end up working in pubs, bars, restaurants and shops, receiving something like £3.50 to £4.50 an hour.

If they stick to the university's recommendation of no more than 15 hours a week, that should bring them an extra £52.50 to £60 a week, but there may be things like tax and National Insurance (NI) to worry about (see below).

**Doing the average 20 hours a week at £4.37 (the National Union of Students' estimate of the average wage), students can boost their income by £87.40 a week before tax and NI.**

If you did that every week, that would put more than £4,500 into the right side of your budget equation, but the fact is that, one way or another, you're unlikely to do it for more than about seven months. Over the summer, you may well not be around and, during May and June, you'll probably have exams to worry about which are definitely more important than paid work.

**So, assuming you can find any work at all and assuming that it pays okay and assuming you can do it enough for hours and weeks to make it worthwhile, then you could hope to earn about two grand a year as a student.**

**But don't rely on it when it comes to calculating your budget (see Chapter 14) until you know what you're really likely to receive.**

## Tips

Working in a restaurant, you might receive a lower basic wage (remember, it's illegal for them to offer less than £3.20 an hour), but there will probably be tips on top of that. If you're taking a job with tips, check out the employer's policy. Some places will let you keep your own. At others, they split them equally and, occasionally, you find a tosser boss who pockets the lot. Sometimes, the boss pockets only the tips on credit card slips and you get any cash.

Tips can double your wages but, of course, don't – we repeat, don't – forget you are supposed to pay tax and NI on tips too. Definitely, supposed to. Okay? So, we told you *not* to just keep shtum. Right? So long as we've got that straight.

## Aiming high

If you're a risk-taker, there are opportunities to make a lot more money – but the risk is that you make less, nothing or even lose out.

For instance, there are selling jobs out there that are 'commission-only'. You get a cut of any sales you make. The problem is, if you make nothing, you get nothing.

It's a mug's game, really, but if you reckon you could sell toilet roll to a constipated deaf man with no arms (or, even tougher, advertising space to small businesses), you might just hit the jackpot and rake in a lot more than most students.

Other high-stakes games including starting your own business. There are plenty of eighties throw-back entrepreneurs out there paying their way through university with their wheeling and dealing skills.

Among the popular ideas are running club nights and events, hiring out evening dress to students for balls, launching magazines and selling second-hand designer gear.

As we said, these are the popular ideas – in other words, other people try them regularly and most fail. Make sure there's a market with a gap in it and minimise your potential to lose big-time.

# Other avenues for work

## UNPAID WORK AND WORK EXPERIENCE

It may sound crazy, but it might pay in the long run to consider working for nothing, especially if looking for paid work is proving harder than hunting for condoms in a convent.

### Work experience

A week or two of unpaid work experience during your vacation doesn't cost you anything but effort and may be prove to be a clincher if you're trying to something highly competitive when you graduate (such as advertising, the media or banking).

Apart from the obvious benefits for your CV, it may boost your morale and, if you make yourself genuinely useful, they may even think of you if anything that pays crops up. Ultimately, it beats chasing non-existent jobs.

Don't let any employer take advantage of you, though. Even if they don't pay you, they should at least give you expenses for travel and maybe even lunch.

Just a quick plug for *Push*'s own scheme – our research team is made up high-flying students and recent graduates. We do pay, but we're the first to admit it's less than the researchers are worth.

Over the years, because we only skim off the cream of students, it's come to be a well-respected feather in your cap as far as employers are concerned – especially in publishing, market research and the media. So, if your cap could do with feathering, check out *Push Online* (www.push.co.uk).

Never, ever use your debit (or credit) card for a 'tab' behind the bar. You'll invariably end up feeling sick, skint and sorry.

### Voluntary work

There are profound advantages to voluntary work that have much greater meaning than money. Spirituality. Inner peace. A sense of giving and knowledge that your life has touched others'.

You don't buy that hippy stuff? Okay. Try this…

**Future potential employers will be very impressed by your obvious goodwill and determined spirit. I mean, volunteering is all very well, but when you're rapidly becoming a charity case yourself, you want to see some benefits.**

But back to the hippy stuff. It really does make a difference to thousands of projects going on in developing countries, not to mention the countless projects all over the UK.

There's everything from conservation work (the National Trust, who look after historic monuments and land) to helping the disabled (the Winged Fellowship Trust), from animal welfare (the RSPCA, animal shelters and other organisations that Rolf Harris interferes with) to the elderly (Help the Aged, who are more than just a song by Pulp).

There are almost always restrictions and conditions involved with helping out any of these schemes and while some organisations will pay general maintenance and travel, don't rely on it. Many schemes (such as Earthwatch, who do cool conservation projects all over the world) will even expect you to fork out big sums in order to be allowed to help.

Even so, it's well worth investigating the options. It's another line on the CV and will give you an inner feeling of harmony, man.

Most students' unions have a Student Community Action group that does work with all sorts of local projects . Some are more active than others. Some are less active than lead.

### INTERNSHIPS AND TRAINEE SCHEMES

Monica Lewinsky was an intern at the White House when she did not have sex with that man. But not every internship promises to teach you quite so many uses for a cigar.

**The idea is that by spending a certain period working in an environment, you get an idea of what goes on and how to do it. There may even be a certain amount of showing you the ropes,**

but as often as not an intern is a fancy word for a gofer (as in 'gofer a cup of coffee, milk and two sugars, please').

Still, an internship or trainee scheme – especially a genuine one – is not only useful work experience. Since they're usually in high demand, it's like having a neon sign on your CV. It may even be a first step towards getting yourself a proper job with the organisation.

Best of all, they're often paid – not brilliantly, but what do you expect?

You may find them advertised in university careers advice centre and there are guidebooks that list them (though the information is out of date almost before they hit the bookshops).

Getting a place could involve an in-depth interview or even a series of interviews (especially if there's a chance that they might end up giving you a job after graduation).

The big, corporate companies are always on the lookout for the next bright young thing, but it's often a case of hundreds of applicants for every vacancy.

## FILLING THE GAP

Back in Chapter 2, we looked at the whole issue of taking a year out – the pros and cons. So this is just a reminder that rather than work as a student when you've got studying to do, there's always the possibility of working first.

There are dangers – the biggest of which is that you get hooked on the idea of having money and decide that you don't want to go back to education.

Alternatively, you may develop expensive tastes in the meantime – or if not exactly expensive, they may not be as cheap as they should be if you want to stay solvent as a student.

The other big danger is that you spend all year working in order to make life more comfortable as a student, yet you don't actually save anything. Or worse, you get a headstart in the debt race. What a waste of a gap year that would be.

**If you're going to spend the year saving, then save. If not, then make the most of it. Travel the world, save the planet – and just make sure you don't get into debt before you start.**

**It is, of course, possible to travel and save. Just about. Find yourself a cushy job somewhere exotic, then have a whale of a time and come back tanned and flushed.**

Meanwhile, back in Blighty, there are plenty of year out programmes that offer work, experience and even, sometimes, the possibility of earning a few knicker.

For example, there is an organisation called **The Year in Industry** that places gap year students with companies all over the UK ,in jobs paying about £150 a week minimum. Getting a temporary placement through this scheme can be a bit of a door-opener and may give you sound business awareness, confidence and practical skills before you even start your university course.

There are regional centres for The Year in Industry all over the place, which schools and colleges usually know about. Alternatively, write to them at the address in the back of this book. We've also listed contact details for a number of other gap year organisations, including BUNAC and Health Projects Abroad.

There are specialist organisations tailored for adventurous students interested in art, science, conservation projects, amateur dramatics, sporting activities, wilderness exploration, teaching... just about anything that floats your boat.

## JOBS ABROAD

If you haven't gone for the Gap Year option and you have a serious case of wanderlust, remember you still have that gorgeous three-month summer holiday from the beginning of July to the end of September each and every year for the duration of your course.

And three months is plenty of time to organise a few weeks abroad, get yourself a cheap travel ticket and hop on a plane to a far-flung destination.

Backpacking and inter-railing are notoriously popular with plucky student adventurers and there's no shortage of cheap travel firms, advice books and organisations.

Assuming you can afford it.

If you've blown your loan months ago, maxed out the overdraft and can't afford a holiday, then you face three options.

First off, don't go. Secondly, spend most of the summer working at some no-brain job and saving up for a week or two at the end.

Or thirdly, get a paid job abroad. You can work on a kibbutz, supervise children on a summer holiday camp, be a nanny or an au pair (even if you're a bloke, if you think you're hard enough), teach, pick fruit, help run a hotel, assist a new business venture, pan for gold…

**If working abroad over the summer appeals to you, make enquiries well in advance and, if you want to join a particular scheme, apply as soon as possible (at least six months in advance) to beat the rush.**

It's a big bonus if you can speak a second language. Failing that, try America, Australia or New Zealand (where they almost speak English).

If you are going to be travelling to a country where you either don't speak the lingo or it's a bit rusty, consider taking a language refresher course – even if it only gives you enough to get by. Many universities offer them cheap to their own students, but often only during term-time – so plan ahead.

You don't even have to have the cost of the airfare to get abroad. BUNAC (details in the back) have introduced a deal to give interest-free airfare loans to cash-strapped students, who can then pay the money back as and when they begin paid work overseas. If you get work on the Summer Camp USA and KAMP programmes then your flights are usually paid for.

Even if you get a deal like this, however, don't leave home without enough dough (or some means of getting cash – such as plastic) to cover you for at least your first month. It can take easily that long for your first pay cheque to come through. If you're going to have to rent somewhere to stay, take enough to cover not only the rent, but the deposit too.

Buy a return ticket (not just a one-way), so if things go pear-shaped – financially or otherwise – you can at least get home.

Working abroad presents a swamp of practical puddles. You need a visa to work in some countries. You may need injections. You may not be allowed to work at all. To get into Malawi, men must have hair shorter than collar length. Honestly.

Preparation is your safety net. Take plenty of passport photos for assorted forms and ID cards.

Talk to other students who've worked abroad. Ask them for tips and contacts. Even if you've no intention of getting in touch with their second cousin once removed who lives on the other side of the country you heading to, it may come in handy to have their number. When you land in jail for inadvertently giving a rude hand gesture when you only meant to hail a cab, it's good to have someone to call.

At *Push*, of course, we have our own useful contacts for you. They're at the back of the book under 'Summer Work Abroad'.

We recommend Usit Campus (www.usitcampus.co.uk). Every years, they put together fact sheets (mostly for European countries) for students, full of practical advice and stories from past students who worked abroad. They can also help with any visa applications and their website has recommended jobs and links.

Save money on central heating by staying in bed throughout the winter.

# Sandwich Courses

Sandwich courses are nothing to do with bread and fillings unless they happen to be sandwich courses in catering.

It's a metaphor. The bread symbolises slices of academic study. The filling is job experience on a work placement. In order to fit in the filling, most sandwich degree courses are four years rather than three.

The metaphor doesn't always work so neatly, because although there are **'thick' sandwich courses** that involve a year or two at university, a year in work and then another year back at university, many sandwich courses involve more than one layer of filling and in only six-month layers. They call these **'thin' sandwich courses**, but if you think about it, many 'club' sandwich courses would be truer to the trope.

We're clearly too hung up on the food thing.

Basically, sandwich courses – thin, thick, club, toasted, whatever – are those that involve an industrial placement as a compulsory part of the course.

**This can be the answer to every strapped student's woes, because they usually get paid for the working part of their course.**

It's rarely as much as they'd get if they were doing the job as a fully paid-up employee, but that's what's in it for the employer. The student gets to do their course and the employer gets someone cheap but capable.

As a result, sandwich students tend to have fewer financial worries than most. Better still, sandwich courses also have a pretty good record of getting students into jobs when they graduate, quite often with a company where they did a placement.

It's not all pay day and high living, though. There are added expenses for sandwich students. For example, you'll probably have to own a couple of smart outfits and there'll be dry cleaning bills to pay (something students normally only have to cover when they throw up on someone's ball outfit).

Then there's the effect on fees, awards and loans to consider.

### AWARDS AND TUITION FEES FOR SANDWICH COURSES

If a work placement takes up a full year of the course, at home or abroad, they'll cut the cost of your fees for that year in half – currently £535. That also means that, in turn, your LEA won't pay an award of more than £535 to cover them.

For anything less than a full year, the full fees will still be charged and the full award will still be available to those who're eligible.

The same rules apply about who's eligible for awards and fees and who's not. See Chapter 3.

### STUDENT LOANS FOR SANDWICH COURSES

Students on sandwich courses get a reduced level of student loan for any year in which they spend more than half the year doing a paid placement. It's just under half the maximum available normally, but at least it's not means-tested.

**YES**

You don't have to be on a sandwich course to get a bite of that particular snack.

Back in the early eighties, Aberystwyth University introduced a highly successful scheme called **YES – the Year in Employment Scheme**, which gives non-sandwich students the opportunity to take a year out in a work placement – whatever their own degree course.

There are over 100 different types of placement and they're more varied than a packet of M&Ms, with several of them being abroad and most of them paid. In fact, unless you're working for a voluntary organisation like a charity, most students on placements get between £8,000 and £20,000 a year.

That sure fills a whole in your bank balance.

The icing on the cake (or sandwich) for participating students, apart from the personal and career development prospects and the financial boost, is that they don't have to pay any tuition fees during the year.

# Student Tax Guide

### INCOME TAX

Taxes are like Alcatraz after closing time. Nobody escapes taxes.

That goes for students, same as everyone. The difference is that although students have to pay income tax, the amount is usually zero. The difference may be subtle, but paying nothing is not the same as escaping them.

**Everyone get a personal non-taxable allowance which is the amount you're allowed to earn before the Government starts taking a cut. Tax years run from April to April (don't ask why – it's something to do with medieval sheep markets) and for the tax year ending 5 April 2002, the personal tax allowance is £4,535.**

So if, between 6 April 2001 and 5 April 2002, you earn or receive income above £4,353, you'll have to pay income tax – although you only have to pay tax on the amount above the allowance, not on the whole lot. The more you earn the more you pay, but at first it's only 10%.

Loans and awards don't count as income. Nor do scholarships or bursaries. So really, we're talking about what you receive from paid work and there aren't too many students doing full-time courses who'll be earning more than four-and-a-half grand in a year.

So if you get part-time work or a vacation job, make sure your boss knows you're a student. They should have the appropriate forms which you'll both need to fill in and sign – they're not complicated, for a change, although you'll need your National Insurance (NI) number.

For temp jobs, the relevant form is called a P38(S) and for term-time work it's a P46. Where they come up with these crazy names, we'll never know.

Once you've filled in the forms, tax shouldn't be taken out of your wages. If you don't, however, it'll be deducted automatically. All is not lost if this happens. You can claim back any tax that you needn't have paid from the Inland Revenue at the end of the tax year, but it's a bit of a hassle and it does mean it's in their account rather than yours in the meantime.

**Give up smoking.**

**Eugene Lewis, LSE**

The students who are most likely to end up paying more than nothing in income tax are those doing work placements (usually as part of a sandwich course, see above).

What they receive from their employer is subject to tax, although there are sneaky get-out clauses for certain money earned by certain students meeting certain conditions.

It's one to check out with your students' union officer or Tax Office.

**Students with savings or investments might also end up paying tax if the income generated takes them over the £4,535 threshold. And if they've got that much stashed away, why not?**

If, however, you have smaller savings, get in touch with whoever is paying interest or returns on those investments and ask that the money be paid gross (ie. without the tax being taken off before they give it to you). That'll save you claiming the money back.

And if you find you're getting near the threshold, let them know and they can start deducting the tax again.

Taxes are one of those things that are a total headache in life. Few people ever get their head round them properly and even if they do, the Chancellor only goes and changes all the rules at the next Budget anyway.

At some time while you're a student, you will almost certainly need advice about either paying or claiming back tax. When those times come, your local tax office is there to help or you can visit www.inlandrevenue.gov.uk, where you might want to get hold of any or all of the following leaflets, each more thrilling than a night in the bath with Dale Winton, a loofa and a packet of ginger nuts:

- Income Tax and Students (IR60)
- Income Tax and School Leavers (IR33)
- Pay as you earn (PAYE) (IR34)
- A Guide to Tax Allowances and Reliefs (IR90)
- A Guide for People with Savings (IR110)

## NATIONAL INSURANCE (NI)

NI is separate from tax although it's collected by the same people at the Inland Revenue. In theory it pays towards your state pension and so on. You can't opt out of it, so it feels pretty much the same as a tax.

It's taken out of your salary by your employer who then pays it to the Inland Revenue (along with a little bit extra they have to add).

It's not much and how much you pay is related to how much you earn, but, unlike income tax, there's no allowance.

Part 2: How much will you have?
Chapter 8

# Scholarships, Sponsorships, Bursaries & Grants

## Money for nothing

The problem with awards is they only pay towards tuition costs. The problem with loans is you have to pay them back. The problem with working for money is, well... working.

Wouldn't it be nice if you could get money for nothing?

It's not quite as crazy as it sounds. There are various ways of getting money, if not for nothing, for very little at least.

**Scholarships, sponsorships, bursaries and grants (sounds like a firm of solicitors) are all different ways of putting the fun into funding. Well, okay, 'fun' may be pushing it, but at least they take away some of the misery.**

You don't hear much about them because it's not as if there's a ocean of money flooding the universities. It's more like a puddle, with too many people jostling to suck it up through straws.

Nonetheless, this puddle is in fact worth many millions of quid a year. That's the kind of puddle I would mind getting splashed by.

However, most of the deals are either incredibly competitive or so specific that most students can't apply anyway. They don't get much publicity because that would only mean even more students being disappointed about not getting money, money that they wouldn't have otherwise known was even on offer.

**What this means, however, is that a little research on your part can go a long way. It's like a lottery that not many people know about. Even fewer can win, but just by finding out about it at all, you've got through the first stage of filtering out the losers.**

Hunting down these sources of funding can be time-consuming, but don't be put off – there are more educational charities, trust funds, foundations and other professional organisations in the UK than you can shake a stick at. Though why you'd want to is anyone's guess.

Most rule out almost everyone from even applying, which means you won't get too many bites at the cherry. But it also means that if you find one that doesn't rule you out from even applying, you may be one of only a few applicants.

It's also worth noting that you can receive up to £4,000 from bursaries and scholarships without it affecting whether you qualify for an award or student loan. Unfortunately, you're unlikely to get anything like that much.

So how do you go about finding one? Start by getting in touch with some of the specialist organisations listed in the back of this book and taking a look at some of the recommended reading. But before you go and do all that, you'll want to read this chapter first to know what it's all about.

Set up a household kitty for shopping and bills. Everyone puts in equally. Then shop, cook and eat with your housemates. It works out cheaper, not only because buying in bulk is cheaper than for one, but also because everyone's competing to get their money's worth so they eat at home more often which is cheaper.

# So what are scholarships, sponsorships, bursaries and grants and how do they differ?

Once upon a time, the word 'grant' used to follow the word 'student' around like a devoted puppy. But since the funding system was shaken up way back in ancient history – the 1990s – there are no student grants any more. Student Grant, RIP. Or not from LEAs, anyhow. (Except in certain circumstances – see Chapter 13).

**2**

These days, 'grant' refers to any kind of money-for-nothing or money-for-not-much kind of deal. It's become a vague word that we shouldn't waste any more time on.

So moving swiftly on. The other three terms are all used fairly inexactly, too. You can use one instead of the other, in pretty much the same way that you don't really need to know the different members of The Corrs. (Just for the record, they're Shouty, Sticky, Fiddly and Ken.)

There are distinctions between them, but there's as much difference between individual bursary deals, for example, as there is between the whole categories of bursaries and scholarships. And sponsorship deals may include bursaries and scholarships may have sponsors and so on.

Having said that you can't really tell the difference, that's exactly what we're now going to try to do, by laying down a few general rules. Just go a bit easy on us when we have to make wild, sweeping generalisations, okay?

So here are some brief explanations to kick us off, with more detailed dissections below...

### BURSARIES

A bursary is a contribution of money – a 'grant', if you like (although maybe we shouldn't start all that again) – given to a student, that doesn't have to be repaid and doesn't require them to do anything special to get it. It may – in fact, usually does – have certain qualifying conditions, but that's all.

Like we said, money for nothing. Conditions attached, but no strings.

120

## SPONSORSHIPS

Sponsorships come from companies or organisations who have something to gain from giving you money, but it may not be anything that they get from you personally. A sponsorship will often include a 'bursary' (told you it got messy) awarded during term-time while you are studying.

Your sponsor may expect you to work for them before, during or after your course. But then they may well pay you extra for that work anyway, so who's complaining?

The strings attached to sponsorship are of varying thickness and can often be untied in any case. Even students on NHS-funded courses, for example, don't have to work for the NHS when they finish their courses.

## SCHOLARSHIPS

Broadly speaking, scholarships plug whoever gives them – like a sponsorship – whilst giving a financial pat on the back to the students who get them for their personal achievements. That's usually the main criteria for getting a scholarship – you've done well at something or you're likely to.

Scholarships don't usually involve any industrial or commercial training or trade-off for favours that come with a sponsorship, but they may not be entirely without other strings.

# Bursaries

We're about to invent another distinction that doesn't really exist – between standard and special bursaries.

By 'standard bursaries' we mean ones that are pretty much open to everyone –so long as they meet the rigid conditions.

By 'special bursaries', we mean ones that are exclusive to particular institutions or one-off arrangements that don't get easily slotted into boxes.

If you're round at someone's house and they leave you alone in the room, check down the back and sides of their sofa and chairs for loose change.

> Try to buy your textbooks second-hand.
> They're cheaper and the good bits are
> probably already underlined.

### STANDARD BURSARIES

Depending on your age, where you're studying, where you live, your background, your status, your personal academic success, your choice of course and probably how often you finished your greens as a kid, you may well be entitled to one of the standard bursaries in the table on the next pages.

The first three are classed as 'discretionary help' and are based on individual circumstances – like being too broke to go to university without them.

The other two (the NHS bursaries) are only for medical courses of different types (see Chapter 10 for the full list of eligible courses and more about the tuition fees involved). If you want an NHS bursary, it doesn't matter if you've already done a degree and received public funding for it, you'll still be eligible.

For other healthcare courses you might get a bursary, depending on whether you can afford it without one.

In some cases, by the way, if you get an NHS bursary, because it gives you money you don't have to repay you won't be able to get a student loan as well or additional help from Access funds (see Chapter 9).

If you want to find out more about careers in the NHS and getting financial help from them whilst studying, call their careers helpline on 0845 6060655 or visit www.nhscareers.nhs.uk.

Also enquire at your university to see if they offer any special bursaries. Some are open to all students, while others will be restricted to high-fliers on a designated degree course. They also have additional awards available including golf bursaries and endowment prizes. Other awards a university might offer are bursaries for law, accountancy, science, engineering and music. Securing an award may require a written exam and/or exceptionally high A Level grades.

| Type of bursary | NHS bursary for medical and dental courses | NHS bursary for health professional courses |
|---|---|---|
| **What is it?** | Bursaries and help with tuition fees for the final years of study. | Grants and allowances to help students on full- or part-time pre-registration course for health professionals. For full details about the help available, call the NHS Student Grants Unit on:<br>England: 01253 332 627<br>Wales: 02920 826 893<br>Scotland: 0131 244 4669<br>NI: 02890 257 777 |
| **Am I eligible?** | UK undergrads doing standard 5 or 6 year medical and dental courses (or those on the four-year graduate entry programmes). | You must be accepted for an NHS-funded place. If you are not eligible for a NHS bursary, you may still be entitled to help from your LEA or university. |
| **How much and how is it paid?** | Depending on your specific course and place of study, you'll get your tuition fees covered for your fourth, fifth and sixth years of study. You'll also be eligible to apply for a reduced-rate student loan for those years (but not till you've completed the first year at least) and a means-tested grant for living expenses. Additional allowances for mature students, single parents or those with dependents or disabilities. | Allowances and awards up to £4,805 are available depending on status, but the NHS will pay your tuition fees in full whether you're studying at degree or diploma level and may give an income-assessed grant for living expenses. Payments are made monthly. |
| **How do I apply?** | If you are offered a place on a NHS-funded health-professional course, your college will tell the NHS Student Grants Unit (SGU). The SGU will then contact you directly with an application pack which you should return to them as soon as possible. | |

| Mature Student Bursary (see also Chapter 13) | Opportunity Bursary | Access Bursary |
| --- | --- | --- |
| An award to help with course-related costs, especially childcare. Many students who received access bursaries in 2000/01 will receive the new childcare grants in 2001/2. | A new award for students studying in one of the Government's 'Excellence in Cities' LEAs in England. | An award for students who need extra help because they have children to look after. Also read about Hardship Funds and Access Loans in Chapter 9. |
| Students over 25. These bursaries are intended mainly for students who got a Discretionary Access Bursary (see above) in their first year. | Available to students between 18 and 21 from families on low incomes if there is little or no experience of higher education within the family. | Full-time student parents (and those studying part-time to be teachers) who do not receive the lone parents' grant or mature student bursary. |
| Up to £1,000, paid by your university. It doesn't have to be repaid. | Up to £6,000 total in bursaries of £2,000 a year. Individual universities decide whether or not to award anything to applicants. | Up to £500 a year. Cases assessed individually. |
| Ask your university's student services department. They'll decide who to award, and how much. (For help, talk to your students' union welfare department). | If your school or college is within one of the targeted areas, they'll have more information. Ask you careers advisor. Alternatively, ask at the university you're applying to. | Ask your university's student services department (or your students' union welfare department). |

## SPECIAL BURSARIES

Most special bursaries and the like are only available at a particular university and some universities have a lot more than others. Since most of them are endowments from charities and ex-students, the longer a place has been around, the more likely it is to have stocked up on the goodies. Something to think about when choosing your university, perhaps.

Often the money has to be spent on something in particular, such as travel or research costs, but, hey, it's their money – at least it's you who gets to spend it.

The catch is that you usually have to meet the right criteria for whatever hand-out is on offer. These tend to fall into three categories – being good at something, being a particular type of person or doing a particular course. Occasionally, there's a fourth: behaving in a particular way. Often it's a mixture of any of them.

So, being good at something. You see? The distinction between bursaries and scholarships is crumbling before our eyes.

The most obvious thing to be good at is studying and there are millions of pounds in awards, scholarships, prizes, studentships, grants and bursaries for the top brain-boxes – especially if they're brain-boxed in a particular subject and they're willing to study it.

But there's also cash available for sports heroes, musical maestros and so on.

Next, being a particular type of person. Pick from the following list: poor; religious; from a particular place (such as local to the university, local to whoever put down the money for the scholarship in the first place or from another country); a parent (preferably single); from an ethnic minority; a student with a disability; or a woman.

Then there's doing a particular course – which is self-explanatory.

And finally, there's behaving in a particular way. This might include not drinking (is it worth it?), agreeing to do missionary work or caddying at a golf course.

Some of these hand-outs can be worth thousands of quid. For example, the University of Aberdeen has an annual Entrance

Bursary Scheme, under which an elite band of really brainy
students get £1,000 a year during their undergraduate degree.
As is often the case, the applications need to be in quite early
(in this case, by the end of March in the year the students want
to start).

These big bounties tend to be the hardest to get – so don't
get over-excited, not least because there are others which are
worthless, sorry that should read 'worth less'. For instance, the
J B Cobb Scholarship (available only to students at Exeter
University) – worth a grand total of £12 a year.

Still, better than nothing.

## Sponsorships

Once upon a time employers were so keen to get graduates on
their payroll that they were willing to fund them throughout their
degree course (or in some cases, higher national diplomas).
Sometimes the students didn't even have to go and work for the
sponsor afterwards.

That, unfortunately, was in the days when you could throw
rocks at a dozen people between the ages of 21 and 25 and not
expect to have stoned a single graduate.

**Nowadays, like the crocodile and the coelacanth surviving
everything evolution could chuck at them over the millennia,
while there are still quite a few sponsorship deals left, they're
the relics.**

**Depending on the deal, taking a sponsorship might be like
selling your soul and, even though you may need the cash, you
should always check what Satan's going rate is these days.**

**In any case, virtually the only courses that attract
sponsorship are the ones where employers have real trouble
recruiting talent.** They tend to be hardcore sciences, technical
subjects (such as engineering), business studies and economics
or vocational courses.

Don't even bother looking for sponsorship to do philosophy,
English literature or sociology. There are some sources out
there, but you might as well spend the amount of time it would
take to find one earning money the traditional way.

## WHAT'S IN IT FOR THE SPONSOR?

Sponsors don't do it just because they're being nice.

They have good commercial reasons and ultimately they hope to gain at least as much if not more from the deal than the student. Highly capable and skilled people with management potential are a limited commodity and sponsorship is a way getting in there before the competitors. It's like jumping the queue at the deli counter because they're running out of taramasalata. Perhaps not.

While it may feel like a great personal compliment if you're jammy enough and smart enough to nab yourself a sponsor, they'll probably be just as chuffed to have nabbed you.

## WHAT DOES A SPONSORSHIP INVOLVE?

Most sponsors expect students to work for them at some point before, during or after their course.

But it's rarely a form of bonded labour. Often they'll pay not only for the time you're studying, but give you a decent wage while you're working for them too. What's more, when you're working the learning won't necessarily stop. Usually there's at least some element of on-the-job training.

This may sound suspiciously like a sandwich course and, sure enough, they're the one of the most lucrative ways to earn while you learn these days. For more on sandwich courses, see the whole section on them in Chapter 7.

However, sometimes you work for you sponsor during your summer breaks instead.

Either way, the employer-cum-sponsor gets a chance to train up and check out its sponsored students while. at the same time, the student gets a shufty at the company's culture and working environment.

Obviously, everyone's hoping the student will want to work for the company and the company will want to employ the student when they graduate – however, there's rarely either a guarantee of a job or a requirement to work for them.

**Some students wouldn't want a sponsorship even if they found one knocking at the door. It can make you feel like your options are closing down around you faster than dot-coms.**

Develop a taste for strong cheap cider.

**You'll have various commitments – such as giving up your summer holiday to work – and it may all be a waste of time, if you decide you wouldn't want to work in that industry anyway, let alone for that company.**

If you don't enjoy working for your sponsor, things could get awkward. After all, you're going to feel obligated to them. You're not going to want to turn round and say, 'You know you gave me that huge bundle of notes? Well, thanks, but now I've got my degree I'm going to take it elsewhere.' It's only natural.

But there's no need to feel bad. If there's no commitment to them, don't sweat it. That's their look-out. You can bet that if the tables were turned and you'd blithely spent your student years thinking you'd waltz into their offices the day after graduation, but they'd decided they didn't want you, they'd have no qualms about slamming the door in your face.

Indeed, most companies will get tough if you don't keep your side of the deal – whatever it may be. They might stop your payments or – as in the case of the Armed Forces, for example – demand you give them back what they've paid you if you don't agree to join them after graduating.

Things like that will be in the contract in the first place, so think about them before you sign on the dotted line. How picky they are will usually depend on how much they're sinking into you. Always check the small print and ask about anything that isn't clear as clean glass.

Having said that, it shouldn't be a big worry because, at the end of the day (or, more usually, several years) four out of five students end up working for their sponsor anyway.

And even if you do change your mind and want to back out, sponsorship's often far from a dead loss anyway. It's almost unbeatable experience, it looks like gold dust on your CV and – with anything from a few hundred quid a year to more than £3,000 – the financial rewards can be sweet as honey-coated sugar cubes.

## WHO MIGHT SPONSOR ME?

There are basically four roads to sponsorships:

### Employers:

Especially the big boys like investment banks, engineering businesses and legal or accountancy firms.

### The Armed Forces:

The Army, Navy, Royal Air Force and Royal Marines all offer sponsorship (although they call them 'bursaries') to potential officers while they're in higher education. They're sometimes called 'cadetships'.

Although the actual conditions vary according to the amount they give you and which service you join, they'll usually demand that your course must benefit them somehow and also benefit you somehow once you've joined them after graduation. So hairdressing's probably out then.

Don't go for a cadetship if you wouldn't have want to serve in the Armed Forces anyway, because if in the end you decide these delights – travelling the world, meeting interesting people, killing them – aren't for you, then you'll need the permission of your commanding officer to leave and they'll want all their money back in full.

The Army also offers gap year students a training programme called the Short Service Limited Commission (SSLC) scheme. Ask at your local Army Recruitment Office.

### Professional bodies:

Engineering students are the prime targets for many sponsors.

### Universities:

On behalf of employers.

Always ask in high street stores, taxis, cinemas, theatres museums — just about anywhere, in fact — if there's a student discount. They'll rarely volunteer the information without being asked.

These groups will see a few students through their education with amounts of money that allow them to live in the lap of luxury compared to other students, but aren't that much in the real world.

Sure, it's partly about competitiveness in the capitalist world, but you might want to ask yourself why they're so desperate. Is it because people like you really are like an emerald among a sea of tinned peas? Or is it that something is putting everyone else off?

### IS IT WORTH APPLYING FOR SPONSORSHIP AND, IF SO, HOW?

In the words of the great Scotty: It's a long shot, Cap'n, but it might just work.

If you're more ambitious than a hedgehog trying to hump a shoebrush and better at your chosen subject than a Mastermind Champion on steroids, then you are in with a good chance, especially if your subject is one of the really sexy disciplines, such as engineering. (Sexy to sponsors, that is.)

There are various books worth looking at that list the likely targets, but make sure you look at a recent edition as they go out of date quicker than boy bands. They're listed in the back of this book. Your school, college, library or careers office will probably have copies and may also have helpful suggestions.

The more you can home in on what you want, the quicker and easier it'll be to compile your list of potential sponsors. Check your facts, compare salary possibilities, investigate the pros and cons and, if possible, talk to other sponsored students to get the inside story.

Above all, ask yourself if you are the right kind of person for the potential sponsor and suitably committed to a future with them. Remember – although there's usually a get-out clause for both parties – choosing a sponsor is tantamount to choosing a career.

Sponsorship doesn't have to start from day one.

It might even start before your course. Sometimes a prospective student will be working for a regular employer one day and the next, they'll have hatched out between them a plan that s/he should go off to university for a few years and that the employer should pay.

Or you might be offered sponsorship following some work experience in the summer before your course starts, for example or during a gap year. Another good reason for doing work experience.

But more often sponsorships are set up during your course, often as part of the process of finding somewhere to do a placement.

Then, sometimes, you'll be doing a placement and it'll be working out very cosily and eventually it turns into a longer deal.

And sometimes it's just a case of sponsor turning up towards the end of a student's university career and deciding they want to muscle in on a bit of the action. By then, they reckon, you've already proved your dedication to your course and they haven't had to shell out for your first few years. Nearly a third of sponsors limit their schemes to final-year students.

If you've already started your course, but you're still interested in a sponsorship deal, just ask at the university's Careers Service – they'll have contacts with employers and will be able to advise you. Some, by the way, have much more intimate relationships with employers, sponsors and business than others.

Indeed, some universities –Warwick, for instance – even have a Student Sponsorship Office specialising in matchmaking those with the money to those who need it.

Most sponsors don't advertise – there's no need. So you'll probably have to try a speculative application or two (or 102). And don't focus only on the 'big name' companies – the smaller ones may be better targets as they'll get fewer applicants (and generally they're friendlier places to work).

Companies local to your home town are often a good bet, especially if you know someone on the inside.

Your choice of course should come before your choice of sponsor. If you're keen to work for a particular company and they say that to qualify for a sponsorship you have to do molecular science, don't jump in to the molecular puddle with both feet.

It's better to match a sponsor to a course than a course to a sponsor. After all, the sponsor might say no and you're stuck doing something you wouldn't have chosen. More than one in six students drop out or fail their courses and for many of them, choosing the wrong course didn't help. Students who flunk are often in the deepest financial crap of all.

Most of the time, the exact course isn't the big clincher anyway. So long as you're in the right ball-park, they'll be more interested in whether you've got the drive, the business instinct and the commitment.

Sponsorship needs to suit you. It has to fit in with what you wanted to do anyway. Otherwise it's just a pain in the neck. For one thing it can make it tricky to change courses if you need to. It can tie you down to what you do and when you can do it. And you'll resent all of that if it's holding you back.

Eventually it stops being worth it for the money. After all, the most important thing is to enjoy being at university and to get the most out of it. If you end up changing course and your sponsor dumps you, so be it.

Bear in mind that for every sponsor there are hundreds of other students probably as keen as you to take their dosh. If you want to be sponsored throughout your course, start sending applications as soon as your UCAS form's done.

Whatever you do, get in there early and keep your expectations realistic.

Also see the section on 'Filling a Gap' in Chapter 7 for details about 'The Year in Industry' scheme – a kind of makeshift sandwich course programme.

Keep a pocket diary handy and make a note of everything that you spend with daily and weekly totals. Living frugally becomes a competition with yourself. It also makes you aware of where it's all going.

## ALTERNATIVES TO SPONSORSHIP

Employers wanting to bribe graduates these days often go for a more direct approach than traditional sponsorship – 'the golden hello' – where they pay thousands of quid to them just to join the company. Sometimes they offer to pay off your student debts.

**In fact, even the Government's got in on the act offering to pay off student loans for graduates willing to become teachers in subjects where there are shortages (if they stick at it for a year or two).**

A warning though: apart from teachers, it's usually only real high-flyers who get the dough from these deals and they're usually attached to very particular jobs.

Recently, a couple of top accountancy firms and management consultants have been doing it. But don't count on it though. They may not be offering it by the time you're ready and you may not get it anyway.

# Scholarships

Scholarships reward students for being brilliant at sport, music, public speaking, writing – virtually anything you can think of. Even academic work.

When we say 'brilliant', in fact you only need to be better than – or even only as good as – anyone else who applies. Indeed it may well not even be an open competition, in which case the word 'competition' would be something of a pessimistic overstatement.

Like special bursaries (see above), apart from being good at something, you'll normally have to fulfil various criteria. You may need to be under 18 on the third Sunday in August, the orphaned second daughter of a doctor or an ex-student of a certain school in Bognor and the proud owner of a pet rabbit called 'Chuckles'. Or something.

Some scholarships aren't fussy about how you spend the money and some are just for tuition costs – but others can get very particular about what they will and won't fund. For example, they may be for travel costs only or to study abroad, to fund some research, even to buy a musical instrument or sports kit.

There are even scholarships that only cough up in book tokens. (What do they think this is? Blue Peter?)

As you'll probably have already realised, a lot of the nuts and bolts of bursaries can be screwed equally on to scholarships and, if they can't, you can be pretty sure that the sponsorships tool-kit will work.

There are four fountains of funds when it comes to scholarships.

### INSTITUTIONAL AID

Institutional aid comes in the shape of a gift to a student direct from the university or college's own funds, usually to promote some special facet of university life and/or study.

Your first point of reference should be the university prospectus, which may give you an idea of some of the awards on offer (or at least a contact name and address), but also keep an eye on department noticeboards once you've started studying.

### PRIVATE FINANCIAL AID

Sometimes – when they're more fussed about getting good publicity than doing direct recruitment – companies opt to offer scholarships rather than sponsoring students.

These may or may not come with conditions about doing work for the company. Whether they do or not, a lot of the same advice about sponsorship applies (see above).

### PHILANTHROPIC AID

Sometimes individuals, charities or trusts decree that students should benefit from a scholarship. Far more important than decreeing anything, they also stump up the lolly.

The reasons why are their own. Sometimes it's the parents of a former student who died and who they want to commemorate. Sometimes it's an ex-student who's gone on to make their fortune and who wants to help others (or just gloat). Sometimes it's a tax dodge. Whatever the reasons, who cares? So long as they show you the money.

In fact, there are over 1,200 charities giving out a over £40 million a year. Most have an application deadline, but may still

keep you waiting for months before responding. Before applying
to any charity, it's worth making a few preliminary enquiries to
find out what they're looking for and if your odds of getting any
dosh are any better than a well-fattened cow's chance in a Berni
Inn Steakhouse.

## Where to get the details

For starters, try your university's admissions office and ask
them what they know about scholarships. and what might be up
for grabs and how to apply. While you're at it, you might as well
find out about bursaries and sponsorships too.

Failing that, you could try The Education Grants Advisory
Service – or EGAS to its friends. It is one of a small number of
organisations that offers advice to undergraduate students
about which charities to contact for grants of any kind.

If you write to them with your details they'll then send you a
list of likely names and addresses and a leaflet about the whole
application process. They'll usually expect students to have tried
other sources first before approaching charities (such as
hardship funds, for instance – see Chapter 9) and generally they
can only help first degree UK students.

For EGAS's contact details and further reading, see the back
of the book.

**Note that when it comes to financial help, most organisations
try to help those who deserve it most. That usually means
either those with the biggest financial challenges – single
parents, disabled students and those from disadvantaged
backgrounds – or those who show the most promise.**

Part 2: How much will you have?
Chapter 9

# Other sources

When it comes to what you'll have to live on, all we've really heard about so far are loans and overdrafts (which you have to pay back), parental contributions (which they may not be willing or able to give), paid work (which you have to earn) and various grants such as bursaries and scholarships (which you're not likely to get).

Frankly, it's a pretty pathetic whip-round. Like the collection plate in a prison chapel, there'll be less at the end than when you started.

So where else does the debt-driven student turn?

Here are a few suggestions. Unfortunately, most of them are either only for the heroically hard-up or come with a day-glo health warning.

## Emergency money

There is an official emergency fund given by the Government to universities to rescue students who find themselves up a certain creek without a paddle, a life jacket or even a piece of driftwood. It's called the access fund and it pays out in three ways: access bursaries, hardship funds and hardship loans.

The amount of money that each university has to distribute depends partly depending on how many students they've got, but only partly. They're free to hand out the money as they see fit within certain guidelines.

Generally they prioritise students from poorer backgrounds and those with particular difficulties – such as a disability or kids (those with kids may not appreciate the distinction). They also tend to favour students who've shown they're really dedicated to their course – by turning up regularly, for instance.

**Subject to the guidelines, the funds are open to all hard-up, full-time, non-fee-paying UK students and to some part-timers – but because of limited availability, the money usually goes on a first-come, first-served basis. Even if you have a genuinely urgent case, you may still end up disappointed, particularly if you leave it till later on in the academic year to apply.**

There are funds available for postgrads (although there are restrictions – of course) and there's a special fund for mature students. See Chapter 8 for more about access bursaries and Chapter 13 about special cases.

### How do I apply?

There'll be a department of the university admin that deals with these funds – usually called something like 'Student Services'. If you can't find out who to ask, try the students' union welfare department.

Student Services (or whoever) will get you to fill out a form that details any money you have coming in and evidence of just how broke you are.

They should give you a decision within a month, although if the situation's really extreme, they might let you know sooner and even let you have a cheque within a few days. That's not the norm, however and it's better to apply before the situation becomes really desperate – it'll only have got worse by the time you see any money.

Buy a beer making kit. It'll save you money and occupy all that time you wouldn't have if you actually turned up to lectures.

## Access bursaries

| | |
|---|---|
| **How much is available?** | Up to £1,000. |
| **Who can get it?** | Parents who are full-time undergraduates with trouble meeting childcare costs. (Not available if you're getting a separate lone parents' grant or mature student bursary – see Chapter 13). Available before you start your course. |
| **What's it for?** | Childcare costs and course-related costs. |
| **What are the terms?** | None. The money's yours to keep. No repayments. |

Sorry, but this isn't anything completely new. We mentioned **access bursaries** briefly in the last chapter when talking about standard bursaries.

## Hardship funds

| | |
|---|---|
| **How much is available?** | Up to £3,500, although the university decides and it'll probably be only enough to bail you out of really deep trouble. |
| **Who can get it?** | It's entirely up to the university to decide who gets what and why, except that you should have tried everything else you can think of first including, normally, applying for a hardship loan first (see below). |
| **What's it for?** | Whatever you like, although the university can lay down conditions if they want and may well give it only for something in particular. |
| **What are the terms?** | Usually given as grants, although sometimes they are given as short-term loans. |

The hardship fund is given to students in crisis, particularly if they've been hit with huge or unexpected expenses. The amount paid out, therefore, is often just enough to cover a particular bill.

**To get any money at all you'll need to prove you're in financial 'hardship'. The definition of that is fuzzy as a night on**

**tequila, so the university is basically free to make it up as they go along. The main limiting factor is the amount they have to give out and how thinly they're likely to have to spread it.**

As a result, you may have to come up with some hard evidence to back up your case, because any money they give you won't be available for anyone else. You may well have to pull out rent books and bank statements and if there's a sorry trail of debits to HMV, French Connection and Pizza Hut, it won't help your case.

If you need to, you can go back as often as you like in a year, but the university's patience may wear a bit thin and, once the fund runs dry, the stream won't start flowing again until the next academic year. All too often, the piggy bank's empty even before Christmas comes around.

**In any given year, about one in 20 students gets some kind of payment from their university's hardship fund, although they pay out in very different ways – some universities pay out very little but help lots of students, and some pay out loads, but to hardly anyone.**

Your own university will give you more information and let you know their own guidelines and policy (if they have one). Alternatively, look at the details for each university in Part 7.

## Hardship loans

| | |
|---|---|
| **How much is available?** | Up to £500. |
| **Who can get it?** | Each university has its own rules and makes the decisions. You must have tried other sources first including applying for as much as you can get as a regular student loan. |
| **What's it for?** | Like the Hardship Fund, what you spend it on is largely up to you, but in order to get it, you'll probably have to prove you need it for **SOMETHING SPECIFIC LIKE RENT OR FOOD.** |
| **What are the terms?** | It's the Student Loans Company that actually pays out the money and you'll have to pay it back along with your student loan in the normal way (see Chapter 4). |

# Borrowing from friends

**As a rule. Don't do it. Ever.**

**Even if your friend happens to be one of those lucky bastards who takes out a student loan just so they can stick it in a high-interest account and reap the rewards after picking up the interest.**

Even if your friend has recently won the lottery, lives in a castle in Hampshire, drives a Ferrari and shops in Harvey Nichols because the student discount shops are frightfully common.

Even if your friend is a friend of royalty – in fact, even if they are royalty, don't borrow from them.

Just don't.

Unless – and this is just about the only exception – you really don't want them to be your friend any more. Because they won't be.

Every day that you're not paying them back, they'll be wondering whether you ever will. They'll be wondering whether you think they're a stupid sap that you've just managed to take for a ride, wondering whether you're really that selfish, wondering whether you're sleeping with their boyfriend/girlfriend too and wondering – no, not wondering – telling people that it's you who never washes up, who always leaves the milk out to go sour and always finishes the toilet roll without ever replacing it.

By then paying them back won't make any difference.

There may well be times when friends will offer to help out. That's what friends are for.

Sometimes, you will have little choice but to accept, such as when you find yourself short of a bus fare at the end of the night or your housemate has done the shopping and you owe them for milk, bread and toilet roll but you can't get any money till next week.

Situations like these provide another exception to the rule. It's okay because it's short term (the shorter the better – it starts to get dangerous after a few hours, literally). They're only bunging you a few quid (the fewer the better). You'd do the same if the roles were reversed.

That's the crunch factor. **Ask yourself if you'd do the same if the roles were reversed. If you're in any doubt, forget it, walk home, ask about a hardship loan, whatever it takes.**

The other possible exception is when your friend can afford it easily and is not a student. (Although they must understand that you will continue to be poor for at least as long as you remain one yourself.)

Even then, proceed with extreme caution and follow the four cardinal rules of borrowing from friends:

- Make sure that both of you know exactly where you stand and that you make no promises or guarantees that you are either unable or don't fully intend to keep.
- Write an IOU. Ultimately, it will count for nothing other than reassurance that that you're as good as your word. The ritual return of an IOU (if carried out within a sufficiently short time) symbolises the return of the relationship to a status quo.
- Always repay your debt fully, promptly and in accordance with your original promise. Oh and when you do, it doesn't hurt to buy a small gift. A drink will do, just something to show you appreciate your debt was more than just the money.
- Never ask to borrow money from a friend and don't be too ready to accept it if it's offered. (And don't insult their intelligence by dropping hints, either.)

These rules are good even after graduation, but while you're a student you should treat them as if they make the Ten Commandments look like the instructions on a packet of Pot Noodles.

Parents are one thing – they produced you and may even be impressed by your promises, however insincere, to pay them back.

But being in debt to a friend is something altogether more horrid to contemplate. It can break up friendships previously thought to be stronger than Carbon-60 (which makes mincemeat out of steel). That even includes boyfriends and girlfriends. People who you think you know well have strange and hidden feelings about money (especially if they haven't got much).

**Give up beer (only joking).**

Likewise, if you're not prepared to borrow from a friend, don't lend to one either, exceptional under the same rules. Even if you trust your mate 100%, there is a good chance that you won't see the money again for a long time, if ever.

It's better just to give them money than lend it. And don't get your hopes up that they might give you some in return one day.

## Credit, Loans and Sharks

There's a whole ocean of sharks out there and not all of them have fins. Whenever you borrow money, know the terms and conditions.

Know when they want it back and how much interest they'll be charging in the meantime. That applies whoever the lender is – your bank, the Student Loans Company, but especially any service not specifically designed for students and recommended by your students' union. (If in doubt, ask the welfare department.)

### INTEREST RATES

**Bear in mind that interests rates are almost invariably 'compound'. In other words, 10% a year on £1,000 may only mean £100 in the first year, but it won't mean £300 after three years. In the second year, there'll be interest on the first year's interest and in the third year, interest on the interest, making £1,331 you have to pay back.**

And that's if the interest is calculated annually. It may well be more often than that. If 10% annual interest is added monthly, for instance, you'd be looking at more like £1,348.18 after three years. If it's added daily, it'll be even higher.

Lenders all use terms like APR, AER and so on. They mean standard things. Don't worry about learning the distinctions, just understand what it means in real terms to you or suddenly a great-looking deal of 5% a month may mean you're paying over 85% a year.

## SPECIALIST CREDIT AND LOAN COMPANIES

**Be particularly wary of taking out a loan or borrowing money from any organisation that isn't specifically geared towards students.** They might be kosher as bagels and chicken soup, but that doesn't mean that their deal will be right for the peculiar circumstances of being a student.

Basically, it's not usually a good idea. The interest rates are often high and you usually need to start repaying long before a student is likely to be ready to do so. The terms of these loans are rarely such that many students could deal with them.

Because students can't usually pay back within the terms of the loan, these companies don't usually want to lend to them anyway. It's not worth it to them to charge you interest you can't pay. That's not how they make money. The best they'll be able to do is send round the bailiffs to take your stereo, your CD collection and your books (which probably won't cover the cost of the bailiffs). (You don't want to think about the worst they could do.)

They're only interested in people with a steady income to pay back what they borrow or people who can guarantee the loan with something worth taking if they need to.

If they're not bothered about such things – be afraid, be very afraid. Unsecured loans are costly as caviar and as risky as naked ferret-farming.

Even those companies that are prepared to lend to students won't offer as good a deal as the Student Loans Company and won't offer such a convenient repayment package. And if they claim to, be very suspicious – there can't be anything in it for them. It's only worthwhile to the SLC because the Government pays them.

If you need it, there's quite a decent personal loan search on www.studentmoneynet.com where you can select 'student only' products along with the amount of loan you require and the terms of repayment.

**Live on campus or near wherever you need to go everyday for your studies.**

### SHORT-TERM EMERGENCY LOANS

If you aren't eligible for the access fund or a hardship loan (see above) or if you've already got it, but are still in deep crap, you may need a quick-fix solution.

Don't be tempted to turn to loan sharks and independent brokers. It's a rocky road to oblivion for anyone and students shouldn't even contemplate going there.

Go to your student welfare department and get advice. It probably won't come to it, but even if you have to drop out of university, it's better than working the rest of your life to pay sums some shark dreamt up when thinking about the population of China.

### A PACK OF CARDS – CREDIT, CHARGE AND STORE CARDS

We're back on vaguely respectable ground here, but unless you're careful and responsible, the dangers are still big as a cockroach in your ice cream.

Cards, however, do have their plus points if used frugally.

They're convenient (especially over the phone or 'net) and, if you only spend what you can afford and always pay off what you owe on time, then you can actually use them as a way of keeping money in your account for as long as possible.

They're also very easy to use and for this reason alone should be treated with caution – the more accessible the credit, the faster the debts will snowball.

#### Credit cards

One in three students has a credit card and the proportion is growing.

Credit cards can be used all over the UK and in many places abroad as well – most shops, supermarkets and restaurants – as well as for a wide variety of internet purchases.

Most banks and building societies now offer student versions of their credit cards, but they usually demand that a parent countersigns the application form as an insurance measure. If you get into trouble with the card, they'll chase your folks for the money. Even if you don't mind that, you may not like your parents seeing what you spent where.

Credit cards such as Mastercard and Visa are issued with a monthly spending limit that you mustn't exceed. (In fact, whatever purchase would send you over the brink may be denied if you try.)

You will probably get a pretty measly credit limit (especially at first) and your own bank's credit card might not be the best deal for you, so shop around a bit.

The interest rates vary quite radically too, from a few special deals at under 10% right up to 25% to 30% a year.

Some charities, political parties and other organisations now (even some universities) now offer their own cards, but these tend not to be designed for students, so check the terms.

## Two popular student credit cards

| College Students credit card | American Express Student credit card |
|---|---|
| No annual fee | No annual fee |
| 25 days grace period (before interest is charged) | 25 days grace period (before interest is charged) |
| Cash access at over 530,000 machines | Cash access worldwide |
| • Choice of 7 card designs<br>• 12 issues of popular magazines free | • Special airline discounts<br>• Online fraud protection guarantee |

Every month you'll get a statement, telling you exactly where you have used your flexible friend and the total damage. It'll also tell you the minimum you absolutely have to pay and by when.

If you pay the whole lot in one go you won't have to pay any interest on the balance. If you don't, however, the interest will grow on the balance like mould on a forgotten cheese sandwich.

**Credit cards are ideal for short-term credit, but don't get carried away – when you first get one it can feel like free money, which it most certainly isn't. In the long-term it's an expensive way of borrowing, but if you use your credit card in moderation you will probably find it is a good way to spread payments for essential purchases and it can help ease temporary cashflow problems.**

Watch what you're spending, though. Keep track of what you owe and, always try to pay your bill in full. Most of all, don't develop swipe-happy habits.

### Charge cards

Charge cards work in much the same way as credit cards, only you pay an annual fee for the privilege instead of paying any interest on money you owe.

The reason you don't pay interest is that you're not authorised to use the card unless you can pay off the whole debt each month. You usually have to set up a direct debit with your bank account, so they can just help themselves to the money when it's due.

The most common charge card is American Express (although they offer credit cards too – see above) and it's only really a way of spreading out your payments.

### Store cards

Store cards also work in much the same way as credit cards, but you can only use them in one shop or chain of stores (or sometimes a group like the Dorothy Perkins Group, which includes Burtons and various others).

Most stores will only issue you with a card subject to a satisfactory credit check. Nevertheless, plenty of shopaholic students would have little difficulty in getting one – or worse, several.

Before even thinking about a store card, answer the following questions honestly. Can you resist a skirt/shirt/other item of clothing if it's a bargain? If you owned four pairs of jeans, would you think you had enough? Do you think it's too much to own at least one album in the charts at any given time?

If the answer to any of questions was 'no', do yourself a favour – go nowhere near a store card till you're earning twenty grand plus.

Resist the sales patter, even if they're offering discounts to card holders. You often pay the extra in card charges or interest anyway and, in the case of many high street fashion outlets, students can get just as good a discount just by flashing proof that they're a student.

**Store cards can be a famously sure-fire way to get up to your ears in debt in lightning time.**

**What's more, you'll find that most stores won't be too sympathetic to the plight of students who can't pay up.** Eventually, they'll come down hard and send round bailiffs to take back what you bought and pretty much anything else they take a shine to in order to pay off the debt.

### Superdebts

People who end up on Kilroy with debts the size of telephone numbers usually managed it with the help of plastic and credit and store cards in particular.

Having more than one card which gives you any kind of credit (as opposed to your bank debit card which transfers money straight out of your account) is like juggling sharp knives coated in oil, not least because some people are tempted to try the impossible and pay off one debt by putting it on another credit card. There's consolidation and then there's just plain stupidity.

See Chapter 14 for advice on how to get the most out of your credit card without having a panic attack every time your statement arrives.

### Kiting

'Kiting' is when someone reports their card as stolen and then in the short period of time between the report and the official recording of the incident (when the card is barred so that shops won't accept it), they go wild in the aisles. They hope they won't be held accountable for the purchases.

The banks and credit companies have wised up to this practice and there are way too many in-store cameras these days, so don't even think about it.

**It is a serious criminal offence that can lead to a massive fine and black-listing at best, prosecution and jail at worst. To cap it all, it'll probably get you kicked out of university.**

# Back to the banks

### OVERDRAFTS

As we said in Chapter 6, a bank overdraft is the cheapest and easiest type of student borrowing – cheaper even than the student loan, at least until they start charging you interest.

Once you've signed up and completed all the necessary forms, your bank should send you written confirmation of your authorised overdraft limit (anything up to about £2,000, but usually less, especially if you are a first year).

If at any point you think you're in danger of going over the limit, get in touch with them immediately. They'll make an individual judgement based on your circumstances as to whether they'll let you have more.

Their decision will partly depend on how well you've looked after your money and how much you've kept them in the picture.

For example, HSBC's standard package means that they'll only increase your overdraft limit each year if you've demonstrated sound money management and have not abused the bank privileges. Barclays' package also provides an automatic 'buffer' of up to £200, but if you want more than that you'll need to complete an official overdraft application.

**Although having an overdraft is the least expensive and most convenient way of borrowing, never get complacent about being in debt to a bank. Treat them as if they were holding the rug under you feet and they could tug whenever they like.**

### PERSONAL BANK LOANS

If your overdraft and the student loan just aren't going to cut it, you can arrange a personal loan with your bank.

You borrow an agreed amount over an agreed period and agree to repayments which are usually agreed monthly amounts at a competitive rate of interest. There's a lot of agreeing to be done, so when choosing your bank check that they offer good terms for personal student loans.

Shop around, as it could save you money in the long run.

In general, banks are not the best bet for long-term borrowing for students – that would be overdrafts and student loans – but they're better than other money-lending companies.

## LOAN ADVICE

Some people think that if they borrow small amounts from a wide variety of different places, spreading their debts around, this will somehow be better than borrowing larger amounts from one or two places. Then again, some people believe in alien abductions and that Elvis really is dead.

**The more debtors you have, the greater the risk – better to stick with the student loan, the overdraft and, if absolutely necessary for specific situations, no more than one other reputable funding source (such as a student credit card for short-term cashflow shortfalls or a personal loan for a big single expense).**

Any more than that and you'll find it hard to keep track of your money and borrowings, not to mention your repayments. If you fail to keep up repayments on just one loan, it could get you 'blacklisted' – which means the word goes round the credit companies, mortgage companies, banks, building societies, TV rental shops, hire purchase firms and probably the local pub, that you're a financial leper who shouldn't be trusted. In can take years to rub the slur from your good name.

Don't borrow more than you can realistically pay back and don't agree to anything that asks you to pay it back any sooner than you'll be able. It's all very well thinking you can worry about repayments later, but when they hit, they'll hit hard.

Some companies will offer to 'consolidate all your existing loans' into one big loan (with 'easy to manage' monthly repayments). The idea's okay, because it's better to have a single payment of a fixed amount taken out of your account at a certain time each month, rather than direct debits of various amounts flying at you throughout the month. In practice, however, they'll probably want a higher interest rate.

So keep to as few lines of debt as possible in the first place and 'consolidation' won't be necessary. If possible, stick to the student loan from the start – the interest rate is microscopic relatively speaking.

For advice on how to make your student loan last and so avoid borrowing from other sources, see Chapter 14.

By the way, Elvis is alive and well and working for a branch of Lloyds TSB in Ormskirk.

## CAREER DEVELOPMENT LOANS

Career Development Loans (CDLs) are a Government-funded scheme to help people who're doing vocational training courses. If it ain't vocational, then you won't qualify.

Most undergraduates don't qualify anyway because you can only get a CDL for a course that the LEA won't fund. (It doesn't matter if you don't get funding from your LEA, just whether the course qualifies.)

However, CDLs can be helpful for some postgrads and students doing courses of two years or shorter. (Or three years if it includes a year's work experience.) If the course lasts longer than that, you may still get a CDL to fund part of it.

The scheme is run through four of the high street banks: Barclays, Clydesdale, The Co-operative and The Royal Bank of Scotland, who will lend between £300 and £8,000 to cover all or part of your course fees (usually 100%, but only 80% if you're in full-time employment) plus any other necessary costs (books and materials). You can only get money for general living expenses if your course is full-time.

The Department for Education and Employment (DfES) is behind the scheme and they pay the interest on CDLs while you're training and for up to a month after you've finished (or up to six months if you are unemployed when repayments are due).

Talk to all the banks offering CDLs before going with any one of them. You don't have to have an account with them already and they do offer slightly different terms and conditions.

A free booklet is available about the Career Development Loans. See the contact details at the back of the book.

Those who still find themselves short of cash may be able to seek sponsorship from their local Training and Enterprise Council (TEC).

Club together with mates on the same course to buy all the main texts between you and share them on a rota basis. Definitely one to try if your university library is a bit thin on the shelves.

# Benefits

We'll let you into a secret. When we were planning this book,
we thought we'd write a whole chapter on benefits, but it took
all of ten seconds to realise it would be a paper-wastingly
short chapter.

Most students are basically excluded from most of the social
security benefits system, not least housing benefits or dole
(oops, Job Seekers' Allowance) during vacations.

However, there are exceptions both to the 'most students'
part – students with kids, for instance, or a disability can get
support – and to the part about 'most benefits' – for example,
there's help for students with prescription charges, not
because they're students but because they're on a low income
(if they are).

For more on special cases, see Chapter 13.

## COUNCIL TAX

Full-time students are usually exempt from council tax unless
they have a second home. Your university will give you a
certificate to send off to the local council to prove you're a
student and that should be the end of it.

# Barrel-scraping ideas

## SELLING AND PAWNING STUFF

Some students, in their blind desperation, will take their most
prized possession – a hi-fi, an electric guitar, a signed
photograph of the Spice Girls – down to the pawn shop and get
as much as they possibly can for it.

The pawn shop acts like it doesn't want that tat, then buys it
(usually at a fraction of what it's worth) and promises not to sell
it for a while. If the student returns within that time and gives
the pawnbroker back their money (plus a handsome interest, of
course), then they can have their goods back. If not, they have
to run the risk that the pawnbroker will sell it to someone else
first.

Then there are other students, bless their hearts, who put an ad in the local paper or the local newsagent offering anything they own that might be worth a few quid.

These are desperation tactics and they should never be necessary.

If you're starting to see some of your precious 'luxury' items as a way of paying next month's rent or the watch your gran gave you for your 18th birthday begins in your head to resemble a good square meal, then you should get down to the bank or the students' union welfare department and discuss less drastic measures.

You should not have to give up the personal things you value just so you can afford to live. Even if you think you'll be able to buy them back eventually, it's not the answer to even the most urgent situation.

Other sources will lend you money more cheaply and without expecting you to give up your belongings before you're even supposed to repay the debt, let alone before you've failed to do so.

Of course, if you have an old pile of textbooks you don't need or a CD collection you no longer listen to or any old junk you think you could flog, there are ways of swapping genuinely unwanted stuff for much more useful stuff – cash, for instance.

Most universities have a second-hand student bookshop, which will give you cash for your old textbooks. Also, check out the websites www.studentswapshop.co.uk and www.books4beer.com – or your university may have a special swap shop scheme of its own.

Just don't go getting rid of anything unless you're pretty sure you won't miss it.

## BEING A LANDLORD
Actually, it's not quite as crazy as it sounds.

Some parents are in a financial position to guarantee a mortgage and, by owning property, not only does the student get the ultimate in independent living for themselves, but while interest rates are low the mortgage payments may work out cheaper than rent.

Meanwhile, the student home-owner can now do the landlord thing and get a few other students in as housemates, charge them a going rent and maybe even wipe out their own contribution to the mortgage altogether. If they're really lucky, the property's value will go up and they can move out when they sell it, clearing their student debts with the tidy profit.

Sounds great, eh?

Unfortunately, it's full of pitfalls. Even the process of buying a property (rather than the property price itself) can cost more than a year's rent and it's a sackful of hassle too. Then there's finding the readies for furniture.

**Also, once you own property, you can't complain to the landlord when the boiler blows up or the roof collapses. You could have a situation where you can't even live there yourself, let alone charge rent to anyone else, unless you find hundreds of quid to mend your plumbing.**

Meanwhile, although being a live-in landlord isn't as bad as just being in it for the money, there's a bundle of red tape over contracts and safety and all the rest.

Finally, as they say in the small print, the value of your investment can go down as well as up.

**Strictly for the wealthy or risk-junkies.**

## GAMBLING

Another one for the risk-junkies. And maybe the maths undergraduates, although most of them will have worked out that the odds are always stacked against the gambler.

Any money you spend on gambling, whether it's the lottery, scratch cards, horses, dogs, slot machines, poker or speculative share trading, should not be regarded as an investment and nor should any money you happen to win be regarded as income. You're too likely to lose it unless you never gamble again.

**Gambling profits and loss belong strictly under the heading 'entertainments' in your budget (see Chapter 14). If you gamble at all as a student, you gamble for fun and since gambling's most fun when there's real risk involved, you should consider it a source of fun you can't afford.**

There have been professional poker players on degree courses, but not as many as there have been students who've thrown away money they didn't have. Definitely not a source of income.

There is one exception to the above, but it hardly has the thrill of true gambling – premium bonds, which, if you want to buy yourself the dream of winning big are the cheapest way to do it because you can cash them in again.

If, however, you have enough money to leave in premium bonds for long enough to make it worth the effort, then you could find much better things to do with the cash that are far more likely to yield a decent return.

## ILLEGAL ACTIVITIES

Now, of course, illegal activities are against the law. That goes without saying, so we're now regretting that we bothered to say it. However, for some students, simply being against the law doesn't seem to be enough motivation not to give them a try.

So if that doesn't convince you, remind yourself why you're at university in the first place. Breaking the law to get money to complete your studies is an utter waste of time because, if you get caught, you'll probably have your ill-gotten gains confiscated and be drummed out of university in double time. And the problem with assuming you won't get caught is that you can't be sure – you won't even have a clue – until it happens.

Some offences, busking without a licence, for instance, certainly don't seem too serious and tend not to carry jail sentences. What's more, you're unlikely to get chucked out of the university for being hauled up in front of a magistrate for playing 'Blowing in the Wind' in the street.

If, however, you choose the wrong patch or your rendition is so bad that it has Bob Dylan leaping into his grave just so he can turn in it, then not only are you unlikely to make much money, but if you also end up with a fine it can undermine the whole purpose of the exercise.

Drug-dealing, however, is, if you'll excuse the expression, a much bigger deal.

We're not going to pretend there aren't students who do drugs. There are.

We're also not going to claim that there aren't a few students who start off just scoring for themselves and a couple of mates who quickly find they've got a lot more friends and a bigger bank balance. It happens, but don't let it be you.

**Students will probably get thrown out just for using drugs if they get caught (and in a tight-knit community like a university, it's pretty easy to work out who's doing what). As for dealing, a university's sympathy will disappear faster than coke up a rock star's nostril and it will often be the university itself pushing the police to bring charges.**

Then there's sex.

A few students – a very few – work in the sex industry and if they're okay with that and they're not breaking the law... well, that's their call. It is not, however, the best way to deal with financial problems. Other less risky occupations pay better and involve less hassle.

There may be good money to be made by young attractive people working for the less sleazy escort agencies and strip joints (as if any strip joint isn't sleazy). But the problem is not knowing what you're getting in to.

Everything might look okay, but in any industry that hangs over the edge of legality, you're always too close for comfort. Whatever pleasant assurances you might be given to start with, you can't know that it's not going to go further than you'd like. Only when it does will you find out and by then you may find you're already in an uncomfortable, possibly even threatening, situation.

As for prostitution, the act itself isn't illegal, but soliciting is. It's also a dangerous environment involving enormous mental anguish for all but the firmest of purpose and medical dangers for everyone (not just those who don't practise safe sex).

Again, the fact that things are against the law shouldn't be your deterrent. Common sense should tell you there are easier ways of getting by.

**As a general rule, if you wouldn't be happy telling your mum, your friends, your tutor and your bank how you got your money, you should think seriously about whether you're not risking or giving up too much for the sake of too little.**

### BODY PARTS, ETC

Many medical students (the male ones, naturally) are wankers. In that they do it for money and get paid for their product, as it were. The reason medical students tend to do it is that they tend to be near a sperm bank.

There's no reason, however, why generations of babies born to women who've gone for fertility treatment should all be the spawn of medical student tossers. Move aside, you trainees doctors and let some others drop their seed into the gene pool.

Sperm donors don't tend to get much for their efforts – around £10 or £20 quid a pop as a rule and you're not allowed to do it too regularly. Quite apart from rumoured damage to eyesight, they need to keep sperm counts up and don't want any particularly hairy-fisted individuals monopolising the market.

Female students don't have the same opportunities. They're not currently allowed to sell eggs (although they can donate them) and while you can act as a surrogate mother you're only allowed to claim reasonable expenses for doing so. It's really not a means to pay your way through college.

Selling organs can't be recommended either. Unnecessary medical procedures tend to interfere with study and... oh yeah, there's some risk to your health.

More realistically students might be tempted to take part in medical experiments, which is also not something to volunteer for unless you're very clear about the risks you face. Whilst researchers conducting any such experiments are obliged to inform you of any known or likely risks, their enthusiasm and indeed the fact that the experiments need to be done at all, mean that you shouldn't have too much faith.

You should have your own independent understanding of exactly what's involved and weigh up the risks on the basis of whether would you do it for free. The fact that you might get paid should only enter into it once you feel safe about it. There's not enough money to make it worth it otherwise, although it's hard to imagine what would be enough.

**Medical experiments usually involve testing treatment procedures and new drugs. The dangers should be obvious. However, not all research is so risky. Lots of research projects, particularly in psychology, involve nothing more hazardous to volunteers than filling in questionnaires and doing aptitude tests.**

Twins, particularly monozygotic twins – that's identical twins to you – are especially in demand. But only if you can persuade your twin to volunteer too.

Again the money's not big bucks, but if it's advancing human understanding, why not? If your university has a psychology department, go and offer you services. The worst that can happen is they laugh at your suggestion and psychologically scar you forever.

# Part 3
# Tuition fees

# 3

# Paying for your course

## Briefly, what are 'tuition fees'?

Higher education doesn't come cheap and somebody has to foot the bill to run the universities, to employ the lecturers, to put books and computers in the library and so on.

Who it should be, however, is a controversial matter.

*Push* has no opinion (or not one that doesn't involve obscenities) – we're only here to tell it like it is.

**At the moment, the Government pays by far the biggest part of any student's tuition costs. They run into many thousands of quid per student per year and, even since the introduction of tuition fees, most students pay only a fraction of the bill.**

**However, for many students affording even that fraction is tough. Especially when the fraction can be as much as £1,075 a year in tuition fees.** (When you've got to find that much, it's not much comfort to know the Government is forking out several times as much.)

**Not every student has to pay the full whack, however. In fact, about a third don't have to pay any fees at all and about another third pay less than the full amount. It's only those who can afford it – or, more accurately, those whose parents can afford it – who have to cough up.**

How much you have to pay is based on your parents' income, their situation (get them to divorce if you can – then only one salary counts), whether you've got brothers and sisters in higher education, how old you are, whether you're married or earning, whether you're from outside the EU and hundreds of other conditions and details that we either already went into in Chapter 3 or that we'll cover either later in this chapter or, if they're special cases, in Chapter 13.

Strictly speaking, in fact, unmarried UK students under 25 without an income and living with their parents aren't usually expected to pay their tuition fees out of their own pocket. Even if the student is the one who actually hands over the cheque to the university, in theory their parents are supposed to be 'contributing' enough to pay the bill, whether it's over a grand or nothing at all (see Chapter 4).

Whatever your situation, how much you or your parents are supposed to pay is worked out by your LEA when you apply for an 'award' (see Chapter 3).

## Explain that again, but in more detail

### WHAT DOES A DEGREE COST?

Students don't normally have to pay the whole cost of their course – which is just as well since most undergraduate degrees come in at a cool four grand a year to run.

That pays for the tutors, the admin staff, the heating and lighting of teaching rooms, the photocopying of course notes, the books and computers in the library, the rubber bands to go on the degree scrolls and so on. Where they start having to pay for high tech equipment and lots of rubber gloves – such as on clinical courses – the bill can be as much as twenty grand a year.

As we said, it's just as well it's not normally the student who pays it.

The bulk of the bill, usually at least two-thirds, is paid by the Government. Often it's actually paid by the LEA, but it's all coming from taxes in the end anyway.

BANK of ENGLAND

`Turn vegetarian.`

## WHAT DO STUDENTS PAY?

Until 1998, students rarely had to contribute anything. Now they do.

**Now about two-thirds of students in England, Wales and Northern Ireland have to contribute something to the cost of their tuition – up to a current maximum of £1,075 but it will probably go up every year more or less in line with inflation.**

The current government's policy is that it shouldn't go up faster than that, but if there's one thing the last twenty years of higher education should have taught us, it's that the policy, the system and everything about it can change.

How much they pay depends, in theory at least, on their ability to pay – or more to the point, their parents' ability to pay.

The idea is that rich students (or ones from richer backgrounds at any rate – rich students are few and far between) should pay what they can, but that poorer students shouldn't be put off the idea of university by the prospect of having to contribute.

In fact, it's estimated that maybe as many as 30,000 people a year since 1998 have decided not to go to university because of the changes to the funding system, although it's doubtful whether it's specifically the tuition fees that have been responsible. It's more likely to be the total levels of debt involved.

## WHAT ARE TUITION FEES AND HOW ARE THEY PAID?

Tuition fees are the yearly cost of a higher education course charged by the university and paid for by either:

- Your LEA
- You and/or your parents
- Or a combination of both.

The university shouldn't demand any other fees for admission, registration, graduation and so on, although don't expect the fees to include your own photocopying, say, or a replacement library card when you lose yours.

Whatever amount you have to pay, you'll have to pay it direct to your university. The exact arrangements for taking money off you vary from place to place, but, don't you worry, when it comes to getting their cash, it won't be something they'll leave you in any doubt about.

They may want the whole amount right at the beginning of the academic year, but most are pretty flexible and will accept it in monthly or termly instalments.

They'll all have some kind of deadline after which they'll try various threats, such as a late payment fine, but ultimately, they'll just chuck you off the course if you don't pay up.

Some also try to persuade you to set up a direct debit (an automatic regular payment from your bank account) which can actually work out easier for you too. They may even try to charge an admin fee if you don't. But if your bank balance is erratic and you're skating on a thin and icy overdraft limit (see Chapter 6), you may prefer to handle the payments in a more hands-on way.

Meanwhile, your LEA (or equivalent) may be paying all or part of your fees if you're a UK or EU student (see Chapter 3).

They'll send their contribution direct to the university, so once you've got it sorted and they've confirmed to you whether they'll pay and how much, then you can leave it to the LEA and the uni to work it out between themselves.

### HOW MUCH DO I HAVE TO PAY?
This is the flip side of the coin of LEA awards that we covered in Chapter 3. Take the total fee (currently £1,075) and subtract whatever the LEA's willing to cough up. That's your share.

It's also the flip side of the coin of parent contributions (see Chapter 5), although this coin seems to have an unfeasible number of sides. You only have to contribute to your tuition fees if your parents (or, under certain circumstances, if you) can afford it, so your share of the fees and your parents' contribution to them would normally be the same thing (although your parents might also be contributing to your living costs).

To decide how much your share of the tuition fees should be, your LEA assesses your parents' income and your status.

162

Details are in Chapter 3 (and, if you haven't already read Chapter 3, you've probably worked out that all this would be so much easier to follow if you had).

Basically, if your parents' residual income (ie. after a few deductions and allowances) is under £20,000, you won't be paying anything. At £20,000, you'll be expected to pay £45 a year and for every extra £9.50 that they earn, you'll have to pay another pound a year. Until finally, when they're on £29,784 or more, you're paying the maximum annual contribution of £1,075.

For married students, they'll usually count your spouse's income instead of your parents' and, for single mature students and lone parents, the LEA will count your own income and you'd normally be entitled to additional help anyway (see Chapter 13).

**Even if you are absolutely certain that you'll have to pay the full tuition fee or even if you might not have to but you're perfectly happy to pay £1,075 a year, apply to your LEA anyway.** It's not just because we take a sadistic pleasure in recommending that people fill in forms (although it is fun for us and we do conduct pointless surveys at weekends as a hobby). It is because, **if you don't, the LEA won't know you're doing the course at all and won't know to pay the bulk of the course costs. You may end up paying them yourself.**

And, as we already said, that's usually at least £4,000 and sometimes as much as £20,000. A fair whack to have to cough up just for not bothering to fill in one fairly straightforward form.

Pick up free condoms from your local family planning centre or the university health centre. (And use them.)

### SCOTTISH STUDENTS
Different funding arrangements apply under the Scottish parliament.

Scottish students studying in Scotland do not have to pay tuition fees and maintenance grants have been restored. However, those starting university from Autumn 2001 will be required to pay a £2,000 endowment once they have graduated – this will be added to their loan repayments.

Certain students, such as mature students, lone parents and disabled students, will be exempt from this Graduate Endowment.

If you are a Scottish student and you want further information, call the Scottish Office on 0131 244 5823 for your copy of *Scottish Higher Education for the 21st Century*. Full contact details at back of book.

## WHO DOESN'T HAVE TO PAY TUITION FEES?

Apart from Scottish students at Scottish universities (see above) and the third of English, Welsh, Northern Irish and EU students who have all their fees paid for them, there are some students whose courses are considered too important to the rest of us for them to have to cough up anything themselves.

Basically, that means medicos of various breeds and flavours and teachers.

In other words, UK and EU students on any of the following courses shouldn't have to pay a penny in fees:

- Postgraduate courses leading to qualified teacher status (eg. PGCE)
- Chiropody
- Dental hygiene
- Dental therapy
- Dietetics
- Most nursing courses
- Midwifery
- Occupational Therapy
- Orthoptics
- Physiotherapy
- Prosthetics and orthotics
- Radiography
- Speech and language therapy

Undergrads training to be teachers – on BEd courses – need to watch out for this, because they'll have to fork out for fees along with everyone else. However, they may get a 'golden hello' – a lump sum when they actually become teachers (see 'alternatives to sponsorship in Chapter 8) – or, if they want to teach a subject in which there's a shortage, they might get extra funding under the 'secondary shortage subject scheme' (see Chapter 13).

If you fancy becoming a teacher – or the fact that you may have an easier financial time as a student may tip the balance for you – give the Teaching Information Line a shout on 0845 6000 991 (or the Welsh Teaching Information Line on 0845 6000 992).

Other students don't get out of tuition fees altogether, but they don't have to pay as much. For students in these three categories, the fees are half what they'd otherwise be (up to a maximum of £535 a year):

- Sandwich students on placements that last a full academic year.

- Part-time students doing their first degrees (see Chapter 13). Part-timers who're studying in a year at least half what they would on a full-time course might get all their fees paid if they are on a low income or if they're claiming social security benefits.

- Students spending a year studying overseas as part of their course, such as on an ERASMUS programme (see Chapter 13).

Keep a finance file with all your bank statements, bills and letters from the SLC and the bank. That way, you'll know where to find what you need when you need it. Also keep receipts and card payment slips in it, and check them off against statements when they arrive.

# Frequently asked questions

**What if I want to change my course or my university?**
Talk about it first – to friends, to parents, to tutors, to the students' union welfare department, to people in the street, priests, Radio talkshows – till you're either bored of the idea or absolutely convinced it's the right thing to do.

The reason you need to take such care is that it will affect you financially and there may be the most horrendous pile of red tape and administrative hassle deal with.

But if you're more sure of yourself than a tabloid columnist with a bad idea, then:

- Tell your university what you've decided to do (generally it's easier to change courses than institutions).

- Tell your LEA. If they've paid out any money for your course, there is a good chance they'll want it back and it's you they'll expect it from. So the sooner you raise the subject with them, the better.

- Tell the Student Loans Company. As soon as you leave your course, you're liable to start paying back the loan unless you are going to reapply and start university again. (The SLC doesn't have to wait a few months, as they would after graduation, if you've left your course early.)

**If you tell everyone as soon as you've decided what you want to do and then you keep them all informed, then, with luck, you may be able to transfer any support you're getting from one course to another, even if it's at a different university. If you don't have to drop back a year (or even, very occasionally, if you do), it may not lose you any funding at all. No guarantees though.**

Your university – in fact, both universities – must first agree to what you're intending to do and there are some standard restrictions on transfers. If you're on a course at a private university or college, you may have to pay extra tuition fees.

All other things being equal, you'll usually still be eligible for whatever amount of support you would have got for either the course you've moved from or the course you've moved to (whichever is longer and/or more expensive), but not both.

So, for example, if you switch from a three-year degree just at the start of the second year to a four year degree somewhere else, but you only have to go back to the beginning of the second year of your new course, then you may well not lose out. Your LEA and the SLC would have been happy enough to support you for four years of study if that's what you'd decided in the first place, so they probably wouldn't object to you doing it this way.

You would have more of a problem if either they'd already coughed up for your second year at the university you don't like or if you had to go back to the start of the four-year course at your new university. In that case someone, somewhere would have to pay for more years study than they would have otherwise and that someone is going to be you.

What's worse is that you may end up paying not only for your living expenses and your tuition fees but, unless you can persuade your LEA, you might end up paying all of the course costs for any extra years.

By the way, if you move into or out of London – either away from home or back in with your parents – then the loan rates will be changed accordingly.

### What if I want to drop out?

If you really aren't happy at university and you are sure that a change of course or scene isn't the answer, naturally you have the option to drop out.

More than one in six students drops out or fails and, although it's rarely the only reason, financial hardship is often a contributing factor.

**Jumping ship, however, may not be the answer to your financial problems. It could make matters worse.** Depending on when in the academic year you decide to bail out, your university may well charge you for the whole year and, depending on your particular arrangement, some LEAs may want their contribution towards your tuition paid back too.

You could end up with the worst of both worlds – not only might you have all the usual student debts, a university on your back for fees and an LEA chasing you for repayment of its contribution, but you won't even have the higher education qualification to show for it and the higher earning potential that brings.

### What if I'm not from the UK or the EU?

Any UK university is going to expect full fees from you. That's not just the tuition fees charged to UK students (with the current maximum of £1,075 a year), but a price based on the total cost of your course – anything from a couple of thousand quid a year up to around twenty grand. They may even want to make a bit of profit out of you.

Contact the university for details of overseas students' fees for individual courses.

There may be help available from your government or from other organisations in your own country.

The UK higher education system is considered to be of a pretty high standard and, since in some countries you'd have to pay all the costs anyway, it may even work out cheaper to study here.

Avoid anything with high interest. Big monthly repayments and a high annual percentage rate spell big trouble. Paying off old debts with new ones generates a vicious cycle. You'll end up with mounting mountains of interest and interest on the interest, ad nauseam.

# Part 4
# Where does it all go?

Part 4: Where does it all go?
Chapter 11

# Where most of it goes

Rent

Shopping

Entertainment

Other stuff

## So, tell me again, how much will I have?

On average, students have between £4,000 and £6,500 a year to live on depending on whether they work part time, whether they live at home, whether they live in London and on how rich and/or generous their parents are. Of this, a large percentage isn't real income, it's a student loan but what the hell, at least it's money to spend.

You can add to that another possible thousand or so in overdrafts from the bank. Again, it's not income, but it's spendable and that's all that counts till you have to pay it back.

That comes at the end when, on average, students are between £9,000 and £14,000 in the red. That figure is not likely to be dropping. In fact, anyone going to university now ought to reckon on being at the top rather than the bottom of the scale by the time they finish.

The thing is, all this 'on average' business undermines a lot of specific advice and makes the prospect of hardship seem less real. You'll have to work out for yourself what you're likely to have. Which is what Part 2 of this book was all about.

**If you think you can easily live on even £7,500 a year – pretty much top whack for a student – think again, pal. Get a grip or else you're going down big time.**

Unless you're way off one end of the bell curve, getting by as a student will be as difficult as everyone says. They're not kidding. They're not boasting about how tough it is for them. Hardship is for real. For almost all students.

# What are the main expenses, then?

The single biggest cost is accommodation. The roof over your head. It's expensive, but an essential.

The next biggest expense may be your tuition fees, depending on how much you have to pay. We'll leave that out of the equation for the time being. Just take a look at Chapter 10 (and Chapters 3 and 5) if you haven't got fees sussed yet.

Other biggies are food, travel, academic costs (like books etc), clothes and bills. All essentials too.

Your entertainment costs are among the top wallet wasters, too, and don't think they're not essential. You can't have a successful time at university if you're hating every minute of it because you're too stingy to allow yourself a penny for fun.

Think of it more as an investment in the wider education that university offers (the education that teaches you how to survive a 9am lecture with the hangover from hell). Or you can think of it as the wise purchase of a support mechanism (otherwise known as 'having friends').

The breakdown on average – again that phrase that tugs out the rug – goes something like this:

| Breakdown | Annual average £ | Percentage of total costs % |
|---|---|---|
| Rent/housing | 2,170 | 32.4 |
| Food | 1,410 | 21.0 |
| Entertainments | 1,355 | 20.2 |
| Phone | 340 | 5.1 |
| Clothes | 270 | 4.1 |
| Local travel | 245 | 3.7 |
| Household bills | 210 | 3.2 |
| Toiletries | 210 | 3.1 |
| Academic - books, photocopying, stationery, etc | 170 | 2.6 |
| Laundry/washing | 160 | 2.4 |
| National travel | 95 | 1.4 |
| Insurance | 60 | 0.9 |
| Total | 6,695 | |

Bear in mind that costs in London (where the total is over eight thousand a year) are dragging up the national average. Outside London, the total is more like £6,250.

Region by region, the breakdown *Push* has calculated the breakdown is something like this:

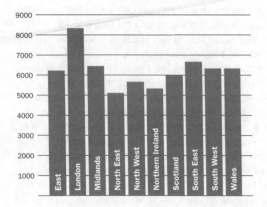

But remember that costs vary not only from one part of the country to another, but from one part of town to another or even within the same university depending on whether you're living in or out, which hall of residence you're in or which course you're on.

Perhaps the most useful way of looking at it is to think in terms of how it splits up what you've got:

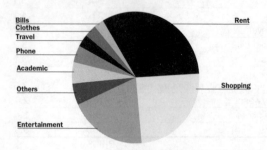

Having added them up, let's break the costs down.

In Chapter 2, we already covered the inside track on how exactly they vary from place to place and how you can stay solvent by choosing your university carefully. Here's a more general idea of where exactly so much money disappears so quickly.

# Rent and Housing

This is your biggest expense – it will eat up a whacking great proportion of your loan, perhaps about half your available income and it will account for about a third of what you spend in a year.

And, unless you are living with your parents or they have gone a step or two beyond the call of duty and actually bought a place for you, it's an expense that cannot really be avoided or minimised.

So be sure to make your dough work hard for you.

**Accommodation costs vary enormously. Depending on location and what you look for, a student might normally expect to spend anything from £35 a week, for a very basic rented room in a student house, right up to £100 a week or even more for some catered or particularly flash digs.**

In London, however, you might end up forking out nearly a hundred just to get the basic rented room that would be rock-bottom of the market anywhere else.

There are two basic alternatives for students – they break down into endless complicated subsets, but let's not spit in the Evian right now, okay?

Students can either live in or out. The 'in/out' bit refers to university accommodation – housing that belongs to your university or college or is at least managed by them. Or at least by someone else on they're behalf. Told you it got complicated.

If you live out, you have to find your own accommodation, deal with your landlord personally and generally get involved in the whole homemaking business for yourself.

If you live in, the university will lay on all sorts of extra benefits. For example, there may be someone who empties your

174

bin and runs a vacuum round the floor every once in a while. They may be a canteen, common room, a bar even. And, what's more, your bills will probably all be included in your rent.

As a rule, living in works out much cheaper. It depends on what the university is charging, but it's rare that once you've allowed for bills, meals and anything else they throw in, that it works out on the wrong side of what's available locally.

Another benefit is that it's usually easier to manage your finances if you live in. Because bills are usually 'all in', you don't have to worry about brown envelopes landing on the doormat threatening to cut off your heating and light unless you pay the electricity bill. (What's worst is they'll probably pick the middle of Eastenders to throw the switch on you.)

You can't always live in. In fact, very few universities offer the chance to live in throughout your student career and, besides, frantic fun though it often is, after a year of it, most students are more than happy to move out.

First years usually get dibs on whatever housing the university has and most students can live in for one year at least.

Living in may be cheaper, but it has its down side. In catered accommodation, you may also have to eat institutional food from time to time. And, depending on the exact arrangements, most students living on campus have to share limited bathroom and catering facilities with a large number of other students – which can be a strain, especially if you value sleep or privacy.

But, then again, what better way of getting to know a strange bunch of people than being stuck in an enclosed space with them for the entire academic year?

There are quite a few factors to consider when choosing where to live.

If going out on the piss, meet up round someone's house first and do most of your drinking there. It's cheaper.

You may not always have total freedom to choose (especially if you live in, as you may simply be allocated whatever's going), which makes it all the more important to know what you want so you can get your money's worth from whatever's available.

**Making the right call about housing – not just where you're going to live, by the way, but also who you are going to live with – is crucial. Most tenancies are for a full year and it's often expensive, inconvenient and tough to find anywhere better if you decide you want to move halfway through an academic year.**

## CHOOSING HOUSING: WHAT TO CONSIDER

### The level of the rent

The cheapest is not always the best. It's just the cheapest.

There is no such thing as a good deal on a ten-foot-by-four-foot room that's cold, smelly and damp, with rickety furniture and an infestation of slugs.

It's far better to fork out a little extra each month for somewhere where you'll be able to sleep, study and just hang loose. If you can't, you'll only end up more miserable and no better off, because you'll be paying costs constantly for the bus to the library and for food and drink when you get there.

When choosing a place to live, sniff about like a dog in a meat-packers. Try talking to someone who's lived there before or is living there now, just to get an idea of what you will be getting for your money, ask about any hidden costs (such as a heating system that uses fuel, but seems incapable of producing heat).

This is another advantage of living in. Universities tend to look after their tenants better than most landlords and it's easier to find out the problems up front and easier too to get something done about them.

If you're living out, the more people you share with, the more the cost of the bills can be spread and the smaller your own proportion of the rent. There is the danger of increased tension amongst housemates, but more people can also mean that tensions are spread more thinly.

A huge factor in the amount of rent you actually pay is how long you're there.

Find out if you have to pay rent during the holidays. Most privately owned, off-campus accommodation requires that you do, but university digs usually have 30 to 38 week contracts that match the length of the terms.

**Unless you absolutely have to, don't rent over the summer break. By not renting for more than nine months of the year, you might save yourself more than £500.**

If you do have to pay rent over the holidays, there's nothing to stop you staying there and finding work rather than going home.

Before saying yes to any accommodation, calculate what it's going to cost you over the year. Multiply the weekly or monthly rent by how long you're actually going to live there and add appropriate amounts for anything that's not included (such as bills or furniture).

### Do you have to share a room?

Students who live in sometimes have to share whether they want to or not.

If you do, your rent should be lower – a lot lower – not least to make up for the cost of having to get on pretty damn well with whoever you're sharing with.

Everyone needs their own space sometimes, so this is not a satisfactory option for most students, especially beer-swilling, chain-smoking hedonists who end up sharing with a younger version of Cliff Richard.

However, sharing isn't as common these days as it used to be, even in halls of residence. And if you state on your accommodation application that you do not want to share, you'll usually not have to.

Even those who do need to share are normally sent questionnaires by the university so they can make roommate matches as harmonious as possible. If one of these drops through your letterbox, make yourself as anti-social as possible. That way they'll probably have to put you on your own (or, failing that, with someone else pretending to be anti-social).

**A word of warning: if you get into university through the Clearing system, you may end up dumped in whatever accommodation the university couldn't foist on anyone else. It's almost always safer to take a year out and apply again the following year.**

If you live out, sharing may make more financial sense because, rather than just getting you a discount, it should actually halve the price.

Some landlords, however, especially if they're providing two beds in one room, charge per person, not for the room. It's immoral, crooked and there's nothing you can do about it.

Never share unless you know you can get on with your roommate. That goes for boyfriends and girlfriends too. Otherwise it can be like living in a room with no heating. You'll end up spending more because you can't spend time at home.

**What's included?**
**When you're working out where to live, work out what's included in the cost. It's no good economising by renting a room at £30 a week if it doesn't include any bills or any furniture. By the time you've made the place habitable, you'll have forked out as much as somewhere twice the price.**

If bills are included, expect to pay about 10% more than without. But check on which bills are thrown in and which aren't. We heard about someone who was told they wouldn't have to pay gas bills. Sure enough, they didn't – because there was no gas supply. The heating was electric and on a meter that gobbled coins like they were chocolate.

Run through the list to see what's included and what's not – electricity, water rates, gas, oil, coal/solid fuel. Most housing doesn't usually need more than water, electricity and, sometimes, gas – but check first.

It's highly unlikely you'll find anywhere where the phone bill is included and don't be impressed if they start talking about council tax. Most students don't have to pay any (see Chapter 9).

If you're living in, the price will almost always include all the bills (except the phone) and may include a cleaner, bed linen and sometimes even a TV (with licence).

Universities will frequently offer catered accommodation as an option (or even as the only option). They may charge you only for the food you eat, either like a cafeteria or as a flat charge for every meal, but it's also common for the food bill to be thrown in with your rent.

Catered accommodation is often around 50% more expensive and it can be a boon or a bane. Check out exactly what meals are provided (lunch usually isn't, nor evening meals at weekends). Also check the meal times. It's all very well having paid for breakfast or dinner (or tea or supper or whatever you want to call it), but not if breakfast is always finished before you get up and dinner's over by the time you get back from lectures.

Also, find out what other options remain when a meal isn't provided. **You don't want to get into a situation where every Sunday night you're ordering a takeaway because there's no meal provided and only a toaster where you can cook anything for yourself.**

Think too about the quality of the grub. Catered accommodation is often a bargain, because at least it's a nutritious square meal and it's already paid for – but if it's inedible, it's just more money down the pan. (All too often quite literally, if indirectly.)

## Location

How far is your accommodation from the university? Or at least, how far is it from whatever part of the university you need to go to most regularly? Bear in mind that lots of universities are based on more than one site – sometime considerably more than spitting distance apart (unless you know anyone who can project a loogie more than five or ten miles).

If you're too far from the action, you're either going to be paying travel costs to get around or spending a lot of time walking and cycling.

If you can't find anywhere close (as is sometimes the case), what's the local transport like? Are there buses or trains and, if so, are they regular and do they operate until late into the night? If not, you just know you'd better put taxis down as a pretty big item in your budget plans.

Obviously the closer, the better – another good reason for living in (although university housing isn't always where you'd like it to be).

**Even if you're on or near campus, are you anywhere near other essential services such as shops, a cheap and friendly pub, a supermarket, an Indian takeaway? Is it a popular student area – will the social scene be good? Again, if not, you'll spend half your time and/or money travelling.**

Also what's the crime like in the area? Steer clear of anything too dodgy, even if the house itself seems pleasant enough. Mistakes like that can be false economies.

### Facilities

You get what you pay for, so if you're getting a big, plush room with en suite bathroom, crystal chandeliers and shag pile carpets, then expect to plunge deep into the debt pool.

In reality, of course, most student houses are notoriously bog standard (and often sub-standard), but occasionally you may be lucky enough to find hints of luxury. Don't laugh, but en suite shower rooms and toilets are becoming pretty much standard in newer housing.

Don't expect to get it for free, however.

**If you're living out, most student houses come equipped with the basics, although if you want a washing machine, TV, VCR, sauna and so on, you'll have to make your own arrangements. (Oh, and if there's no plumbing for a washing machine, check that you won't have to carry your dirty kecks halfway across town to find the nearest launderette.)**

You may well also need to provide your own kitchen equipment – everything from knives and forks to pots and pans. But not usually including the kitchen sink.

If you go in with a sizeable group of housemates, you may all want to chip in to buy or rent a microwave and/or a freezer if there isn't one provided. Renting one is usually pricier in the long-term (see below) and if you own it, you can at least sell it on to the next bunch of students when you leave. However, rental, does avoid arguments about whose TV it is – especially if it gets nicked.

You should expect central heating, with fully functioning radiators in every room. Your room should have, at the very least, a bed, a radiator, a desk, a chair and a wardrobe. Fashionably spartan rooms (I believe the word is 'minimalist') are the norm and don't expect brand new spine-friendly mattresses or top quality furnishings. Expect orange carpet, purple curtains and brown walls.

It's up to you to give it your own personal makeover to make it feel as homely as possible, but ask the landlord's permission before doing anything expensive or you may end up paying again to reverse it.

## RENTING TIPS FOR LIVING OUT

Most universities have an accommodation office that helps students find a suitable place to lay their weary head, but if there's high demand they won't be able to do much more than help you realise a bit quicker how hard it is to find anywhere affordable.

If you aren't using your university's property service to find accommodation, at least get them to check out your tenancy agreement before you sign it. In fact, nag them with questions if there's anything to do with your living arrangements that bugging you.

Get your landlord/lady to give you confirmation that everything's in satisfactory working order (a boiler certificate, for example) before you sign anything and whenever something goes wrong pester them till they sort it out. Especially if it's dangerous or causing you expense. Tenants have rights and you shouldn't have to put up with faulty plumbing, blocked drains, a leaking roof or rising damp.

Make sure you get an inventory of everything that's there when you move in and make sure it doesn't have anything on it that isn't.

Your landlord will check it all when you leave and if there's anything missing, they'll charge you for it.

**Before you move in, you'll have to pay usually a month's rent in advance plus a deposit. The deposit is usually the same as a month's rent (if it's more than two months, get suspicious) and it's there as protection for the landlord if you either trash the joint or do a runner. You won't normally have to pay a deposit if you live in.**

Despite what a shocking proportion of landlords seem to think, it's not there as a bonus for them to keep when you move out.

All things being well, you should get the deposit back at the end of the year. However, in the meantime, it can make hole of several hundred quid in your bank balance.

Apart from checking the inventory, another way to protect yourself is to take photos of the place when you first move in – especially if there's any dodgy decorating or anything broken. That way you can prove what's got worse while you've been there.

A reasonable amount of wear and tear shouldn't cost you your deposit, but specific breakages and party damage will. It's also not a deposit-losing offence if the roof falls in or the boiler blows up, unless it was clearly your fault. (So hide the elephant afterwards.)

When negotiating your tenancy, try to get the landlord to put the deposit in an account held jointly in your name and theirs. That way neither of you gets the money at the end of the year without the other party agreeing it's fair.

Never hand over any money (for deposits, retainers, rent or anything else) till everyone's happy with all the terms and conditions and has signed on the line. A verbal agreement is not good enough.

**Don't be fooled by wily, charming or – worst of all – apparently vague landlords or property agencies: they're business people after your money. And it's not as if there's much to go around.**

**Don't give it to them until you know exactly what you will be getting and firmly believe it is right for you.**

*The Young Ones* is not a documentary about student house-sharing and should not be regarded as a guide to student living. Cleanliness may not come naturally to you. It may not even be your top priority, but you don't want to get a call from the landlord saying they're popping by tomorrow if that's okay and then have to splash out on a professional house-cleaning crew in order to protect your deposit.

Nor do you want the place to become a health hazard, for that matter.

Speaking of surprise visits, depending on your contract your landlord normally has to give you notice if they want to come round. But usually it's only 24 hours and, besides, it can be hard to say no in case they ask why.

Your landlord isn't usually allowed to put your rent up more than once a year, so if they try, tell them you won't pay the increase. Then don't. So long as you pay your old rent, they won't be able to do anything.

Read your tenancy contract and don't do anything you're not allowed to. Then you should be fine. And don't stand for any crap from your landlord that's not in the contract. Always be as friendly and polite as possible and only as rude and firm as necessary – that's the way.

Complain, a lot. Whenever you get a bum deal or anything that's off. Apart from the fact that you can't afford the waste, you'll often get more than just a replacement. Some companies will give you your money back and/or coupons too, effectively meaning you get what you bought for free.

# Food

Food will probably take the next largest bite out of your budget.

It's perfectly feasible to eat healthily, sensibly and cheaply all at the same time, but students tend to concentrate most on the last of those three. Or they do until the pub closes and then they're more worried about eating fast.

As a result, students have a tendency to be junk food junkies. If you can't order it with fries or bung it in a microwave or a toaster, it's simply too much hassle for most. Okay, so we can't all be Jamie Oliver, but there are plenty of cookbooks on the market written especially for students.

**Healthy eating on a budget is not as tedious as it sounds. In fact, learning to cook is one of the most useful skills you can acquire as a student (stuff all that computers and foreign languages nonsense). It's also the best way of keeping you costs down.**

Take ready-made garlic bread for instance. Even the economy brand costs more than a quid. You can make your own for half the price in about the same time. Honestly. Try it. Mix garlic puree, butter, dried parsley, spread it in a French stick, slam it in the oven, 200°C, ten minutes. As Jamie would say, pukka.

**The real key, however, is not to make your own versions of fast food, but to work with fresh ingredients.** Fruit and veg are nutritious and a lot cheaper than meat or packet foods. Eating healthily is not only best for you – it works out relatively cheap and, once you've got into it, tastes damn fine too.

Here's another one for you. Get some vegetables (courgettes, tomatoes and peppers, say, with a bit of garlic), chop 'em up, bung the lot in the oven for 20 minutes with a little oil, salt, pepper and some herbs. Serve with pasta and cheese. Cracking nosh at next to nothing.

A lot of students go veggie (if they're not already), which, so long as you get a balanced diet is healthier and cheaper. (Even cutting down on the dead flesh makes quite a difference.)

There's also the appeal of it being more sound. In fact, buying politically correct products is often no more expensive, especially if you know where to shop. Many student shops on university campuses stock a decent range of sound groceries from trade-fair choc to biodegradable washing powder that are cheaper and just as good as leading brands.

Organic foods do tend to be more expensive, however – at least for the moment. But even the organic products at the market can be cheaper than the stuff blasted with chemicals at the supermarket.

For packet foods, own brand stuff is almost always cheapest. Most supermarkets even have an own economy brand which is really cheap. They're often not noticeably inferior, they just package it like that to make you feel good about spending more. Don't be fooled.

**If you're spending more than about £40 a week on food (£50 in London), you're probably spending too much. (There's a proper budget plan in Chapter 14.) Remember that your food budget isn't just what's on your supermarket receipt. Don't forget to count snacks, teas and coffees in the campus cafeteria and any takeaways.**

You can ignore eating out when working out the weekly food budget, so long as you remember to count it under your entertainment costs.

What you spend on grub is bound to depend on where you live, what you eat and how much, but set aside a realistic nosh dosh allowance and stick to it.

If you're lucky, your parents will pack you off to uni with a big box of basics: longlife milk and fruit juice, coffee, tea, pasta and so on. But students cannot live on basics alone and this lot won't last long anyway.

Just remember that odd little snacks throughout the day do add up, so take the long route home from lectures, the one that avoids the coffee shops, the newsagent and the snack-crammed vending machine.

Don't rely on your next loan cheque to pay off what you already owe. You'll need it for your rent and food next term, so what'll you do then?

## TOP TUCKER TIPS

An hour or two before closing, supermarkets mark down some of their goods, usually stuff that's heading fast towards its sell by date.

Like hyenas to the waterhole, scavenging hoards of bargain-hungry students have been known to descend on Tesco of an evening in the hope of bagging a few half-price items. But make sure you eat them before they go off.

Also, look out for tins that are marked down because they're damaged. So long as you can still get a tin opener latched on, there's nothing wrong with the contents.

What's more, supermarkets always have various special offers going, but some are more special than others. Keep your eyes peeled for those that are actually worth something, especially 'bogofs' (buy one get one free).

**Don't shop while you're hungry – you'll end up with twice as much stuff as you need in your basket.**

Collect coupons from magazines, flyers or from the sides of packets – or anywhere so long as it cuts the price. Remember to take them with you when you go shopping.

On the other hand don't buy stuff just because it's marked down or on special offer or you've got a coupon. It's not enough that it's cheaper than usual. It's got to be cheaper than other things. A reduced price frozen pack of macaroni cheese is probably still three times the price of one you could make for yourself.

Most supermarkets (not Safeways) offer a loyalty card of some sort which in the end gives you money off. Some even have special loyalty cards for students. They're all a bit of a rip off, because presumably you end up paying for any loyalty card deals by paying higher prices in the first place, but that certainly doesn't mean you shouldn't use the system. Why should you be the one who pays extra for everyone else's discounts?

Don't over-order at restaurants – the 'eyes bigger than belly' syndrome. Of if you do, ask for a doggy bag.

If you're eating out, exploit all-you-can-eat buffets to an almost criminal degree. However, don't starve yourself so you can eat more. It doesn't work. A Warwick maths student friend once fasted for a day before gorging on ten pepperoni pizza slices and three servings of cold pasta salad for the bargain price of £4.99. He spent the evening with his head in the toilet bowl getting no nutritional value from his food whatsoever.

Any ready-made sandwiches that cost more than 50p are a con. You can make your own with whatever fillings you want for just a few pence.

**Share cooking and shopping with housemates and split the bills. Don't fuss about who's eating more. You're all subsidising each other anyway because it works out cheaper than buying for one.**

**Learn to cook before you leave home and don't try to save money by eating less or only eating plain pasta. Food is your fuel. Try putting lighter fluid in a Formula One car and you won't get top performance.**

Team up with housemates to form a cooking syndicate. Cooking for one is expensive and. besides, a rota means that you only have the hassle of cooking once in a while. What's more, if you only know how to do spag bol, you might get to try someone else's speciality once in a while.

If a cooking syndicate doesn't appeal (it may turn out that your housemate's idea of cordon bleu is cremated bread with spaghetti hoops), how about cooking in bulk – make big casseroles that will last you a few days. Especially good if you've got a freezer and/or a microwave.

Remember to refrigerate leftovers, especially if they contain meat. Then remember to eat them before they go off.

Although eating like a veggie is a good option, even on a budget the devoted flesh-feeder doesn't have to give up sausages and bacon.

Rice, beans, lentils and pasta are words that most carnivores do not use very often, but they're a staple in most students' diet. They contain lots of carbs and goodness, they're very versatile and, when you get used to the taste, actually quite yummy.

# Household Bills

To some students – if they've not lived away from home before – bills can come as a shock. (The electricity bill would be an electric shock, we guess.)

From the start, make an arrangement with your housemates to avoid future tension. Perhaps you could make a different person responsible for each bill and divide the costs equally between you from there.

When you're living out, the bills that are likely to come dropping through the door are as follows:

### TV Licence

If you have your own TV set or have bought or rented one with your housemates, you'll need to get a licence.

It's currently £104 for a colour telly, which isn't so bad if it's divided between several people. It's definitely not worth risking the fine and a criminal conviction.

### Telephone

If you want a land line, make sure you get a good deal (perhaps one with an internet package included).

BT offers its 'Family & Friends' discount deal, among others. If you use the internet from home, make sure you ISP's number is down as your best friend. It may feel particularly sad to have the internet as your best friend, but forget pride, this is serious. It's about money.

BT aren't the only phone company around, so do a little research to find the best deal, especially if you make many international calls.

**If you're sharing a line with housemates – which you probably will – have a notepad by the phone on which everyone writes down all their outgoing calls. That way you can minimise the arguments when the bill comes. (Oh, and make sure you get itemised phone bills.)**

Since basic line rental is quite pricey, students who don't need to connect to the 'net increasingly go for mobile packages, particularly 'pay as you go' deals.

## Gas, electricity and other fuel

Depending on how many of you are sharing, how many electrical appliances you have between you, how much you all enjoy heat and steamy baths and the time of year (rates will naturally be higher in winter), expect to pay £5 to £15 per month per person.

Gas is generally a bit cheaper, but an efficient electric central heating system is cheaper than an old gas boiler.

In rural areas you may still find you need to use oil or solid fuels (such as coal). It's not common and they're a total pain in the butt – not too mention dirty, environmentally unfriendly and inconvenient when you run out of fuel.

See Chapter 14 for tips on how to keep the bills down.

## Water rates

Your landlord will often pay these for you, but find out where you stand because if they don't, just having running water will usually add between £200 and £300 a year to the household budget. Students are usually able to split the costs as housemates, but still, it's more money you haven't got.

**Some houses now use water meters that measure exactly how much you use. Unless you're compulsively clean and take one hell of a lot of baths and do a load of washing every day, for students these tend to work out cheaper.**

## Hire and rental fees

If you choose to rent kitchen appliances or entertainment equipment, it's best to go with a recognised outlet such as Radio Rentals or Granada who will probably offer student deals at branches in university towns.

There are plenty of budget rental shops, but some of them are a bit suspect and their kit often has a tendency to break down on an exhaustingly regular basis.

Average rental for a washing machine (or washer/drier) runs at around £15 to £20 a month. Compared to going to the launderette, it's a little more expensive, but in terms of hassle it's like comparing a hover mower to cutting grass with nail clippers.

For a basic TV/VCR combo you're looking at about £20 to £25 a month, including insurance. If you consider what you might otherwise spend on entertainments if you didn't have a TV at home, it can actually be quite a cheap form of amusement (even when you factor in the TV licence – see above). It's cheaper still if you can persuade your housemates to split the cost with you.

**You won't need a separate insurance policy for rented stuff if you've already got household contents insurance (see below), but you'll have to take your insurance documents to the hire shop to prove you are covered.**

### Others

Students do not have to pay council tax, but there may be other expenses such as maintenance costs (for flats) and general household repairs to watch out for.

If you choose to host a party, there's almost always a sacrifice to be made to the great party god. If anyone breaks a window or puts their head through a wall, say, it's down to you to get it fixed and such unexpected costs can be pretty expensive.

**4**

Always go to Freshers' Fairs even when you're no longer a fresher or even if they're not at your own university. You can pick up loads of freebies — food, toiletries etc — stock up enough and you won't need to shop for a year.

Kiki Enobakhare, UCL

### BILLS TIPS

If you leave a bill long enough without paying it, it goes red. Well, metaphorically speaking. What usually happens is that a few weeks after you get the first bill, you get a reminder (that often is, literally, printed in red).

They don't warn you again. After that, they cut you off. Phone, electricity, gas, it doesn't matter – someone at head office flicks a switch and you're powerless. Literally.

To get reconnected, you have to pay not only the original bill, but a slap-on-the-wrist charge for being so naughty.

Therefore, it's best not to let the bills go red in the first place.

It's so tempting to ignore bills when you have so many other financial pressures on you, but the best policy is to pay up promptly. Ultimately, it's not just a matter of being cut off – you could be evicted by your landlord for not paying utility bills or end up with a court summons.

Decide with your housemates who is responsible for which bills. Don't leave it to each other on the assumption that someone will deal with it. Someone rarely does. If a red bill turns up, check what's going on with whoever was supposed to pay it and, if necessary, work something out. But whatever you do, get it paid.

Ideally, keep the bills low in the first place, not just for your benefit but for the environment too.

**Switch off lights and don't heat the house when you're not there. That kind of thing makes a big difference (see Chapter 14).**

Some people like to keep a household kitty which everyone chips into and which you use to pay for communal things like bills and possibly even shopping for food (or for essentials like bread, milk, tea and coffee, at any rate).

In some households, for whatever reason, kitties don't work – they just cause more arguments and friction.

If you all have the same attitude to money, the communal approach is more likely to work and by pooling your resources you could save money and get bills paid on time. **Unfortunately, it's usually only after you've lived with someone for a few months that you realise what a selfish git they really are, how they never wash up and how they never pay up their share on time even though they always seem to have money for their copy of *Loaded*.**

Sometimes, rather than a kitty, a rota for paying bills works out better (and a rota for household chores is usually a good move, too).

# Washing, laundry and household sundries

That fateful straw that cripples the poor proverbial camel is not from some super-heavy GM crop.

Likewise, it's the more mundane and easily-overlooked costs that can dump you in debt just when you thought you were in the clear. It's a looking-after-the-pennies thing.

Washing powder, cleaning products, toiletries, kitchen towels, toilet paper... again these are areas where a household kitty could come in handy. They may be little things, but, as anyone who's ever realised they've run out of toilet roll at a critical moment should recognise, they're not expenses you want to skimp on.

**You can economise by not using Clinique and designer smellies. To paraphrase L'Oréal, you may be worth it – but you can't afford it.** Body Shop was pretty much invented for students (ethically sound, not too expensive), but if you're comfortable making your own soap from the bins out the back of the liposuction clinic (*á la Fight Club*), go ahead.

Laundry costs can be considerable though there is, of course, the option of never washing or doing laundry. It has been known for students to get four days' wear out of their pants through 'quartering' (wear them for a day; turn them back to front, wear them for another day; inside-out, another day; inside-out and back to front... voilà, four days' wear). However, this route to cost cutting can mean you need to spend more on your social life to keep any friends.

And, by the way, have you ever experienced the mindless tedium of trying to iron your clothes? In fact, do you even own an iron? (Most university rooms will have a communal ironing board that doesn't stay up and an iron that doesn't work. In which case you can pick up a perfectly good iron for under £20. Oops, there goes another pony.) Time to go back home for the weekend and tell your mum how much you love her...

# Clothes

**Two words: charity shops.**

They really do give you the best of both worlds – you get to maintain that archetypically scruffy student image for a fraction of the price, whilst helping out some worthy cause.

But seriously, it's not all tasteless tank tops, corduroy dungarees and flamboyant flares. Just because you're Oxfam's most loyal customer doesn't mean the fashion police will be after you. On the contrary, you'll have more clothes in your wardrobe and more cash in your pocket. You can sashay past the big department stores in your battered old 99p Green Flash trainers with your head held high.

It does matter where you live, however. Not every charity shop is a resting home for retired designer wear, so it's well worth trekking across town to charity shops in the posher or trendier areas to find a better class of old tat.

Two more words: January sales.

If you don't mind risking death by crushing crowds and suffocation, these are often a good bet. The discounts are sometimes unmissable – 75% off or even more…

Then there are markets and stalls. Most are cheap – well, cheaper than high street shops at any rate. Places like Camden Market in London and the retro shops in the Laines in Brighton are renowned as treasure troves of cheap chic.

Second-hand and cheap gear sellers also often visit students' unions and set up a stall.

Of course, nothing's cheap if you buy more than you need of it, so don't get blinded by the bargains. If necessary, only take a certain amount of cash with you to stop yourself just having to snap up another pair of eight-inch pink glitter platform trainers – a snip at only £90.

Shopaholism is a recognised ailment in modern society and students are sadly not immune from this terrible affliction.

Students from the 'big cities', especially fashion-conscious London, are particularly susceptible. All their self-control seems to wither away whenever they pass a fashion store. Which is why credit cards and store cards are potentially so dangerous (see Chapter 9).

**On the whole, new clothes are hardly cheap, although there are plenty of relatively inexpensive fashion stores knocking about on the high street (Top Shop/Top Man, New Look, Bay Trading, Miss Selfridge, Madhouse, Byrite to name but a few) and some will give you discounts if you show them your student union card.**

Watch out for the impulse purchase. If you see a bargain, ask yourself: is it really such a good deal? How often will you wear it? But try to buy decent quality – clothes made of good material that'll last longer than the next rinse cycle as you'll want to get a fair amount of wear out of anything you buy.

There are some special occasions when you'll want to splash out (see Chapter 12), but as a rule don't buy anything unless you have tried it on first and know you'll be able to wear it regularly for many months before it falls off you in rags.

It's not that you have to give up on image. It's just that you'll need to exercise a bit of imagination to create it.

Don't be tempted to update your wardrobe on a whim every couple of months (or every time you split up with a partner) – learn how to mix and match a few versatile items of clothing to create a range of different looks. Wear layers so that you can get use out of your summer outfit all year round.

**Only treat yourself when you can afford to, which means sticking to your budget (see Chapter 14). Whether you like it or not, clothes represent an area of your spending on which you can cut back, so it's best to see how finances are going first.**

Most students spend between £200 and £500 a year on clothing. To put this into perspective, Posh Spice allegedly spends £2,000 a day – but that's probably a smaller percentage of her income than £500 a year would be of yours.

As you can see from the figures above, anything over £270 is pushing at the edges of the debt envelope – but you can decide to spend whatever you like so long as when you add it all up, it's within what you can afford. Then you need to stick to it.

Distinguish between wants and needs and prioritise from there.

And how about making your own clothes?

You don't have to be a fashion student to create something unique and wearable (and even stylish). You can always buy something from a second-hand shop and modify it to suit your taste.

You could tie-dye a shirt (sooo 90s), embroider some old jeans, hack up a skirt or print your own designs on plain T-shirts. There are a number of books on the market about how to clothe yourself on a budget and you don't have to be Vivienne Westwood to step out in homemade style.

Supposedly, Lawrence Llewellyn-Bowen makes a lot of his own clothes, but don't let that put you off.

> You may be covered by insurance, but minimise the risk of having your stuff nicked in the first place by keeping expensive-looking items away from windows and always locking internal doors where you can. Insurance premiums will be lower if you have a personal lock on your bedroom door.

## Insurance

Not everybody bothers with insurance, but if you don't it'll probably cost you many times as much in replacing everything or bailing yourself out of whatever crisis you find yourself in.

Basically, if you can't afford to buy everything you currently own, you can't afford not to be insured. There are many different types of policy about and lots of special student packages available. There's a policy search facility and more info at www.insuranceforstudents.co.uk.

### POSSESSIONS INSURANCE

Don't fall into the trap of thinking, 'I'll be okay, so long as I always lock the door.' Students are notoriously common victims of burglaries. It doesn't matter whether you live in or out, it only takes a minute to grab a hi-fi or walk off with a computer.

Another trap is to think that you don't have anything worth nicking. You'd be surprised what people will take if they can't find anything valuable. If they're stupid enough to go thieving other people's stuff in the first place, they're stupid enough to think your clothes, your homemade music compilations, your books and even your mugs and half-used toiletries are worth taking.

**Even students who don't have a computer, a TV or even a stereo are often surprised at how much their combined possessions are worth. Unfortunately, they only usually stop to work it out when it's been pinched and, because they thought insurance was an unnecessary expense, they're now forking out to replace it all.**

If you are in halls of residence you may find that your rent charge includes a comprehensive insurance policy to cover all the students living there. But don't assume that it does.

Failing that, check your parents' home insurance policy. Quite a few of them cover your belongings even though you're living away from home (but sometimes they exclude student residences, so read the small print).

If after checking all these options, it turns out you're not insured, you can get basic personal cover from pretty much any general insurance company or bank.

There are companies that specialise in students, most notably Endsleigh, although other companies such as Norwich Union often have packages that are just as good, depending on where you're living.

For total possessions up to a value of £2,000, premiums will usually be around £20 to £30, with higher rates for those in private rented accommodation off campus. Two grand isn't actually all that much and if you've got a computer or any expensive bit of kit, you'll need to talk to the insurer about either increased cover or insuring that item separately. (You might also want to cover certain items for accidental loss or damage.)

If you're living out, your landlord should already have building insurance (to cover fire and structural damage), but it won't cover any contents of the building that belong to you.

You'll need to take out either your own policy or a joint policy with your housemates. It's likely to be a little more expensive than if you were living in, depending on the security measures (window locks, alarms and so on) and, most importantly, exactly where you're living.

**If you live in a dodgy area and have thousands of pounds worth of stuff in your room, there will be no avoiding a sky-high premium – but it's worth it anyway. It's higher precisely because you're more likely to be robbed.**

Generally, possessions insurance shouldn't set you back more than £100 a year tops. If it does, either get another quote or see if you can leave some of your more valuable possessions back at home, especially things like jewellery.

Just because you're insured up to the hilt, don't get complacent about security. Not only is making a claim a real hassle, but replacing stuff takes time and is never 100% satisfactory.

Besides, there'll probably be an excess on your policy – a sort of buffer zone of anything from £50 to £250 to stop you making pathetically small claims. This means that whatever your claim, you have to meet the amount of the excess yourself – you always lose out.

Just taking out insurance isn't enough – be aware, too. Lock doors and windows when you go out (or even when you're in) and if you live on campus and see someone you don't recognise wandering down your corridor in halls, ask them if they need any help (especially if they're carrying anything valuable).

They may just be visiting a friend. On the other hand they could be on their way to your room, to help themselves while you're in the kitchen making a coffee.

## WHEELS

### Cars

Amazingly enough, quite a few students are car-owners, in spite of the massive costs involved in running a car and the havoc the metal monsters reek on the planet.

After buying the car itself, the biggest expense is the insurance and new drivers under 21 are unlikely to have much luck finding anything that doesn't blow their student income out of the water.

Endsleigh Insurance do a special deal for students that can work out relatively cheaply, depending on the make, age and model of the car, your age and status and where you live. It might be cheaper to take out car insurance from your home address rather than your university address or vice versa.

**Whether your car is shiny and new and sexy or clapped out and rusty, fully comprehensive car insurance for students is likely to be at least £600 a year and more than double that in some cases.**

Shop around for the best deal – you can save several hundred quid.

If your car's more than 25 years old, you may qualify for classic car insurance which cuts the cost like a machete through a mango. It's still outrageously expensive, though, and hardly any student who cared about the state of their finances would ever even consider owning a car.

### Bicycles

Bike insurance is pretty pricey too, believe it or not. Mainly because the student who doesn't have their bike nicked at some point is probably the student who doesn't own one.

Endsleigh have teamed up with the National Cycle Register (NCR) to offer a special insurance scheme for bikes worth up to £2,500. You register with the NCR and are given a unique number so you can make faster claims and have a greater chance of getting your bike back if it is stolen.

Some of the banks offer good insurance deals also. If you're getting a bike – which, by the way, is a fantastically economical thing to do as a student (so long as you use it) – best to stick with one that doesn't look too flash.

It's also worth splashing out on the most intimidating padlock and chain you can find. (And, by the way, you can buy a metre of saw-proof chain at a hardware store much more cheaply than a tailor-made bike chain). And try to get a bike with a removable saddle.

Bike insurance ranges from about £40 up to £240, although premiums usually take a hike every year. Always check the terms and conditions of your insurance documents very carefully.

**Travel insurance**

Whether you're travelling in the UK only, around Europe or all over the world, get yourself a good insurance policy. They're not that pricey and since it's so easy for things to go wrong when you're budget travelling, it's important to know there's a safety net to cover delays, cancellations, theft, lost luggage, medical bills and all your other nightmares.

Every policy's different, however, so make sure you get the right balance of cover for your needs and shop around till you get it at the right price.

If your course includes time abroad, you'll have to manage your finances to cover extra travel expenses (see Chapter 13).

# Travel

**LOCAL TRAVEL**

If you live out, you'll probably have to get to campus most days (perhaps every day if you're on a science course). That will almost certainly mean using public transport, for which the operators have an annoying habit of charging fares.

Even if you live in, you'll want to get off campus once in a while, if only to do the shopping – campus life can get a bit like nomination time in the Big Brother House and sometimes getting out and about is the only way to preserve your sanity.

**So whichever university you attend. and wherever you live, you'll have to put aside a certain amount for local travel, probably anything from a few quid a month up to, in London, potentially £50 or more every week (see below).**

Check out the cost and frequency of local buses to and from the university campus, the time of the last bus – perhaps you'll have to fork out for a taxi after midnight – and the safety of the area in which you live. If it's not safe to walk home at night, you'll either be looking at self-imposed house arrest after sun-down or yet more cab fares.

Living on campus obviously cuts your travel costs, but even if you can find somewhere within a mile or two you will protect your pennies and what's more you'll keep fit what with all the walking, cycling or even jogging you'll be doing back and forth.

As soon as you get to university, one of your top priorities should be to find out about local travel passes. There'll often be some kind of pass for buses and/or trains for students and/or young people.

Passes are often restricted to a certain number of trips or to a specified period of a day, a weekend, a week, a month, a year – or sometimes even a term – and sorting it out near the beginning of term will ensure that you get the most out of it. They can also cost so much that you'll want to get the expense out of the way before you're too broke.

### Travel in London

Most public transport in London makes burning money look like sound investment practice. Thanks to recent price reductions the buses are actually quite reasonable, but they still take forever to get anywhere. The same goes for the whole public transport system, actually, but that's partly because London is just so damn big.

The sheer size of the place also makes walking impractical for a journey even a relatively small way across town. As for cycling, again the distances are a challenge and if you survive the traffic and the fumes you may just make it to your destination.

As you probably know, even if you're not a Londoner, public transport consists mainly of the Underground ('the Tube') and red double-decker buses. There are also overground trains and other smaller networks like the Docklands Light Railway and the River buses (which are boats that hardly anyone uses).

There's a whole pack of Travelcards for buses, Tubes and trains. They're for different people, for different periods of time and even for different modes of transport (you can, for example, get passes for buses only).

Most importantly, they're for different zones. Zone-wise, London is split into concentric rings with a circle in the centre. The circle is Zone 1 and the rings going out are Zones 2, 3, 4, 5 and 6.

If you only need to travel within a single zone, travel is relatively cheap, but cross the line and prices start climbing.

**Unfortunately most of the universities in London aren't in residential areas (or not areas that students can afford) and it can be tough balancing the cost saving of cheaper accommodation with the cost of getting from there to college and back again every day.**

For example, a monthly Travelcard for Zones 1 (where most of London University's buildings are) to Zone 3 (where the rents are more likely to be student-friendly) would set you back £86.10 – or £60 with a Student Card, for which you get an application form from your university.

Don't be tempted to resort to black taxis or minicabs. You could easily blow your weekly travel budget on one trip. Even late at night, you shouldn't have to. The night bus network – although interminably slow and full of drunk teenagers (as well as drunk students) – will get you home eventually.

When you send letters, packages and birthday cards, write between their name and the address 'FREEPOST'. 99% of the time the Post Office doesn't check and, if they do, it's the recipient that pays anyway.

Rhymer Rigby

## NATIONAL AND INTERNATIONAL TRAVEL

The further you live from home, the more it's going to cost to get there and back. So either pick a university that's not too far away or give up on the idea of making it back for your mum's Sunday lunch every weekend.

Bus and coach services are usually quite a bit cheaper than the trains, but you may be looking at a much longer journey. Unless, of course, the trains don't get any better over the next few years, in which case you'll be sitting in a stationary carriage for hours anyway.

Either way, you'll want to get either a Student Coachcard (for National Express and other coach services) or a Young Person's

Railcard. You could get both, but once you've picked your mode of travel, you might as well stick with it. They charge a one-off fee after which you get big travel discounts – although sometimes you'll find you can only travel on double apex supersaver trains on Tuesdays when there's a 'z' in the month and you've had a rabies shot. The basic deals are as follows:

- **Young Person's Railcard:** a third off most rail fares in the UK, plus a third off all-zone underground travel in London. You can get a Young Person's Railcard even if you're no longer a young person, so long as you're in full-time education.
- **Student Coachcard:** All students aged 17 and over can get a third off National Express and Scottish Citylink fares. For info phone National Express Call Centre on 0990 808080.

As for travelling abroad, most universities have their own travel bureau on campus. They're usually pretty cheap and specialise in student deals, but if there's either a Campus Travel or STA Travel bureau nearby, you may want to check out fares with them too.

There are discount cards galore for the international traveller – most of which cost money and usually only one of which will be worthwhile (and that not until you need it):

- **The International Student Identity Card (ISIC):** Up to 30% off international airfares and access to over 15,000 discounts in 90 countries worldwide.
- **Under-26 card:** Many perks and benefits for intrepid student travellers.
- **Go 25:** Much the same.
- **YHA Membership (Youth Hostel Association):** Access to over 5,000 budget youth hostels across 64 countries.

Also available are Interail tickets (cheap tickets for a month's unlimited travel on the railways of Europe) and the Freedom Pass (unlimited travel in the country of your choice for a short period of time).

## TRAVEL ALLOWANCES

The level of the student loan assumes that you'll spend £255 (£155 in Scotland) on travel in a year. But if your expenses are higher and you are lucky enough to fall into one of the following categories, then you can claim more:

You're disabled, especially if you are unable to use public transport and have to rely primarily on taxis (see Chapter 13)

You need to get to another establishment as part of your medical or dental course

You're attending an institution abroad as an essential part of your course (see Chapter 13).

## CARS

**Why the hell are you reading a book about student financial survival if you're even contemplating owning a car. You must have money to burn if you think you can afford it. You can't. 'Nuff said.**

Oh, alright, we'll say a little more, but only a little.

If you own a car, as we already said, the single biggest cost after the vehicle itself will be the insurance (see above). Then there's petrol, which ain't cheap either (approximately £30 to fill a medium-sized tank), plus you've got road tax (£105 annually), maintenance and an annual MOT test on top of all that. If (excluding the cost of the car) it doesn't costs you an extra £1,000 a year, you're very lucky or you're using it so little you probably don't need it anyway.

Should you be crazy enough or rich enough to have a car as a student, you could always offer lifts to friends and get them to chip in for the petrol – so long as it's less than the price of a bus or taxi, everyone should benefit.

However, don't set yourself up as a minicab unless you've got a licence. It's illegal and they'll take away your driving licence if they catch you. Then you'll be sorry.

Apart from the expense, possibly the biggest problem with owning a car is that it's always you who has to drive whenever you go anywhere with your mates and that means you can't drink.

## Academic Costs

You might think that once you've paid your tuition fees, you should get everything provided – exercise books with you name written on them, a pencil, some crayons – just like primary school.

But no – unfortunately, your tuition fees are just the start of it.

For a start, even though we're at the start of the 21st century, books are still a vital element of every degree course.

**Strangely enough some students, when confronted with a long reading list of academic titles, get a bit over-excited and rush out and treat it as a shopping list. Don't be tempted. You certainly won't need them all and, even if you do, that's what a library is for.**

With any luck, the list will be prioritised. There'll be main texts and secondary texts. You may well want you own copy of the main ones.

If so your first port of call should be the university's second-hand bookshop (if it has one). If you're lucky you'll get everything you need for half the usual price – maybe even less. Don't worry if someone's already written notes in the margins or highlighted bits. They may save you a lot of trouble.

**Get hold of your reading list as early as possible, so that you can look for pre-enjoyed books before everyone else on your course buys up the complete stock, leaving you to buy your books new.**

Whether you buy your books cheap or not, you'll probably spend more on books during the first term of each year than at any other time.

Many students feel they need a computer for typing up essays and for email and internet access. Or for programming or spreadsheets if that kind of thing is part of their course.

All universities have computers available for student use, so you may be able to get by without having your own, but often there aren't really enough to go around or the opening hours don't fit in with your through-the-night attitude to essay crises.

**A buzzing, whistling, DVD-playing, CD-rewriting, tea-making state-of-the-art computer will set you back thousands of pounds, but you can get a pretty good second-hand one for a few hundred.** It's your call whether you really can justify the expense, but if you're going to think about a personal bank loan for anything (see Chapter 9), a computer may be the right thing.

Then again, that's what birthdays and Christmases are for. Getting computers as presents.

As we already said back in Chapter 2, your choice of course has an impact on what academic costs you're going to face.

Whether it's a lab coat or an easel, oils and canvas, each course has its own cost implications. Art and design courses tend to be most crippling, but most have costs hidden in there somewhere.

Get an idea from your department of what the costs are and whether they know of any help you might be able to apply for (including, for example, bursaries – see Chapter 8).

Whatever you study, there are some basics you'll need: piles of notepads, files, folders, pens, paperclips, staples, highlighter pens, printing paper – and lots of dividers so you can spend your time organising your work rather than actually getting on and doing any of it.

Make a specific allowance for photocopying. Seriously. You'll have to do that much. If the maintenance and running costs weren't so high and if it weren't for the fact that you'll need to do most of your copying in the library, it would probably be worth buying your own copier.

It isn't, though. We only said that to make you realise quite how much money we're talking about here. Serious bucks.

**To limit your academic costs to the £170 listed in the table near the beginning of this chapter, you'll have to take a lot of care.**

**Your course, however, is obviously pretty damned important. So don't skimp more than you have to. Where possible, buy second-hand. Or better still, borrow.**

# Entertainment & socialising

Perhaps the only element of your budget that has any more give in it than a frozen pencil is entertainment.

Don't imagine that you can just cut the whole thing, however. You will need to have fun from time to time. Apart from the fact that you'd fairly swiftly go psycho if you didn't go out and kick back occasionally, you'd also miss out on a good chewy chunk of what student life is all about.

But if something's gotta give, it's gotta be the finances for fun.

When you come to work out your budget (see Chapter 14), you'll need to allow generously for the cost of everything you can't predict exactly. What's left is what you can allow yourself for entertainment.

With a bit of luck you'll be under budget on other things and therefore be able to loosen up on your own spending restrictions, but it's better to do that once you're in the clear than spend first and ask questions later.

**Where possible, apply for your student loan early and have it put into your account in three instalments throughout the year.**

**Still, if you want to have a good time, but need to do it cheaply, at least it's easier if you happen to be a student.**

For a start, if your students' union is affiliated to NUS, you'll get a free NUS card at the beginning of your first year. It'll carry your name, NUS number, the students' union's stamp and an invariably unattractive mug shot.

This is your passport to discounts in clubs, pubs, cinemas, theatres, in fact just about anywhere where students will be welcome bums on seats.

Within your university, too, the students' union will be responsible for putting on ents ranging from regular club nights to hypnotists, from movies to plays – you name it.

As we said in Chapter 2 (and I'm sure you were paying attention), the quality, quantity and the kind of entertainment varies from place to place – and even if it weren't for those variations, the differences in costs would probably be wider than a hamster eating a frisbee.

As it is, what you spend on entertainments will depend entirely on where you're living, what's available, what tickles your giggle stops and how often you do it.

**Taking all this into account, you're probably looking at a good-time budget of around £30 to £50 a week. This is to cover the usual: drinks, entrance to clubs, gigs and concerts, more drinks, movie tickets, eating out (if you don't count it under food; see above), a few more drinks and morning-after painkillers.**

Drinking in student bars is almost always cheaper than regular pubs and if you get your drinks in during happy hours, you can squeeze even more alcohol out of your notes.

Always be on the look-out for free entry and cheap deals. If you're a girl, practise your seductive smile and the blokes might just buy your drinks for you. If you're an easily-seduced bloke, try not to get taken in too often.

# Miscellaneous expenses

### CIGARETTES

If you have a twenty-a-day habit, that's £30 a week on bad breath, smoky hair and a hacking cough. That's more than £1,500 a year. Hardly spare change.

Roll-ups are cheaper, but just as unhealthy and almost as expensive. Give up the cancer sticks and you can free up that £30 for something healthy and fun, like windsurfing or Swedish massage.

Loads of students smoke just because it's sociable, but why not get together with a mate who smokes too and resolve to pack it in together?

No more student loan up in smoke (literally). You'll feel better, look better, smell better and save money. What more incentive do you need?

### MOBILE PHONES

Pre-pay mobile phones are popular with students and are two-a-penny these days.

Well, not quite that cheap perhaps, but they're an attractive alternative to sharing a single land line with your housemates. You get your own personal number and the cost of calls isn't too high if you don't go crazy (about 5p to 50p per minute, depending on the time of the call, who you're calling and the network you use).

A £50 pre-pay voucher should last you at least an entire term or even longer if you keep your text life under control and avoid peak-rate calls.

Contract mobiles are generally more expensive, even with the free off-peak minutes included in most packages. But keep looking out for special mobile offers advertised in newspapers; sometimes you can get the latest model handset with free connection and other benefits for a very good monthly price.

Whatever deal you opt for, keep an eye on what you actually spend. You may want to either switch tariff or learn to talk quicker.

### CHILDCARE

If you have a child in registered day care, you can get some kind of help with the expense. It might not cover all of it, but there are also supplementary grants available to students with dependents. See Chapter 13 for more guidance for student parents.

## And finally...

In Part 6, The *Push* Guide to Penny Pinching, there's even more advice about budgeting and stretching your money till it's a mile long.

Part 4: Where does it all go?
Chapter 12

# Costs from out of the blue

It's all very well planning your finances like a military operation, but sometimes Lady Luck likes to shove an oar in and remind you who's boss. She'll dump an unexpected expense on you that makes all your finely tuned preparation look like doodles in the sand.

**Nonetheless, whilst it may be a contradiction in terms, part of financial planning is to plan for the unexpected.**

It's a bit like your mum buying clothes two sizes too big when you were a kid – you were probably only going to grow one size till you'd worn out that jumper, but she went for two sizes just in case. If you were like me, that meant your clothes were either worn out or too big. But that's another story. The point is to leave room for costs to expand more than you think.

One way is to get insurance (see Chapter 11), but there are also certain seasonal costs you can predict. 'How?' you might ask. Because *Push* is going to tell you, that's how.

## Starting Out

### FRESHERS' WEEK

One thing about student life can be more or less guaranteed – the first week will the most expensive of your entire university career.

During the first week – or, as it's more commonly know 'Freshers Week' also 'Orientation Week', 'Week One', 'Week

Zero', 'Intro Week' and so on) – there aren't usually any academic commitments, just an endless stream of social events and red tape.

There are three functions of Freshers' Week:

- **Social:** to break the ice and establish a social life
- **Environmental:** to get used to the new situation and find your feet (the end of your legs is a good place to start the hunt)
- **Administrative:** to get you to fill out a million more forms and have described to you in tedious detail everything from how your course will be taught and assessed to what to do in the event of a new ice age.

To get the most out of Freshers' Week, it's a good idea to keep all three of these in mind.

And because you're going to be focusing on those three, it's dangerously easy to just spend, spend, spend during the first week.

In fact, it's pretty much impossible not to shell out a quite disturbing proportion of the money that's supposed to last the whole year.

Just for starters, you'll probably have to pay your tuition fees (if you have to pay any), plus your rent for the term or at least your first month's rent and a deposit. That's several tonners down already.

Then there'll be...

- all the clubs, societies and sports teams you want to join (about £3 to £15 a pop)
- drinks to buy – and believe me there's a whole lot of drinking going on in Freshers' Week what with unmissable ents on every night
- pubs and clubs to check out
- people to impress
- new kitchen cupboards to fill up with grub
- plants and posters to make your room feel less like an asylum cell
- books, paper and pens to buy
- endless passport photos to get for all the forms and ID cards.

Allow yourself some extra for Freshers' Week. At least an extra £20 for entertainments alone (let alone all the one-off expenses like mugs and a hole-punch). Fresher's Week is one of the few times it's okay to push the boat out a bit.

**Splashing out is part of settling in, getting to know the people (biblically, in some cases), consuming cheap beer like it's going out of fashion. It's almost an initiation ritual – after a week of binging and parties, you wake up with a hangover, late for a lecture and completely broke. You are now, officially, a student.**

But after this initial spurt of justifiable madness, it's time to take a chill pill and review your financial status before drinking yourself into a false sense of security.

Even during Freshers' Week there are some reins to pull on. Don't pay out money for anything unless you know you'll benefit from it.

For example, don't join every student society that looks more interesting than belly button fluff – join only those where you think there's a genuine chance you might actually turn up to something they do in the next few years. (But be open-minded – you'd be surprised what strange and perverse pastimes you might find yourself drawn to.)

And don't feel like you have to be a big spender to make friends or impress anyone. If you insist on getting all the rounds in, you'll look like a prat because everyone's in the same boat financially. (In fact, students often don't bother with buying rounds at all.) You'll end up with everyone taking advantage of you for a week and then being too poor to go out again all year.

`Don't shop while you're hungry — you'll end up with twice as much stuff as you need in your basket.`

There are a couple of saving graces about the finances of Freshers' Week.

Firstly the goody bag. NUS usually organises a plastic bag full of free stuff for new students. The free stuff comes from sponsors desperate to get your custom and includes everything from dog-flavoured Pot Snacks to new guarana and amphetamine flavoured drinks.

You'll also be given a whole load of money-off coupons for more of the same which, when you discover the stuff is disgusting, you should throw away rather than waste money.

There should also be some useful stuff in there, like toiletries, condoms, coffee, crisps, chocolate, even beer – you know, the essentials.

Secondly, there's the stuff you bring from home. Many parents won't object to your raiding the cupboards before setting off to university. Some will even help you load up.

Freshers' Week is also the time parents are most likely to give you some extra cash.

You'll presumably have already worked out between you how the formal parental contributions deal is going to work (see Chapter 5) and many parents want to stick rigidly to the formula. Fair enough. However, even they often feel tempted to shove £20 in your hand as they wave you goodbye.

If they can afford it, don't stop them. Just say thanks and tell them you'll see them at Christmas. (You can tell them you love them too, if that's the kind of stuff you do with your folks.)

In fact, if your parents can afford it, you can even tell them from us that even if they think giving you the odd tenner here, the occasional twenty there, is a bad idea – something we wouldn't disagree with – we think this is the one exception.

### SETTLING IN

Freshers are particularly susceptible to 'loan arrival frenzy' – when the first instalment of your loan hits your bank account, it's tempting to delude yourself into thinking you are rich. But that apparently huge lump sum has to last the entire term and it won't take much budget planning to see that it'll barely stretch across the bar, let alone across the term.

**Budgeting starts from day one. If it doesn't, then that first, reassuringly sizeable stash of cash will disappear like water down a plughole, leaving no more than few hairs and some gunk behind.**

In fact, it's worse than that – even if you do budget, you'll watch as your bank balance after the first week turns into a pale imitation of its former self by week two and after the first or second month the accumulated rent, bills, books, food, drink, taxi fares etc will almost certainly have beaten it down to minus figures.

In any case, your budget for the first few weeks should be on the high side. For one thing, for several weeks you'll be making one-off payments for stuff you need like a kettle, a cheese grater and a second set of underwear.

Also you'll also need to get the lie of the land. Where's the best place to shop for food, stationery, books and so on, weighing up the pros and cons of distance, price and quality? Where's the nearest laundrette? Where the best place for new clothes, because your first attempt at the laundrette turned everything pink?

These reconnaissance missions can in themselves become impromptu social events, either as collective outings or as debriefings from various scouting parties.

There are also likely to be some costly abortive attempts at new recipes, unnecessary travel expenses till you find out about the right bus pass and, until you realise why no one else ever goes there, visits to the more expensive kebab shop.

## Main Events

There are a few events during student life when you will feel the need to spend an obscene amount of money for something really unusual, special or just plain stupid.

University balls, for example. Most of them are basically just a big dinner and a disco – the difference being that you wear posh frocks and pay a posh price tag. Usually, there'll be more by way of entertainments than simply a couple of decks and a few flashing lights. There may be cabaret acts, a casino, fun fairs, bouncy castles and loads of bands – sometimes even has-beens you've heard of. (Hot Chocolate do a lot of balls – and we mean that in every sense).

Some universities go for balls in a much bigger way than others. Some have them once or twice a year – modest affairs at £30 a head.

**Other universities (Oxbridge especially) seem to have them almost every week and some of them are outrageously decadent bacchanalias more reminiscent of a Hollywood wedding than a student shindig, whose tickets sell like hot cakes at over a hundred quid each.**

Add to the ticket price the cost of far too much alcohol (some will probably be included in the ticket, but usually not enough), obligatory dress or tux hire (or even purchase if you plan to go to several of these jamborees).

The whole thing can end up costing the same as several weeks' rent.

Then there are job interviews.

Especially in your final year, you'll want to have an outfit that says, 'I scrub up alright and can look smart if I have to'.

The good news is, you may be able to get some help. In the case of a job interview, your bank will often make allowances and allow you to extend your overdraft (but not by much, mind and don't forget to ask first), so you can buy a suit.

For any other special events, you may just have to ask your parents or put in a few extra hours at your job if you have one – just one extra shift might earn you enough.

Remember that you may need to look smart at quite short notice. You may be able to predict family weddings or christenings a few months ahead of time, but if you have a funeral to attend, you'll probably have other things on your mind than what to wear.

At the end of it all, you may want to look a bit dapper for graduation day. Maybe not – plenty of students have collected their scrolls wearing jeans and a T-shirt under their gowns. But even they had to pay to hire the gown and, if they wanted it, the poncy photo for gran's bedside table.

## Spoiling yourself

Jewellery, perfume or aftershave, magazines, cosmetics, weekend breaks... now and then you need something to pep up your pecker – so long as you're sensible the rest of the time and when you do take a weekend break you spend it in a youth hostel in the Lake District rather than the Hilton in Hawaii, you should be able to afford the occasional treat.

See how much you have left each week after all the necessities have been paid for. If it's more than nothing, decide if you deserve a treat now or later, or just put more into your entertainment budget for next week.

The same goes for holidays. Except you'll need to save up all year.

If you work, however, you may even be able to put a little aside to save up for something really special, whether it's an air ticket to India, a leather jacket or a scooter.

The secret is to learn to recognise a luxury item before you pay for it – distinguish between what you want (the stuff you can live without) and what you need (the things you can't). Shoes are a necessity, for instance. Ten pairs, however, are a luxury.

**Prioritising expenditure is a central part of good budgeting sense. Stick luxury items on your Christmas and birthday wish lists and make sure the list does the rounds at the right time.**

**Buy fruit and veg from market stalls, not the supermarket.**

## Gifts

Every now and then (usually when you're down to your last penny), some bastard so-called friend will decide to have a birthday and expect to be bestowed with lavish gifts.

Okay, so if you're all students you know that your mates can barely afford the wrapping paper, let alone anything to put in it. So improvise a bit – give your mate that scratched, battered old CD they gave you for Christmas or make them something *Blue Peter* style out of an old toilet roll, a cluster of cotton buds, a tub of glitter and some sticky-back plastic.

Better still, convince them that the new Stereophonics album is quite simply the best thing since sliced bread and then buy it for them after cheekily recording it for your own collection. That way, you've treated yourself as well as the naturally delighted recipient.

**Improvisation is the key here along with, again, a good eye for the bargains. If it's your mate's birthday, find out what he or she really wants and then club together with some other friends to buy it.**

When it comes to family birthdays and anniversaries and Christmas, you'll probably have to use your common sense and maybe a little bit of artistic licence to come up with a novel gift idea.

It's not as if Christmas should come as a surprise. Apart from falling on the same date every year, you may find subtle hints of its approach in shop windows and TV trailers from late September onwards.

Even with a big and demanding family, you should be able to plan and limit the expenditure and the good news is that however many presents you have to give, you probably get about the same number back. Make this work for you by putting out the word on what you want good and early.

Also, when the January sales come around, seize the opportunity to buy some reduced Christmas cards and half-price pressies.

Better still, make your own cards – the ones in the shops aren't cheap considering they're just bits of folded card. Making your own will give it that special 'individual' touch, even if you don't have a single creative bone in your body.

After all, it's the thought that counts. Although we've always found that just thinking about buying a present is rarely quite so warmly received.

Nevertheless, if you can find something really thoughtful for 50p, it'll often go down better than something impersonal for a lot more.

Oh, and don't forget birthdays. A card on the right day is worth more than a hurriedly bought present three weeks late.

# Medical costs

For some people medical costs are an ongoing expense, particularly if you wear contacts or are diabetic or asthmatic. Generally, non-prescription stuff like contact lens solution is just going to have to be part of your budget.

However, all too often, extra medical costs come as a nasty insult added to the injury of being ill or hurt in the first place.

Fortunately the NHS, despite all the complaints, is still both free and offers a pretty high standard of care. A lot better than anything most students could afford in the world of private healthcare, anyway.

Nonetheless, there are charges for prescriptions, eye tests and dental appointments.

**Students are no longer automatically exempt from prescription charges and the like, but you may be entitled to help with charges for eye tests, prescriptions and dental treatment through the NHS Low Income Scheme.**

Take a look at the booklet HC11, *Are you Entitled to Help with Health Costs?*, available from your local benefits agency and probably from the students' union welfare department and the university's health service. Or you can call the Health Information Service on 0800 66 55 44.

If you're eligible, you will need to fill in a HC1 claim form, which you can get from a Social Security Office or your doctor. Once you've filled that in and sent it off, you'll get an HC2 certificate which entitles you to full help with health costs.

If you've forgotten to go through all this palaver or you've already had to pay out for treatment or prescriptions, keep your receipts – you might still be able to claim a refund for part of it.

# Part 5
# Finance for
# real people

5

Push

Part 5: Finance for real people
Chapter 13

# Special interest groups

## What about me?

It's easy enough to talk about students as an amorphous
collective blob, to say this is how it is if your parents earn this
or if you live there – but students are more than case studies.
Students – yes, even students – are real people.

And, because they're all individuals and it follows that there
are so many exceptions to any rule we might try to describe, it
can seem as if the only rule is: there are no rules.

This part of the book, therefore, is dedicated to the
exceptions – to the individuals who, one way or another, actually
make up about half the student population.

## What about postgrads?

As the number of undergraduates has risen over the past ten
years, so has the number of postgrads. And it's not just a
simple percentage game.

As more people realise the career benefits of having a
degree, they rightly assume there are even greater benefits if
you distinguish yourself further by having more than one degree.

Unfortunately, however, more people wanting to take up
postgrad studies means more pressure on the sources of
funding to support it. New funding possibilities have sprung up,
but not enough to make life easy.

To choose to be a postgrad is almost to say: 'I don't mind
continuing to be poor for at least another few years' (and quite

possibly, if you become an academic, never having a great deal of money).

However, postgrads don't usually live like undergrad students. Apart from tuition fees, postgrads should reckon on their costs being about 25% higher than undergrads'. Living in halls, for example, is hardly conducive to the kind of hard study and long hours most postgrads need (and want) to put in.

Being a bit older, as a rule, they'll often want somewhere on their own – or less of a dive, at least – and they'll be fed up of living on baked beans and pasta. In particular, their academic costs (books, computers, periodicals and so on) are much higher.

Nor is postgrad poverty quite like regular student poverty. It's in a different league and you don't even enter into it unless you can see a way out. The way out might be through funding that comes with your course or it might be that you expect to earn a lot when you finish and are therefore willing to take out a considerable loan.

Increasingly, postgrads combine their studies (often part-time themselves) with part-time or full-time work.

There are a number of sources of funding available to postgrads, but it isn't as straightforward as the undergraduate system and the competition is fierce.

The course you want to study and your academic brilliance make a big difference to your chances.

Instead of spending your important beer money unnecessarily, pop down to your local Burger King and fill up a bag with free sugar, salt and milk. Voila: accompaniments for a cuppa, a bowl of cornflakes, and a tequila slammer.

Leigh Koscan, University of Liverpool

The best odds are in courses that have a clear benefit to the country or to a company. Postgrad courses fall into two categories: taught courses and research degrees. Some funding sources only apply to one type or the other, but taught courses often have a specific use and so whomever it's useful to may be willing to pay.

As a ludicrously broad generalisation, research degrees only get funding if they have a practical application, but if that application makes money for someone other than the student, they may well get support. So science, technology and business courses attract much bigger bucks than, say, research projects on Shakespeare entitled 'To be or not to be: Should Hamlet have phoned a friend?'.

If you're outstanding in your subject area, you're also more likely to get some kind of support, even in the arts (in which case that support it may be only a pat on the back and a few luncheon vouchers). This works as a kind of ad hoc filtering system. You should only be doing postgrad study if you're up to the considerable academic challenge. So, the better you are, the more likely you are to get a place on a course (or find a supervisor for your research) and to get funding to do it.

**Postgraduates always have to pay towards their own fees or find someone to pay these for them. Different courses cost different amounts, although the standard going rate is currently £2,805 a year. Quite a few are more expensive – MBAs, for example, are £8,600 a year.**

Like the undergraduate fees, the fee is usually only a contribution to the total cost, the rest of which is paid for by taxpayers. Overseas postgrads pay full fees, which range from just under £7,000 for arts to over £17,000 for clinical courses.

**As for your living expenses, they're your own problem too. Unless you are taking a Postgraduate Certificate in Education (PGCE) you can't apply for a student loan.**

There is, however, some good news: postgrads who find themselves in a quidless quandary can appeal to their university's hardship fund for help. But that's only useful to get you out of a hole, not to stop you falling in it.

Nevertheless, there are funds out there to help pay both fees and the costs of living. The most important are laid out below and your university will also be able to give you advice.

University careers offices often produce leaflets about postgraduate funding and where to get it and most universities publish special postgrad prospectuses.

Talk directly to a tutor in the relevant department where you want to study. They'll tell you more about their work and may be able to give you pointers about raising the readies.

It's also worth taking a look at the 'Gradfund' page on Newcastle University's website (www.newcastle.ac.uk/services/finance/gradfund).

You can search for the right source of funding by using pull-down menus to pick the relevant subject, your nationality (some awards are available to all nationalities, but some are specific) and what exactly you intend to do (research, etc).

The website then searches its database and comes up with suggestions. If you have no luck, you may need to be more general with your criteria.

### GOVERNMENT FUNDING

The Government is (indirectly) by far the biggest bill-footer of postgrad study. Last year, through its award-making bodies, it gave out over 9,000 awards to students doing masters or doctorates and to full-time students doing professional or vocational training.

These awards might pay for your fees or your maintenance (living) costs, some allowances (for children, for example) or some additional expenses such as travel, but probably not all of them.

Depending on what you're studying, how many years you've already been studying it, where you're living and which award body you're asking for the money, most awards will be between £3,000 and £10,000, although some are even higher.

You might also be able to wheedle additional funds such as a support grant for research training.

All awards are made on a competitive basis, so it's hardly worth bothering unless you can boast a pretty rocking result in your undergraduate studies – usually a good 2:1 or a 1st.

The awards come in three flavours:

- **A Research Studentship:** Usually a three-year full-time or five-year part-time award for students doing doctorates (PhD or DPhil).

- **A Collaborative Research Studentship:** For example, Cooperative Awards in Science and Engineering (CASE) where a company contributes to the costs of a postgraduate research project and usually offers the student some valuable experience, plus some extra cash on top of the basic award, if they feel like it.

- **Advanced Course Studentships:** For taught courses lasting at least six months (usually for one to two years), usually leading to a masters – MSc, MA – or other qualification.

Check with the university department about how to apply. Sometimes they handle the application themselves – although by no means all courses or departments attract funding. Just because you've been accepted to do a course or research that is eligible for studentships, don't assume that you personally will receive one.

Often you'll need to contact the award-making body directly. There are now eight of them handing out the Government dough, comprising six **Research Councils**, the **Arts & Humanities Research Board** (AHRB) and the **Central Council for Education & Training in Social Work** (CCETSW) which doesn't give any of the normal flavour awards, only small means-tested bursaries for diplomas in social work.

Each body gives funding for separate subject areas, so make sure you're going to the right one and if they turn you down, don't bother trying the others.

Before you apply, contact before applying to check that they cover the right subject and to get full details about all the various strings attached to the money they might or might not give you.

### AHRB

As its name suggests, the AHRB funds arts and humanities students, but it doesn't have as much money as most of the Research Councils (see below). Even so, if you're lucky and get in there quickly, you might be considered for a grant for large-scale collaborative research projects, an award for research leave or a small grant in the creative and performing arts.

For contact details, turn to back of book.

### Research Councils

There are six Research Councils, each covering a different subject area – five for sciences and technology and one for economic and social sciences. You should apply to whichever is most appropriate for whatever you want to study.

- Biotechnology and Biological Sciences Research Council (BBSRC);
- Engineering and Physical Sciences Research Council (EPSRC);
- Economic and Social Research Council;
- Medical Research Council (MRC);
- Natural Environment Research Council (NERC);
- Particle Physics and Astronomy Research Council (PPARC).

The Research Councils have to report back to the Office of Science and Technology in the Department for Trade and Industry, which should tell you where the balance lies between education and commerce as far as the funding is concerned.

### COMPANIES

Employers sometimes sponsor their staff through courses, especially MBAs.

Alternatively, businesses often fund particular research projects and any postgrads that work on them. Sometimes, this'll be run as a collaborative research studentship through CASE (see above).

## TRUSTS AND CHARITIES

Trusts and charities are worth investigating. They will probably not be in a position to offer full financial support, but you may get a small award if you apply early enough. Contact EGAS (see Chapter 8) or look in the various directories and registers of charities and grant-making trusts.

Some charities, for example The Wellcome Trust, may fund particular research in the same way that businesses do.

## LEAS

Local education authorities (and their equivalents in Scotland and Northern Ireland) do not have to give any money to postgrads, except those on teacher training courses (see below).

Even so, if there's anything left in the kitty after they've given out what they must to undergrads, some do provide 'discretionary funding'.

Usually, you're only likely to get such funding for vocational courses that lead to certificates or diplomas (things like law, journalism, accountancy, computer science) and it'll depend on what other income you might have available (back to the parents again).

LEAs decide their own criteria for discretionary awards – but being early in the queue and being thoroughly deserving will usually help.

## UNIVERSITIES

Many universities have a limited number of studentship awards available for specific courses which usually cover fees and maintenance. Criteria and deadlines for applications vary, so do your research well in advance with the admissions officer of the university you want to go to.

Individual university departments may also be able to help in one of two ways.

The first is just to ask – it's a long shot, but if you're a complete star in your chosen subject you might just get lucky.

Your best bet for funding direct from your university or department is having a specific tutor take up your cause individually, which is most likely to happen if you stay in the same department where you've already done an undergraduate or lower postgrad degree.

They'll probably be championing your cause because they want you to become an academic, however, so expect to take on some tutoring responsibilities.

The second option is to get a job within the department more formally as a research assistant. You'll get paid and so long as you write up your research appropriately, it'll be assessed for a qualification.

The jobs are usually advertised in the normal way, although if you're already in a department keep your ear to the ground, just in case you can get in there early and persuade them to look no further. Otherwise, check *The Times*, *The Guardian*, *New Scientist*, *Times Higher Education Supplement*, *Lawyer Magazine* etc.

## BANKS

Banks aren't a formal part of the funding mechanism for postgrads, but many students rely on them more than any other source.

Banks have special loan packages for postgrads, mostly with a lower than standard rate of interest and repayments deferred till you finish your course. See 'Graduate Packages' in Chapter 6 for some of the current offers.

The Government backs the Career Development Loans scheme, but they're only available to students doing vocational courses. See Chapter 9 and then phone 0800 585 505 for a booklet about CDLs.

Since most postgrads have particular needs and reasons for doing what they're doing, not to mention their own situation in terms of what security they can offer, banks usually consider each case on its own merits (or lack of them).

So go in, have a chat and see if you can't wangle yourself a big fat loan and a nice free overdraft. (It's unlikely you'll get both, but either is a possibility and it's worth a try.)

# What about mature students and part-timers?

### MATURE STUDENTS

The definition of a 'mature student' varies, but it doesn't necessarily mean someone who wears a cardigan and slippers and who drinks a nice cup of cocoa before a sensible bedtime. For the purpose of student finance, 'mature' means a first-time undergraduate over the age of 25.

Under that definition, they may be able to claim a special bursary of up to £1,000 to cover course-related costs (see Chapter 8). However, you can't get it if you're already receiving a Childcare Grant (see below).

There's also a Mature Students Incentive Allowance of £1,550, but this time 'mature' means 26 or over by the 1st September before your course starts.

Almost any full-time student – mature, youthful or just plain childish – is entitled to the student loan up to the age of 50 (or 54 if they intend to go back to work after qualifying).

If you're thinking about going back to studying and becoming a mature student, as a first step you might want to get in touch with your nearest educational guidance and information centre by phoning LearnDirect on 0800 100 900. Alternatively, call in at the local Citizens' Advice Bureau.

### PART-TIME STUDENTS

Two-thirds of mature students study part-time and all part-time students studying at least half as much as they would on a full-time course can claim each year £500 or more as a loan (from the Student Loans Company) to help with course related costs. This was introduced a couple of years ago specifically with mature students in mind.

Part-time students on benefits or a low income may be able to get their fees paid – ask at your university.

Other than that, part-timers have to pay their own fees and, so the thinking goes, since they've got time to work for a living, they don't need other financial help.

**MARITAL STATUS**

If you're a single full-time mature student, you get an extra tax break on your income – the Inland Revenue doesn't count the first £7,500 at all.

If you're married, however – and this applies to students under 25 too – your husband's or wife's income will be assessed in much the same way as parents' incomes would be assessed for most students (see Chapter 3). However, the kick-in point at which you have to start contributing to fees (and ultimately to living costs) is lower (currently £17,200).

Again, as with parental assessments, there's a top limit to how much they're expected to help out and allowances are made if you've got kids.

# What about teachers in training?

The UK needs teachers at the moment like Railtrack needs a good kick up the arse. As a result, there's rarely been a better time to give teacher training a whirl.

The Government has been offering greater incentives for trainee teachers, especially for postgrads on PGCEs.

To be a teacher you have to have Qualified Teacher Status (QTS) and a PGCE is the most popular way of getting it. PGCE stands for Postgraduate Certificate in Education and, as the name suggests, you need to be a graduate to do the course which covers initial teacher training.

PGCEs normally take a year (or two, if you study part-time) and you won't have to pay a penny towards fees. In fact, you'll get paid a training salary of £6,000. It's not a loan. It's not means-tested. It's just loot.

And there's more. If you're training to teach a subject at secondary school level where the shortage is particularly severe (ie. maths, science, modern languages, design and technology, IT, music, religious education or geography), you might get an additional bursary of up to £5,000 (or up to £7,500 if you're over 24), although they'll assess your situation to see how much you need. Even overseas students can apply.

Also, graduates specialising in any of these subject areas can expect a further £4,000 'golden hello' at the end of their first year working as a teacher and they'll gradually have their student loans repaid by the Government so long as they stay in teaching.

In Wales, this scheme is called the Priority Subject Recruitment Initiative and they add Welsh to the list of shortage subjects. For more info, contact The National Assembly for Wales Education Department on 029 2082 5831.

If you're interested in being a teacher, visit the Graduate Teacher Training Registry at www.gttr.ac.uk or the Teacher Training Agency at www.canteach.gov.uk.

The Teaching Information Line has full details of money available while you're training: call 0845 6000 991 (the Welsh Language Teaching Information Line is 0845 6000 992).

Support for Teachers and Trainee Teachers may be found on the following websites: www.teachernet.gov.uk (the full range of relevant government info and sources), www.teacherline.org.uk (free and confidential teacher support network for all teachers and trainees in primary and secondary schools in England and Wales) and www.teachers4london.com (created to try to get people into teaching in London schools).

Details of new training salaries and support for the latest Graduate Teacher Programme are available from the DfES's Public Enquiry Unit on 0870 000 2288 or at www.go4itnow.com

You can also get your QTS by doing a (usually four-year) undergraduate course of teacher training that leads to a first degree – normally a BEd.

But we don't recommend it right now as you or your parents will have to pay the normal fee contributions (subject to assessment) and all you'll get to live on is the normal student loan. Better to spend three years on any old interesting degree and then do a PGCE afterwards. The demand for teachers is such that the Government is unlikely to drop the sweeteners for a while yet.

# What about students with kids and dependents?

If you've got someone who depends on you financially or for care – whether it's your child, someone else's, a husband, wife, parent or some other adult – then you could be eligible for certain extra money, even if you're still dependent on your parents yourself.

### The Dependents' Grant.

The maximum amount for a full year is £2,175 for the first and main dependent, with up to an additional £1,740 per year for any others, depending on age and circumstances.

### Childcare Grant

This is a new means-tested grant that replaces the Discretionary Access Bursaries for mature students and the previous flat-rate Lone Parents' Grant.

But never mind what it replaces – you're eligible for it if you're a student with children in childcare (it has to be the real thing, registered and accredited). The idea is that it covers those costs of up to £100 a week for one child and £150 a week for two or more.

The DSS won't count this grant when they're working out your social security benefits so there's nothing to lose.

### The Lone Parents' Grant

This has now been replaced by the Childcare Grant above, but you can still claim up to £1,075 as an extra non-repayable allowance if you began your course in 2000/1 or earlier and don't get the Childcare Grant.

### Others

There are various other little bungs, such as a travel, books and equipment grant of up to £500, a grant to cover the cost of school meals for each child and, of course, don't forget to check whether you can get an Access Bursary or Hardship Loan.

Universities also often have crèches and nurseries – which may be subsidised or just plain cheap – and there may be a student parents support group.

# What about students with disabilities?

Just because you have a disability, it doesn't mean you should have any less choice about where and what to study and all universities have a policy statement which outlines the support and facilities they offer, financial or otherwise.

Get a copy of these along with prospectuses when you're thinking about applying. It's a good idea to check the place out in person if you're serious about studying there, to assess your needs and attend a 'special needs' interview to discuss them with the university's disabilities officer (assuming they have one – if they haven't, well, that tells you something).

Generally, everything we've said elsewhere about fees, loans, blah-de-blah still applies. In fact, even if your disability is severe and is likely to affect your earning potential after graduation, it doesn't affect your right to claim the same student loan as everyone else.

The Student Loans Company will also ignore any benefits you get because of your disability when working out when you should start repaying your loan and how quickly.

There are other sources of income you may be able to tap too.

If you have a disability or a medical condition that directly affects your study (sight impairment, for instance), you may be entitled to a Disabled Students' Allowance (DSA) of up to £1,420 a year basic (£1,065 max for part-timers).

The DSA can be used to pay for a care helper, Braille books, adaptations to accommodation and so on.

In fact, there's up to £4,255 available for specialist equipment over the length of your whole course and up to £10,755 a year to pay for a non-medical helper (£8,070 max for part-timers).

However, the DSA isn't supposed to go towards costs that you'd still have if you weren't at university.

Your need for financial support is assessed on the nature of your disability and what type of course you're studying. There's also usually a bundle of other conditions that may seem like a pointless hassle.

For example, you'll often need to provide medical proof of your disability, such as a letter from your doctor. Or if you're dyslexic, you should get a letter from a recognised specialist.

One way or another, you'll need to convince your LEA that your disability means you actually need the extra money to study. Ask them what they'll want to see before you send in your application, because if you don't make them happy in the first place, they may expect you to undergo the extra hassle of an independent assessment.

For a copy of the DfES's booklet *Bridging the Gap*, which answers commonly asked questions about DSAs, call their information line on 0800 731 9133.

You may also be able to get extra help with travel costs if, for example, you can't use public transport because of your disability.

And there's an allowance of up to £5,120 per year for full-time and part-time postgrads with disabilities.

None of the various allowances for students with disabilities are means-tested and they don't have to be paid back, but if you're claiming for a particular expense most authorities will want to see a receipt or a quote before they'll pay up.

Although most students can't claim any benefits, if you're getting Incapacity Benefit, say, you'll probably still be allowed to claim while you're studying.

There is a free and confidential Benefit Enquiry Line for people with disabilities and their carers. Call 0800 882200 (minicom users call 0800 243355).

It's also a good idea to contact SKILL – the National Bureau for Students with Disabilities. Their number is 0800 328 5050 or you can email them on info@skill.org.uk.

Their full contact details can be found in the back of the book, along with those of other relevant organisations. They publish various information booklets, including *The Higher Education Guide for People with Disabilities and Disabled Students' Allowances*.

## What about Scottish students?

For starters, you won't be dealing with your LEA, but the Student Awards Agency for Scotland (SAAS) and if you've got any questions, they're the ones to ask.

There are some other significant differences in arrangements too, the most famous of which is that Scottish students studying at Scottish universities don't have to pay tuition fees. At all.

In fact, nor do other EU students studying in Scotland.

However, new Scottish students who've escaped having to pay the fees will now have to pay an endowment when they graduate. It's two grand at the moment, but it'll go up each year with inflation. Also, it applies only to degree courses, not HNDs or HNCs.

Scottish students already at university won't have to pay any endowment. Nor will mature students, lone parents or students with disabilities.

The endowments will be collected along with student loan repayments, which are basically the same as the rest of the UK.

There are loads of ifs and buts to all this – who exactly counts as Scottish and so on – so it's best to check out SAAS's website (www.student-support-saas.gov.uk) or get hold of the booklet they produce called *Student Support in Scotland*.

Even if you won't have to pay tuition fees, it's just as important to apply to the SAAS for support or else, as in the rest of the UK, you could end up paying not only fees, but your entire course costs.

Meanwhile, Scottish students will probably become a rarer sight in future outside Scotland, where they'll have to pay tuition fees like everyone else.

There are specific bursaries available to Scottish students whether they're mature students, part-timers or from poorer families (up to two grand for the most needy cases).

Being Scottish is also one of the factors that might qualify you for all sorts of charitable scholarships and bursaries.

For more information, SAAS's full details are in the back of the book and we've already given you their website address. If you prefer, you can call them on (0131) 476 8212.

## What about students from Northern Ireland?

Basically the system is much the same as England and Wales. The only remotely significant difference is that the things that are known as LEAs in the England and Wales are called Education & Library Boards (ELBs) in Northern Ireland.

The Department of Higher & Further Education, Training & Employment (DHFETE) runs the show and can be phoned on (02890) 257777 or virtually visited at www.dhfeteni.gov.uk

## What about overseas students?

### EU STUDENTS

#### Tuition fees

EU students applying to British universities have to pay tuition fees contributions in the same way as UK students.

If applying through UCAS, they'll be sent an application form for help with tuition fees when they're offered a place on a course. Otherwise, they should ask their university for an application form.

The completed form goes off to the Department for Education and Employment's European Team, Mowden Hall, Staindrop Road, Darlington, Co. Durham DL3 9BG. You can surf on into their website at www.dfes.gov.uk/eustudents for further info.

#### Living Expenses

EU students can't apply for a UK student loan, supplementary grant, Hardship Loan or Access Bursary. Well, they can apply but they'll be turned down, so there's not much point.

The SOCRATES-ERASMUS and Leonardo Programmes all splash out grants to promote the exchange of students and academic staff around Europe (see below).

## STUDENTS FROM OUTSIDE THE EU

Most students from countries outside the EU will have to pay the full cost of fees, although not for nursing or midwifery courses.

Living expenses are your own problem, too.

Bear in mind that, depending on your status, you may not be allowed to work in the UK to fund yourself – even part-time.

> Apply to be a resident tutor – most universities halls have them and they live rent free or for very little. Also you're then above suspicion when food thefts are rife.
> Bonnie Dixon, UEA

## GENERAL ADVICE FOR INTERNATIONAL STUDENTS

Before coming to study in Britain, find out what you're letting yourself in for, particularly costs-wise.

UK course fees may look good value (and most of them are), but the cost of living in Britain may be higher than you're used to – even for Americans and Europeans.

Get the latest advice and guidance from your local British Council office and take a look at Chapter 16 to see how costs vary from place to place. Your chosen university will probably send you more info on local costs if you want it.

Keep an eye on fluctuations in the exchange rate – they may suddenly make the whole thing unaffordable (or much cheaper, if you're lucky).

Apply for funding and scholarships long before your course starts (at least a year) – deadlines vary and competition is tough, so get organised well in advance.

Look into whether you can get any funding from the UK university you're applying to – some offer scholarships to international students for specific course and/or from certain countries. Also try the relevant departments of your own government, the British Council in your own country, the European Commission and perhaps even various voluntary organisations.

Don't start a course in the UK until you've calculated all the expenses and are sure you can still comfortably afford to live. It's both a pain and a challenge to get any financial support once you've left your own country and it can cost a lot just trying.

In order to get into the country, especially if you're from outside the EU, you may need to prove that you'll be able to cover the full costs of your course. It's just one of those immigration things.

A booklet called *Investing in the Future: Help with Tuition Fees for European Union Students* is available from the DfES. Or *Studying in The UK: Sources of funding for international students* is available free from UKCOSA – The Council for International Education (call 020 7226 3762). Also, visit www.britishcouncil.org/education/index.htm or email education.enquiries@britishcouncil.org

# What about studying abroad?

If the UK's so expensive (see above), why should even British students study here? Why indeed?

There's a lot to be said for studying abroad, not least if foreign languages play any part in your plans either for your course or your career. (Don't bother going to the USA for the foreign language skills. That particular strange lingo will remain a complete mystery to all Brits however long they spend there.)

In fact, for many students (especially those studying a foreign language) studying abroad is a necessary part of their course.

Living costs in different countries swing like monkeys from a tree – with Japan and Switzerland being among the most expensive – and your financial entitlements will be adjusted accordingly.

You're still entitled to your student loan if you study abroad and if you need to be there for eight weeks or more as part of your course, you may even be able to claim a larger loan, depending where you are studying.

Many students will also be entitled to a grant to cover travel costs over a certain amount (currently the first £260) and, if you have to take out medical insurance, you can often claim a refund on the premium.

However, if you spend a year or part of a year abroad as part of your studies, you'll still have to pay tuition fees to your UK university, albeit a reduced amount (see Chapter 10).

Unless, that is, you're on an ERASMUS exchange, in which case you are exempt.

The SOCRATES-ERASMUS scheme is a European study programme that gives students the chance to live and study somewhere else in Europe for a while – generally a year or a few months at any rate. If you're interested, you'll need to talk to your course director at your university to find out whether you can apply. Not every course has opted to get into the scheme.

Some students on ERASMUS can claim a grant, but it is not very much and it's not an automatic right.

The Leonardo programme is another EU scheme, again giving students (or graduates) the chance to live in another country for up to a year, but this time the scheme is based around vocational training with an employer.

For details of the UK SOCRATES-ERASMUS Council, ask at your university or take a look at www.erasmus.ac.uk or www.esn.org (Erasmus Student Network). European Training Services can be contacted on 01543 414549.

Individual universities also have bursaries or scholarships to send their students out of the country. Usually it's only the cost of travel that's covered, but occasionally there are awards, bursaries and prizes that fork out for all sorts of strange things like fees at overseas institutions, living expenses or T-shirts that say 'My friend went to Padua and all he got was a few extra CV points'.

You could also try seeking out scholarships not restricted to your university. Or perhaps try contacting the embassy of the country you want to visit – see if there's anything your host country can offer you.

If you want to do your whole degree abroad, there's a couple of books: *Awards for First Degree Study at Commonwealth Universities* and *Commonwealth Universities Yearbook*, both published by the Association of Commonwealth Universities.

# What about anyone else?

There's a handful of other Government-backed funds, two of which we detail below – but for any others, try contacting your Local Education Authority as a first step.

### Care-Leaver's Grant

This is an allowance for full-time students who are in care on their 16th birthday or afterwards for at least three months and under 21 at the start of their course. It's supposed to help with accommodation costs during the summer holidays (up to a maximum of £100 a week) and it's paid by the LEA to you or to your landlord.

### Two homes allowance

If you have to maintain another home in addition to where you live during your course, you may be entitled to apply for this funding, up to a value of £750.

This is not designed for the owners of holiday homes – there has to be a good reason why you own two homes, such as commitments to dependents.

5

# Part 6
## The Push™ Guide to Penny Pinching

# Balanced Budget

The reason they call it a bank balance is because it's a question of getting the scales to tip the right way.

Ideally, what comes in is heavier than what goes out (unless it's paper coming in, copper going out – but you get the idea). As a student, unfortunately, your expenditure almost invariably squats heavily at one end of the scales as your income is lightly perched at the other. It's like pitting a stick insect against a walrus.

This is not, however, any reason to give up. Indeed, it's all the more reason to put the walrus on a diet and get the stick insect pumping iron.

**The two keys to student survival are planning and priorities. Know what you have to spend – even if it's borrowed (which is like borrowing a couple of sheep to join forces with the stick insect). And know what your spending priorities are.**

**Maximise what comes in. Minimise what goes out. And be extremely pessimistic about both.**

To do this you need to work out how much you can afford to spend on any one thing and then stick to it. Or if it's not possible, either make cutbacks elsewhere or somehow get hold of more money.

**You can't do this unless you plan, however. You can't know what you can afford until you've worked out what you've got. And you can't make cutbacks until you know the figure you're cutting.**

**It's all just a matter of balancing the books** – a tedious business at first, but once you've done it, the whole being a student thing seems a lot less like living under a rock that hangs by a thread. You can start to enjoy it – student life that is, not balancing the books.

**Feeling secure and confident about your finances will boost your overall morale, help your studies (yeah, for real) and although you're unlikely to ever be rich while you're a student, so long as you can make ends meet, you'll have much more relaxed and stress-free existence.**

If or when the whole lolly lay-out has gone doolally, you need to be able to see it quickly before it has a serious detrimental affect on your studies and your health – which it will if you're not able to seek help before it gets too serious. **There's nearly always a straightforward solution to every problem, if it is dealt with in time, so don't just ignore it and hope it will go away.**

# Making a budget

So, how do you work out what to spend on what?

Over the next few pages and looking back over the rest of the book, you can work out what you're going to have to spend and what you're going to have to spend it on.

We've kind of roughed out the range of possibilities but, ultimately, your finances are your own. Not only will your income and costs be unique, but, much as we'd love to play the part of personal exchequer to each and every student in the land (yeah, right), it's important to work out your budget for yourself, know it inside out, own it. (Nice cop out on our part, don't you think?)

**6**

### THE RANGE OF INCOMES

Your loan is a big chunk of what comes in – but how big it is and indeed your whole income, depends largely on your parents. What they're supposed to give you. Whether they give it to you. Whether they give you more.

Beyond that, you need to make the call about what you want out of student life. If you simply want to study and are not too bothered about a social life, you will probably scrape by on your student loan and overdraft without having to supplement your income with work.

But, let's face it, after a fortnight of that, your good intentions will probably pop down to the student bar and take you with them.

Those students with a fiercely independent streak (or a clearly severe shortfall in their budget) will probably seek term-time work as soon as they start their course. It has to be said that earning your own money gives you a greater sense of financial freedom and takes the strain off your parents, while giving you that all-important work experience.

However, it's even more important to ensure that you never compromise your studies. Maximise your disposable income as much as possible – but if you feel you are taking on too much work, you will have to look at minimising outgoings instead.

This is what budgeting is all about: if you haven't got the funds coming in, you should aim to cut down on what you are spending.

But let's take a look at the range of annual incomes. The maximums involve parents in the highest income bracket and paid work for 10 to 15 hours a week and/or in vacations.

Bear in mind also that there are so many ifs and buts involved in these figures that they'd read like a stammer if we bothered with them all. We've dealt with them in the other chapters already. Go figure, okay?

| Source | Maximum Highest income families | | Minimum Low income families | |
|---|---|---|---|---|
| | London £ | Elsewhere £ | London £ | Elsewhere £ |
| Student loan | 3,525 | 2,860 | 4,700 | 3,815 |
| Parental contribution | 6,591 | 6,000 | 0 | 0 |
| LEA award | 0 | 0 | 1,075 | 1,075 |
| Overdraft | 1,250 | 1,000 | 1,000 | 1,000 |
| Paid work | 2,500 | 2,200 | 0 | 0 |
| **Maximum total** | **13,896** | **12,060** | **6,775** | **5,890** |

Most students won't get either the minimum or the maximum.

They're more likely to have something around the £6,000 to £10,000 mark (£7,000 to £11,000 in London).

Following the rule about being pessimistic, it's best to work from the bottom up. Take the column on the right and add to it anything extra you know (or at least are pretty sure) you're going to get. For example, if your parents will be giving you an agreed amount each term.

It's best not to count on earnings until you've got a job at least. At some universities, they're not so easy to come by.

## THE RANGE OF COSTS

In Chapter 11, we dished the dirt on the average costs.

For calculating your own budget it may be more useful to look at the following figures, which give the realistic range – the fat bit of the bell curve, for those who like their statistical terminology.

Of course, the exact budget for each cost is as different for individual students as they are. Some may splash out big time on designer gear while another gets kitted out for less than the cost of a night on the tiles. Some will have crippling rent to pay all year round and others will live rent-free at their folks. We know these things vary more than Geri Halliwell's waistline stats – we're only trying to help.

| Breakdown | London | | Elsewhere | |
|---|---|---|---|---|
| | Minimum £ | Maximum £ | Minimum £ | Maximum £ |
| Rent/housing | 1,750 | 4,500 | 1,500 | 3,500 |
| Food | 1,000 | 1,400 | 1,000 | 1,250 |
| Entertainments | 1,000 | 2,500 | 800 | 2,250 |
| Tuition fees | 0 | 1,075 | 0 | 1,075 |
| Phone | 100 | 600 | 80 | 600 |
| Clothes | 250 | 750 | 150 | 500 |
| Travel | 350 | 1,000 | 200 | 500 |
| Household bills | 300 | 400 | 300 | 400 |
| Toiletries | 150 | 300 | 100 | 300 |
| Academic - books, etc | 150 | 500 | 125 | 500 |
| Laundry/washing | 100 | 200 | 75 | 175 |
| Habits, hols and others | 500 | 1,000 | 500 | 1,000 |
| Insurance | 0 | 120 | 0 | 80 |
| **Total** | **5,650** | **14,345** | **4,830** | **12,130** |
| **Average** | | **9,600** | | **7,325** |

Note that we've put the minimum tuition fees down as nothing – but if you want to count it like that, you'll have to cut the £1,075 from your income (see above) because you only get that money if you need help paying your fees. You have to count it in and out or don't count it at all.

Compare this against the range of incomes, however, and you can see that things don't look good. It's not impossible though. So that's something.

> Get a part-time job with lots of benefits. Working at a cinema, I got free tickets and popcorn for me and my friends. British Airways sometimes take on students part-time and they get the same discounts on flights as everyone else. At a very minimum, restaurants tend to give staff a free meal.
>
> Eleanor Harris, Durham University

## A Sample Budget

But how do you put all this into a budget?

Here's one way of doing it. Work out what you have coming in. Work out the costs of essential items. See what's left. Split that appropriately between your other costs – the ones where you could economise if you really have to.

By way of example only, that's what we've done here. It's a budget for a fictional first-year student, whose parents earn £34,000 a year and who intends to study outside London and live in a shared house (for nine-and-a-half months from mid-September to the end of June).

His/her (we haven't filled in too many of the character details here) academic year is made up of three terms of ten weeks each (30 weeks over the year) – the rest of the time, s/he'll go home.

Of course, s/he – let's say he's a she, shall we? In fact, let's call her Penny, er, Penny Pinching – Penny can exercise some control over some of the essential costs and some of the variable costs aren't altogether avoidable, but the breakdown helps.

| Part 1 Income | Amount per year £ | Per term 1st £ | Per term 2nd £ | Per term 3rd £ | Per week £ |
|---|---|---|---|---|---|
| Parental contribution to tuition fees | 1,075.00 | 358.50 | 358.50 | 358.00 | – |
| Parental contribution to living expenses (LEA's suggestion) | 400.00 | 133.50 | 133.50 | 133.00 | 13.00 |
| Extra help from parents | 100.00 | 100.00 | 0 | 0 | – |
| Student loan | 3,415.00 | 1,138.50 | 1,138.50 | 1,138.00 | 66.00 |
| Overdraft facility (maximum) | 1,000.00 | 470.00 | 380.00 | 150.00 | 30.00 |
| Bar work (at £5/hr, 10 hrs/wk) | 1,200.00 | 500.00 | 500.00 | 200.00 | 50.00 |
| **Maximum total available** | **7,190.00** | **2,700.50** | **2,510.50** | **1,979.00** | **159.00** |

| Part 2 Essential costs | Amount per year £ | Per term 1st £ | Per term 2nd £ | Per term 3rd £ | Per week £ |
|---|---|---|---|---|---|
| Rent | 2,055.00 | 810.00 | 810.00 | 435.00 | 50.00 |
| Tuition fees | 1,075.00 | 358.50 | 358.50 | 358.00 | – |
| Bills | 360.00 | 135.00 | 135.00 | 90.00 | 12.00 |
| Insurance | 60.00 | 60.00 | 0 | 0 | – |
| Food | 1,200.00 | 400.00 | 400.00 | 400.00 | 40.00 |
| Travel | 300.00 | 100.00 | 100.00 | 100.00 | 10.00 |
| Laundry/washing | 150.00 | 50.00 | 50.00 | 50.00 | 5.00 |
| **Total essential costs** | **5,200.00** | **1,913.50** | **1,853.50** | **1,443.00** | **117.00** |
| Maximum remainder | £1,990 | £787 | £657 | £536 | – |

6

| Part 3 Variable costs | | Amount per year £ | Per term | | | Per week £ |
|---|---|---|---|---|---|---|
| | | | 1st £ | 2nd £ | 3rd £ | |
| Emergency money | 10% | 199 | 65 | 65 | 69 | 6.50 |
| Academic costs | 10% | 199 | 100 | 45 | 44 | 6.50 |
| Clothes | 10% | 199 | 70 | 80 | 49 | – |
| Entertainment & socialising | 50% | 965 | 350 | 350 | 265 | 30.00 |
| Freshers' Week extra | | 30 | 30 | – | – | – |
| Toiletries | 7.5% | 149 | 50 | 49 | 50 | 5.00 |
| Phone | 7.5% | 149 | 65 | 42 | 42 | – |
| Miscellaneous | 5% | 20 | 7 | 7 | 6 | 0.50 |
| Christmas & birthdays | | 80 | 50 | 15 | 15 | – |
| Holiday | | 0 | 0 | 0 | 0 | – |
| **Total variable costs** | | **1,990** | **787** | **653** | **540** | **48.50** |

Can we just take you through what Penny did there?

**Part 1: Income**

This is what she reckons will be her income.

Presumably, she's already applied to her LEA and been told what she can expect by way of support (no award, 75% of the full loan) and what she should expect from her folks.

Presumably, she's also talked to them about it and the amounts she's put down are based on safe assumptions.

That bar work, however, might be a problem. If Penny knows that she's got the job already, then she's safe. If not, then it may be a bit risky to suppose that there'll be any work going.

The amount she's allowed for the bar work – £1,200 – highlights another potential problem that it looks as though she's accounted for. Chances are that there'll be at least a few weeks in the summer term when she can't work at all because she needs to focus on her exams.

She's reckoned on six weeks when she won't be earning. She may make up some of that with vacation jobs or occasional overtime, but she's right not to count on it.

## Part 2: Essential Costs

Next, Penny worked out what she'll need for costs that, basically, she can't do much about. Her rent, for example, is just what it will cost. Her travel shouldn't be too bad because she's on campus, but she need to go into town to do her weekly shopping and, since she's not paying for any rent over the vacations, she'll need to go home at the end of each term.

As it happens, she thinks she won't need that much for food and hopes to keep bills to a minimum – but when making a budget it's best to assume the worst. At least that way you're prepared for it if it happens and, if it doesn't, you've got money to spend on something else (or not to spend at all and therefore end up less far in debt).

She's also spread the costs appropriately. She's allowed more for bills for the first two terms, when the weather's colder and she'll need the heating on more. She's also shoved all the cost of insurance right up the front when she'll actually have to pay it.

Meanwhile, she's spread her rent unevenly between the three terms because she's allowed enough rent money to take her through the short winter and vacations too.

Having worked out her costs in Part 2, she's calculated the maximum remainder she'll have left over. Of course, in the income section, she had to factor in an overdraft from the bank of £1,000. If she can get away with it, she'd rather not borrow that much. That's why this is a *maximum* remainder.

## Part 3: Variable Costs

**The variable costs are the ones where, if necessary, Penny will have to find a way of economising.** Even her academic costs may have to be cut. She'll need to spend a certain amount on pens, paper and so on – but if it comes to it, for books, she'll just have to spend longer in the library rather buy her own or photocopy them.

She's worked out how much to give herself under each heading by allocating a percentage of the remainder to each heading. She's chosen these percentages for herself, based on what they're likely to cost and the priority she puts on them.

By only giving 10% to academic costs, it doesn't necessarily mean she'll ignore her studies, just that she thinks they won't cost her as much as, say, entertainments. She's also put most of the costs in the first term when, presumably, she's planning to do most of her book buying.

She's spread other costs, too, out unevenly over the year to reflect when she's actually going to have to shell out. For example, she'll have to do her Christmas shopping at the end of the first term, so she's allowed £35 more than the rest of the year.

She's done something really sensible – that's our Penny for you – by giving herself nearly £200 emergency money. She'll try not to touch that, but it means she won't automatically blow the whole schedule if she needs to rush home unexpectedly, or loses her job, or has her bike stolen and needs to pay an excess on her insurance, or aliens land and make her give them her lunch money.

If, at the end of the year, she hasn't used her emergency money, she can put it towards the holiday she clearly wants (after all she's given it a heading even though she seems to have worked out that she can't afford it) or she can just be grateful she didn't have to borrow up to the max that year.

## CASHFLOW

Under 'Entertainment and socialising', Penny Pinching put a sub-heading for Freshers' Week, where she allowed herself an extra thirty quid to have a good time. (In other words, double her regular weekly ents allowance.)

However, it looked like she hadn't allowed herself anything else for settling in – to cover all the stuff she'll discover she forgot to bring with her (see Chapter 12) and for a big splurge at the supermarket to get her kitchen cupboards off to a good start.

That doesn't sound like Penny. Not Penny who is sensible in a way that only fictional people can be.

Sure enough, she has thought about it. Apart from breaking it down into three terms, Penny has also worked it out for every week of the year. Perversely diligent person that she is, she's even done a spreadsheet on a computer.

Her weekly allowance for food, for example, is £40 average over the year, but if you were to look at her cashflow spreadsheet, you'll see she's allowed herself an extra fiver each week for the first four weeks and one pound less a week for the second two terms.

This weekly breakdown tells her at the end of any week in the year what her bank balance should be. She can then compare it with what it actually is and decide immediately what to do.

If she's over budget on her 'food' heading, say, she either has to just make do on the food she's already laid in for that week – which isn't satisfactory if it means missing meals – or find somewhere else to make a saving – probably one of the variable cost items. In other words, she decides she can't afford to go out tonight.

Alternatively, she can ask her boss at the pub if she can work extra hours.

If, however, she's under budget, she might decide she can afford to treat herself to a takeaway tonight, or put money aside for that holiday. (We understand she intends to go to Switzerland, home of banking – not to mention the cuckoo clock.)

By keeping a check on her cashflow, she's not only counting the money out, but counting it in.

Most students find budgeting very difficult because their money arrives in two or three large chunks during the year, whereas outgoings are constant (and relentless) over every term.

Penny knows when to expect big movements either way and she has an early warning system long before any problems crop up.

Apply to your LEA before going to university even if you don't think you'll qualify for any financial support. After all, you may be wrong – but, more importantly, if you don't, you may end up having to pay more.

> Try to persuade your parents to get
> divorced or at least to separate. Not
> only might you get more Government
> funding, but it also puts you in a great
> position to use emotional blackmail to
> sting both parents for money.

## FLEXIBILITY

**Penny also has a little notebook in which, for the first term at least, she intends to write down every penny she spends. That way she can work out how she's really doing with her budget headings.**

Realistically, she knows she won't keep track when she's out for a night on the piss, but that doesn't matter. Just so long as, the next morning, she knows what she spent in total. The whole lot goes down under the entertainments heading as 'night out £9.24'.

Every couple of weeks, she can tot up what she's spent on what and compare it with her budget and cashflow.

She knows perfectly well that some of her estimates are going to be way out.

**By monitoring what she spends closer than a cat watches a tin opener, she'll be able to adjust her budget as she goes along.**

Having put so much effort into the budget in the first place, this may seem like sacrilege – but to Penny, it's part of the whole point. If the budget's not working, rather than live a life of misery because you can't afford to go out because you're £5 over on your food, just juggle the figures.

However, Penny shouldn't have to. **She even has money for emergencies.**

Nevertheless, while you can expect the unexpected, you can't always predict exactly what shape it'll come in. For Penny, as for every student, there are imponderables – and there's no such thing as typical student budget that will always work for everyone.

If she's over budget, she looks for somewhere where she's under budget. And if she can't find anything, she works out where she can get more money – more hours working at the pub, a heart to heart with the parents, or even asking the bank.

**If Penny takes her budget and cashflow along to a meeting with the bank, they'll extend her overdraft, no problem.** Even if something's gone seriously wrong and she's in a monetary mire, they'll that see she's the kind of person who'll find her way out in the long run through careful financial planning.

**Going as far as Penny may seem extreme, but actually, it's not so far from what should be basic budgeting procedures.**

Even with all her efforts, according to her own calculations she's going to end up more than £13,000 in debt at the end of a three-year course. That's about average at the moment.

At the very least, you should do a budget like Penny's for yourself and keep revisiting it until it works. Then revisit it again every time you get major new information (such as finding part-time work).

And then look at it at least once a month while you're at university to see how you're doing. Stick it on the wall above your desk. If necessary, make changes to keep it current.

It's like a revision timetable, however – it's not just a chart you spend hours colouring in and then ignore prior to last-minute panic. It's a relevant guide to what you can and can't spend if friends, for example, ask you to join them for a drink. If you've spent your weekly entertainment allowance already, the answer is, unfortunately, 'no'. Everyone has to give it a miss sometime. Study instead.

There's nothing crazy in any of this. All we're talking about is looking after your finances.

They're skills that everyone has to acquire sometime – even ridiculously wealthy people. How do you think they became wealthy in the first place?

It's a bit of a deep end experience if you're learning to budget when you're really strapped, but if you want to get anally retentive about the process, it's the best time to do it. And remember, it's better to be anal than sorry.

# Priorities

**Don't think of budgeting as a negative thing. Think of it as positively expressing your priorities.**

It really is worth losing the luxuries and the wild weekends if it means getting by financially in the long run.

It's no fun living on marmite sandwiches and Tesco's Value orange squash for a month after squandering the last of your cash on a couple of over-indulgent Saturday nights. You'll realise with the infallible clarity of hindsight that it just wasn't worth it (however much fun it was at the time).

Doing a preliminary budget is all very well, but sticking to it is the difficult bit. In theory, it's easy – in practice, it's a different matter. Despite your best intentions, you may still find yourself up to your neck in debt, wondering how the hell you got there.

**Don't worry about being in debt – that's normal. Worry about being in too much debt or being in debt too soon. Some debts are necessary. Others you can do without.**

As the debts get bigger, don't panic or give up trying to keep them to a minimum. Even if you find, despite your best efforts (or even because of a lack of any effort), that you're in a debt ditch, there are ways of climbing out. And, for what it's worth, there are thousands of others in exactly the same situation.

However, if you can't pay for tedious but compulsory house-related costs or if you get behind on your rent, your housemates may well start seeing you as a liability. You can't expect others to bail you out or lend you the money to cover your share of the bills.

The key is to *prioritise*. See that the necessities are covered before you get on with the less mundane side of student life.

Departments normally put on parties for freshers. It's your only opportunity to get free alcohol at the department's expense — and what's more, they'll even be grateful if you turn up.

R Alston, Royal Holloway

## 30 Steps to Solvency

**1** Work out your budget and get an idea of your cashflow situation before you even pack to go to university. Do it as soon as possible. Preferably sooner.

**2** Economise right from the off. If you blow big bucks at the beginning of term your fast and loose spending will only leave you miserable and bored by the end.

**3** Don't buy anything you don't need, if you can't afford what you need. Paying your rent on time and having food to eat are more important than anything else.

**4** Keep your budget under regular review and make adjustments for any costs you miscalculated.

**5** If you need a little extra to tide you over, try to get a job if you can, but don't assume when budgeting that you'll be able to get one immediately.

**6** If you've got a job, but you're still feeling the pinch, try to get a few extra shifts but not at the expense of your course.

**7** During a 'typical' week at university (or, even better, a whole month or a term), keep a record of everything you buy (by cash, card, direct debit and cheque), and how much it costs – pints, snacks, cab rides, fetish outfits, etc. Cheque stubs, receipts and bank statements can all help you draw up a comprehensive record of total expenditure.

**8** It may seem like a hassle, but you can use this information to help you draw up a realistic budget. The little things you don't think twice about buying are often overlooked, and after the big birds like fees and rent have flown from the nest egg, they suddenly seem a whole lot bigger.

**9** Anyone on a low income should avoid anything with high interest payments. That means you. Big monthly repayments and a high annual percentage rate spell big trouble. Paying off old debts with new ones generates a vicious cycle. You'll end up with mounting mountains of interest and interest on the interest, ad nauseam.

**6**

**10** Only have the heating on when you really need it – even in winter just a few hours in the morning and a few hours at night will see you alright. Other energy-saving rules: have showers instead of baths, always turn the light off when leaving an empty room, only fill the kettle as much as you need to, don't leave the telly on standby.

**11** Share cooking and shopping with housemates and split the bills. Don't fuss about who's eating more. You're all subsidising each other anyway because it works out cheaper than buying for one.

**12** Buy fruit and veg from market stall, not the supermarket.

**13** You may be covered by insurance, but minimise the risk of having all your precious things nicked in the first place by keeping all expensive-looking items away from the windows and always lock internal doors where you can. Insurance premiums will be lower if you have a personal lock on your bedroom door.

**14** Get a friend to cut your hair – preferably one who knows what they're doing. Alternatively, find your nearest hairdresser and ask if they want any models. You'll only pay about £5 and get just about whatever haircut you want. For a bit extra you can get colour and perming too. Toni and Guy always require models to find your nearest call: 0800 731 2396.

**15** Check out 'bargain basement' shops such as Poundland (everything's a pound!) You can get all sorts of necessities in there – household cleaning products, shampoo, lightbulbs, notepads, novelty pens, etc, etc. All for... er, a pound. Be warned though – these places are full of tat you don't need, and not everything's a bargain. Some stuff is actually less than a pound elsewhere.

**16** Be on the look-out for special student nights at clubs, pubs, cinemas etc. Carry your NUS card with you everywhere – it can get you so many discounts it could be your most valuable bit of plastic.

**17** Pick up free condoms from your local family planning centre or the university health centre. (And use them.)

**18** Make calls and surf the net during off-peak times only. Usually after 6 or 7pm and at weekends, but check.

**19** If you must have a credit card, choose one that offers money back (instead of points for freebies). And use it as if it were made of glass. Don't use it unless you know you can pay the monthly bill in total. Cut it up if you find you can't.

**20** Don't spend all your money on drink and drugs. If going out on the piss, meet up round someone's house first and do most of your drinking there. It's cheaper.

**21** Go out in groups of four or five (or more). Get in a round each (or buy your own drinks). Don't take more cash than you're willing to spend and only take your cashpoint card for emergencies. Swap it with one of your friends for safe keeping. (Don't tell them the PIN.) Leave enough money for getting home. When you're all drunk and raucous enough at the end of the night, pile into a taxi together and split the cost.

**22** Where possible, apply for your student loan early and have it put into your account in three instalments throughout the year.

**23** Pay regular bills automatically by direct debit or standing order. Not only does this avoid the problem of ignored bills going red and then the electricity strangely cutting out, you also usually get a discount. But keep track of what's coming out of your account each month and when. Take it into account in your budgeting and don't believe the balance the cash machine tells you if a payments due.

**24** Keep a finance file with all your bank statements, bills and letters from the SLC and the bank. That way, you'll know where to find what you need when you need it. Also keep receipts and card payment slips in it and check them off against statements when they arrive.

**25** Club together with mates on the same course to buy all the main texts between you and share them on a rota basis. Definitely one to try if your university library is a bit thin on the shelves.

**26** In a perfect world, your overdraft facility would only be a last resort. In this world, you'll almost certainly need at least some of it. If you are having trouble sticking to your agreed limit, talk to your bank manager or student adviser immediately. Don't risk getting a snotty letter by going over your limit and hoping nobody will notice – they will notice, and that snotty letter will come, complete with fine.

**27** Always ask in high street stores, taxis, cinemas, theatres museums – just about anywhere, in fact – if there's a student discount. They'll rarely volunteer the information without being asked.

**28** Don't rely on your next loan cheque to pay off what you already owe. You'll need it for your rent and food next term, so what'll you do then?

**29** Don't get stressed out over your finances. You'll only make it worse. A calm approach with good planning will see you alright. You'll be in debt, but, hey, so's everyone.

**30** The Access funds exist as a safety net for those who are experiencing problems. Ask if you need help – you shouldn't have to suffer in silence if your situation has got to the stage where you are depriving yourself. Try asking, even if you don't think you'll get anywhere. The worst they'll do is give you free advice.

# In the red

## Handling Debt

Students have always complained about being broke. Chaucer even makes gags about it in *The Canterbury Tales*. Honest (and what a hoot they are too).

**But in the last 15 years or so, the situation has gone from one where students faced the challenge of merely staying out of the red to one where even the official funding system acknowledges that they're likely to graduate with the worst part of £10,000 in debts.**

As it happens, the average debt on graduation is about £12,750 and while there are some who make it through without borrowing anything, there are also plenty more who wind up owing over £20,000.

Try telling that to someone with a mortgage and they probably won't be too impressed – but, if you have a mortgage, you probably have property to show for the hole in your finances. You probably also have a salary to support your repayments.

Most students have neither.

Does this sound a tiny bit negative?

So sorry.

It shouldn't put you off. We've been through that. It's only money after all and as the great Bob Dylan once said, 'What's money? A man is a success in life if he gets up in the morning and goes to bed at night and in between does what he wants to do.'

Bloody hippy. Someone go tell him that a degree's an investment.

The good news is that it won't be a problem if you follow the rules.

**The key rules: borrow wisely; spend according to need rather than want; keep tabs on your bank balance; don't get behind with bills; tap every available resource; and get yourself a good holiday job.**

During holidays, try to get some work so that you can pay off all or part of your overdraft – you will then have the facility available to you once again when you begin the next term. It's not much fun to start term in the red and with your next loan instalment cheque inexplicably delayed in the post. Prepare yourself for the unexpected.

**Don't let debt take over your life: it will only become a problem if you let it and ignoring red bills and letters from creditors or applying for more loans when you can't pay off the ones you already have is just asking for trouble.**

Don't be complacent and assume it won't happen to you: even the meanest misers, penny-pinchers and prudent puritans are often amazed at the flash with which their bank balance transforms from healthy wealth to black hole.

## SAFE & UNSAFE DEBTS

Your student loan and your overdraft are **safe** debts, virtually unavoidable and the cheapest money that money can buy.

The interest on both is very small (the overdraft is usually free if you stay within your limit) and you don't have to worry about paying them back until after you have graduated.

However, any other borrowings are a **risk**. If possible, avoid taking out other loans altogether. Credit card frivolity, too.

If you run up debts and end up missing or delaying repayments, this will not be good for your future credit rating and you'll end up with pariah status amongst the entire financial fraternity.

Unauthorised debts – for example, exceeding your overdraft by writing rubber cheques or stretching the debit card a bit far – are also unsafe.

Stick to the safety zone.

## Stress-busting tips for the poor and disgruntled

So how do you stop debt becoming a problem?

Debt is undoubtedly a hassle and, in fact, while you're a student one of the main problems with debt is not that you don't have any money, but what worrying about it threatens to do to your head.

Hopefully, after all our wise advice, you'll stay in the relative clear, financially speaking – but as Nick Ross would no doubt put it, after all the horrors we've described, 'Don't have nightmares'.

Getting into debt and not getting out is not something you can do much about until you graduate and nor will anyone expect you to. So don't waste nights staring at the ceiling fretting about it.

So long as you can pay your way in the meantime, do what you can and be cool about it.

That's all very well for us to say. Now you're going to worry about worrying about it.

Just don't go down that road.

**If you are having difficulties, whatever they are – drawing up your budget, getting by on what you've got, negotiating with your bank, filling in forms to apply for funding, worrying about debt, chasing the SLC for your loan payment – talk to your student welfare officer.**

They're usually based in either the students' union welfare department or the university's. Often they'll both have complementary advisors and a specialist debt counsellor or financial adviser too.

They'll offer guidance and, if you need it, sometimes even practical assistance – ie. they've got the keys to the access fund safe.

Remember to refrigerate leftovers, especially if they contain meat. Then remember to eat them before they go off.

## POMMIE

Where would we be without mnemonics? (Actually I used to know the answer to that, but I couldn't ever come up with a way to remember it.)

The central principles of a stress-free university career (at least as far as money management goes) can be expressed in the almost delightfully uncatchy acronym pommie:

**P**   **PRIORITISE:** Buy what you need first (eg. food and shelter) – what you want comes second.

**O**   **ORGANISE:** Plan your budget, check your balance regularly and keep a record of all financial correspondence.

**M**   **MAXIMISE:** Make sure you are getting all the income you're entitled to.

**M**   **MINIMISE:** Keep expenditure to a minimum without depriving yourself unduly.

**I**   **IMPROVISE:** When you can't afford something, be creative about alternatives

**E**   **ECONOMISE:** Stick to first five rules and buy cheaply when you can.

**For want of a better reminder, stick to the POMMIE principles and remember why you're at university in the first place – to better yourself, to improve your prospects and ultimately to embark on the career you want... money, success, blah, blah, blah.** You know the script by know.

**The message is, essentially: you don't need money to have a good time.**

Students don't stay poor forever and the loudest voices saying that students shouldn't complain are often graduates themselves. A few years down the line, you too will probably wonder what you were so worried about.

Of course, debt and hardship is like a ripe zit on the end of your nose. While it's there, it's horrible – it's as if the world revolves around it – but with the correct procedure, in a shower of pus, normality is restored.

Indeed, it's better than that. The money management skills you pick up at university are not only just as useful when you have more money of your own, but in any profession involving any contact with budgets – ie. almost all of them – they're as useful a skill as being able to suck up to your boss.

If you need help and advice:

| | |
|---|---|
| Credit Action Helpline | 0800 591084 |
| Debtcall | 0800 9805060 |
| National Debtline | 0121 359 8501 |
| Department of Social Security | 0800 666555 |
| Educational Grants Advisory Service | 020 7254 6251 |
| Money Advice Association | 020 7236 3566 |

# After University

All good things will come to an end. Falling asleep in nine o'clock lectures, cheap beer, exam stress, being unable to afford a new pair of socks...

Eventually, all being well, you'll get kitted out like Batman with a black square on his head and pick up your scroll.

After that, you might be thinking that all the hard slog is out of the way, but the problem now is that you'll have to earn a living and start to pay back what you owe.

**Some debts – such as your overdraft – you won't be able to delay long before you start making repayments. Most banks won't let you swan along for too long. They want to see their investment in you start to ripen.**

**As for others, mainly the student loan, the longer you put off being in a position to start making good, the more interest you'll end up paying.**

Besides, after three years of it or more, most people have had quite enough of poverty.

So try to get earning pretty sharpish. If the thought of going straight for a long-term career fills you with dread, try temping or make enquiries about jobs abroad (see what we said about 'Filling the Gap' and 'Jobs Abroad' in Chapter 7). Lots of graduates take a year between finishing uni and landing a long-term job, especially if they didn't take the opportunity before university.

If you do intend to up sticks and leave or even wait a while before stepping up to the start line of the rat race, check first on what your bank and the Student Loans Company want you to do about your debts. You should be able to defer repayments on your student loan, but your bank may want you to come to some arrangement.

**Don't indulge in 'solvent abuse' — ie. teasing people because they're not in debt. It's not big and it's not clever. When it comes to student debt, you should be more proud of keeping it small than having a big one.**

## EMPLOYMENT

Towards the end of your student career, the whole employment issue will raise its short-haired, neatly coiffured head.

Your university's careers service will help. They differ in size, effectiveness and what they'll offer to do for you and you'll want to mastermind the hunt for yourself anyway.

**Job Fairs and Graduate Recruitment Fairs will most likely become a regular fixture in your life. Employers have stands where they try to convince you to work for them and you try to convince them to employ you.** Despite how it sounds, people and jobs don't pair up quite as easily as you might think.

The name 'fairs' makes them sound like summer fêtes and, sure enough, they're most prolific in June and July, but that's where the similarity ends. If you're after a rural metaphor, they're more reminiscent of cattle markets, only most of the livestock are wearing suits.

Strangely enough, the cattle theme continues – these fairs and mini-fairs at individual universities are known collectively as the 'milk round'.

There are general fairs for jobs across the board and specialist ones for different industries or fields. Each offers seminars and advice and they provide a unique opportunity to meet hoards of potential employers all in a flock.

Make an irresistible CV and take plenty of copies along with you. Dress up smartly and sell yourself. Be prepared for an interview on the spot.

Even if you don't end up with a job, you can scout the territory, find out about different jobs, different companies and how to get in to what you want to do. You can also network – get names, numbers, contacts – and pick up on the leads later.

You can find out what fairs are where in the Graduate ('Rise') section of *The Guardian* every Saturday, which also is the probably the best paper for most graduate vacancies.

After graduating, if you're not walking straight into a job, take the opportunity to pick up some office and IT skills or to improve on what you've got.

If you're not completely sick of education, you could even enrol on a short training course. There may be yet more costs involved, but there are quite a few schemes to help out.

For example, the Independent Learning Account is a Government attempt to get people learning skills that are in short supply in Britain. It's run by the DfEE, which pays up to 80% of the fees on some courses. Contact your local job centre for more info.

If you're lucky, you may even find an employment agency that's willing to give you some free, basic training – even if it's nothing more than improving your typing speed or introducing you to a software package. Don't knock it. Keyboard skills and computer literacy are often a decider when it comes to getting a job. They also make life easier once you've got one.

# Part 7
# In the back

Push
...like it is

7

Part 7: In the back
Chapter 16

# The universities

## How to use this chapter

So, having read every word of this book – indeed, in a fit of enthusiasm, you've probably learnt it all by heart – you now know everything worth knowing about student finance.

Except that doesn't help you choose a university.

In Chapter 2 we said – in fact, we couldn't have made it any clearer – not all universities are the same. That's as true about differing costs as it is about differing names and addresses.

Exclusively, **The Push Guide to Money** brings you this chapter – the only comprehensive university-by-university guide to the different costs at every UK university. To get an even fuller picture of every aspect of student life at each university we recommend, strangely enough, our sister publication **The Push Guide to Which University**.

For each university, we've spilt the beans on the major money variables and broken them down into bite-size chunks.

### DEBT

**Average student debt:** The amount per student owed for each year of study other than to the Student Loans Company. So most of the money will be bank overdrafts, but some may be to credit cards, parents, bank loans, hardship loans and so on.

As with several of the other figures that change radically from year to year, you shouldn't take this one too literally. Its main use is as a measuring stick for putting one university up against another. Although at present average debts can vary considerably from one year to the next, their levels relative to other universities can still be very useful information.

**Access fund/successful applications per year:** These figures tell you how much the university has each year in each access fund, and how many people it is spread amongst. Not only will this give you an idea of how big the pot is, but also whether their policy is to give big help to a small number of students or small help to a big number.

**General debt info:** A brief run-down of the other help available – bursaries and the like.

## EMPLOYMENT:
**Employment:** Ultimately, you can afford to dip deeper into the den of debt if you're more likely to land a job. We tell you what proportion managed it in the past, and anything useful about the university that might stand you in good stead.

**Paid work:** Meanwhile, since more and more students work their way through college, we tell you what your chances are. What are the opportunities and what will the uni do to help you find them?

## TRAVEL
Details of the national and local travel links and what they cost.

## ENTERTAINMENTS
Alcohol may not be the only cost when it comes to finance, but it's a pretty good indicator of what the fun market's like. Push's exclusive Booze Index is a price calculated by averaging out a series of drinks in both student bars and local bars, weighted according to where the students drink.

Apart from that we also reveal the shocking differences in price between staying on campus for a few pints of beer or glasses of wine, or drinking the same locally.

The prices usually go up year by year, unfortunately – but, like the average debt, the figures are good for comparisons.

**7**

## ACCOMMODATION
The biggest cost in your budget. What proportion of students live in, and what they pay for what, and for how long. And, of course, local rents for those who live out.

## UNIVERSITY OF ABERDEEN

University of Aberdeen, Kings College, Aberdeen, AB24 3FX.
Tel: (01224) 272090.  Fax: (01224) 272576.  E-mail: srs@admin.abdn.ac.uk

**DEBTS:** • Average debt: £1,550
• Access fund: £236,137 • Successful applications: 927
About 150 endowments, bursaries, external grants and trusts for school leavers coming to Aberdeen University. Some are very obscure: for one, applicants must be from Cabrach (a village 40 miles away) and promise not to drink or smoke.

**EMPLOYMENT:** • Unemployed after 6 months: 4%
**Paid work:** A free job agency has the usual part-time and vacation work. Students can sometimes find work in the oil industry, especially if their studies are relevant.

**TRAVEL:**
**National:** Despite being so far north (the same latitude as St Petersburg), rail connections are quite good, if expensive. Among others, services are offered to London (£52.15), Glasgow (£19.15) and Dundee (£10.55). National Express coach services to for example, London (£37), Glasgow (£19.50), Dundee (£9).
**Local:** Good buses around the city from 35p, useful for getting into the centre.

**ENTERTAINMENTS:** • Booze index: £1.75
**Town/City:** • Pint of beer: £1.90 • Glass of wine: £1.80
**University:** • Pint of beer: £1.60 • Glass of wine: £1.50

**ACCOMMODATION:**
**Living in:** • Catered: 14% • Cost: £74-88 (32wks)
• Self-catering: 21% • Cost: £41-63 (32-50wks)
**Living out:** • Ave rent: £50

## UNIVERSITY OF ABERTAY DUNDEE

University of Abertay Dundee, 40 Bell Street, Dundee, DD1 1HG. Tel: (01382) 308000. Fax: (01382) 308081. E-mail: iro@abertay-dundee.ac.uk

**DEBTS:** • Average debt: £1,600
• Access fund: £223,000 • Successful applications: 462
Other sources of financial assistance (administered by the Student Services Unit) in the form of local trusts and legacies. There is a centenary scholarship (£1,000) and a few bursaries for part-timers and overseas students.

**EMPLOYMENT:** • Unemployed after 6 months: 2.3%
The University Careers Service offers a service called SCOPE (Student Centre for Opportunities and Part-time Employment) which assists students in finding part-time work, casual or vacation work.
**Paid work:** See University of Dundee

**TRAVEL:** See University of Dundee
**Local:** Dundee station is 10 minutes' walk from the University. The very comprehensive local bus service is well used by students. The bus fare from the halls to the University is 80p.

**ENTERTAINMENTS:** • Booze index: £1.80
**Town/City:** • Pint of beer: £1.80 • Glass of wine: £2
**University:** • Pint of beer: £1.30 • Glass of wine: £1.50

**ACCOMMODATION:**
**In college:** • Self-catering: 21% • Cost: £36-54 (36-56wks)
**Externally:** • Ave rent: £45

**UNUSUAL COSTS:** Students can buy a £13 card giving free or cheap access to Council sports facilities.

## ABERYSTWYTH, UNIVERSITY OF WALES

University of Wales Aberystwyth, Old College, King Street, Aberystwyth, Ceredigion, SY23 2AX. Tel: (01970) 622021. Fax: (01970) 627410.
E-mail: undergraduate-admissions@aber.ac.uk

**DEBTS:** • Average debt: £1,000
• Access fund: £216,000 • Successful applications per year: 400
The Student Financial Support Office provides help and advice for all matters fiscal. 90 scholarships are available (worth up to about £3,000 apiece) by sitting the Uni's own exam. There are also music bursaries at £400 per year.
**Banks on campus:** HSBC Bank.

**EMPLOYMENT:** • Unemployed after 6 months: 5.8%
**Paid work:** Somewhere as small as Aberystwyth can't provide jobs for 6,000+ students, but things improve in the summer, when the tourists move in. A shopping complex provides opportunities for retail operatives (ie. shelf-stackers).

**TRAVEL:**
**National:** Trains: Aberystwyth station is about $1/2$ mile from the main campus. Direct main-line connections to London (£29.55), Birmingham (£21.65) and Manchester (£23.15). Coaches: Trans Cambria and National Express services – London (£18.25), Birmingham (£15.25), Cardiff (£14.80).
**Local:** Reliable local buses till 11pm and from station every 20 minutes (50p).

**ENTERTAINMENTS:** • Booze index: £1.45
**Town/city:** • Pint of beer: £1.70 • Glass of wine: £1.40
**University:** • Pint of beer: £1.40 • Glass of wine: £1.34

**ACCOMMODATION:**
**Living in:** • Catered: 19% • Cost: £54-67 (30 weeks)
• Self-catering: 37% • Cost: £42-54 (30-48 weeks)
**Living out:** • Ave rent: £45

**UNUSUAL COSTS:** £18 for an Athletics Union card gives access to all sports facilities. Parking permits £15 a year.

## ANGLIA POLYTECHNIC UNIVERSITY

(1) Anglia Polytechnic University, Chelmsford Campus, Bishop Hall Lane, Chelmsford, Essex, CM1 1SG Tel: (01245) 493131 Fax: (01245) 495419
E-mail: angliainfo@anglia.ac.uk
(2) Anglia Polytechnic University, Cambridge Campus, East Road, Cambridge, CB1 1PT Tel: (01223) 460008 Fax: (01223) 356558

**DEBTS:** • Average debt: £1,600
• Access fund: £691,486 • Successful applications per year: 1,600
Small welfare fund for short-term loans.

**EMPLOYMENT:** • Unemployed after 6 months: 5.4%
**Paid work:** University employment office with bar work, restaurants, etc.

**TRAVEL:** For Cambridge, see University of Cambridge
**National:** Trains: From Chelmsford Station (2 minutes from campus) into London Liverpool Street (£5). Change for Manchester (£30.35) and other destinations. Coaches: National Express from Chelmsford to London (£6), Bristol (£23), etc.
**Local:** Buses and Network SouthEast trains.

**ENTERTAINMENTS:** • Booze index: £1.68
**Town/city:** • Pint of beer: £2 • Glass of wine: £1.60
**University:** • Pint of beer: £1.50 • Glass of wine: £1.30

**7**

**ACCOMMODATION:**
**Living in:** Cambridge • Self-catering: 15% • Cost: £63-68 (40 weeks)
**Living in:** Chelmsford • Self-catering: 15% • Cost: £46-62 (40 weeks)
**Externally:** Cambridge • Ave rent: £55
**Externally:** Chelmsford • Ave rent: £42-70

## ASTON UNIVERSITY

Aston University, Aston Triangle, Birmingham, B4 7ET. Tel: (0121) 359 3611. Fax: (0121) 333 6350. E-mail: prospectus@aston.ac.uk

**DEBTS:** • Average debt: £600
• Access fund: £276,000 • Successful applications per year: 728
Guild hardship fund (up to £3,000 per person), two other hardship funds, help with childcare costs. There's the opportunity to get a bursary before you even start your course and there are emergency loans.
**Banks on campus:** NatWest, Post Office, Barclays and Link cash machines.

**EMPLOYMENT:** • Unemployed after 6 months: 3%
The vocational nature of the courses, as well as the business placements scheme, gives Aston students a definite edge.

**TRAVEL:** See University of Birmingham

**ENTERTAINMENTS:** • Booze index: £1.67
**Town/city:** • Pint of beer: £1.90 • Glass of wine: £1.50
**University:** • Pint of beer: £1.65 • Glass of wine: £1.60

**ACCOMMODATION:**
**Living in:** • Self-catering: 45% • Cost: £49-71 (40-52 weeks)
**Living out:** • Ave rent: £42

## BANGOR, UNIVERSITY OF WALES

University of Wales Bangor, College Road, Bangor, Gwynedd, LL57 2DG. Tel: (01248) 351151. Fax: (01248) 370451. E-mail: admissions@bangor.ac.uk

**DEBTS:** • Average debt: £1,150
• Access fund: £311,000 • Successful applications per year: 278
Help may be sought from a small welfare budget in emergency cases. Otherwise there are scholarships for the brilliant only.

**EMPLOYMENT:** • Unemployed after 6 months: 5.6%
**Paid work:** Apart from the usual bar work and restaurant waiting, there's the local Outdoor Pursuits Centres and other tourist spots which offer jobs to the early bird. Student Services runs a Student Opportunities Centre with employment bureau and volunteer agencies.

**TRAVEL:**
**National:** Trains: Bangor station is half a mile from the main buildings. To get almost anywhere, it's got to be via Crewe (£16.65). London (£35) is possible without changing. Buses: National Express services to London (£26), Birmingham (£18.25), Cardiff (£35.75) and other destinations.
**Local:** The buses are fairly regular and for a quid it's possible to get about 6 miles out of town till 11pm. They also go all over Gwynedd (the county). Trains run every hour to towns all along the coast of north Wales.

**ENTERTAINMENTS:** • Booze index: £1.85
**Town/city:** • Pint of beer: £2.05 • Glass of wine: £1.90
**University:** • Pint of beer: £1.60 • Glass of wine: £1.80

**ACCOMMODATION:**

| | | |
|---|---|---|
| **Living in:** | • <u>Catered: 15%</u> | • <u>Cost: £67-74 (31 weeks)</u> |
| | • <u>Self-catering: 29%</u> | • <u>Cost: £41-56 (37 weeks)</u> |
| **Living out:** | • <u>Ave rent: £40</u> | |

**UNUSUAL COSTS:**
Parking permits are required and cost 70p per month.

# UNIVERSITY OF BATH
University of Bath, Claverton Down, Bath, BA2 7AY. Tel: (01225) 826826. Fax: (01225) 826366. Email: admissions@bath.ac.uk

**DEBTS:** • <u>Access fund: £271,888</u> • <u>Successful applications per year: 220</u>
Students who have to do vacation and field study can apply for special awards. There's a hardship fund.
**Banks on campus:** All 4 major banks also have branches on campus (with cash machines).

**EMPLOYMENT:** • <u>Unemployed after 6 months: 3.2%</u>

**TRAVEL:**
**National:** Trains: Bath Spa station offers services to London Paddington (£19.80), Bristol (£3.10), Birmingham (£17.80) and beyond. Buses: National Express and Badgerline services from Bath to various destinations including London (£11), Bristol (£3.25).
**Local:** The SU has negotiated a bus service which operates between the town, Bath University and Bath Spa.

**ENTERTAINMENTS:** • <u>Booze index: £1.82</u>

| | | |
|---|---|---|
| **Town/city:** | • <u>Pint of beer: £2</u> | • <u>Glass of wine: £1.80</u> |
| **University:** | • <u>Pint of beer: £1.50</u> | • <u>Glass of wine: £1.90</u> |

**ACCOMMODATION:**

| | | |
|---|---|---|
| **Living in:** | • <u>Self-catering: 42%</u> | • <u>Cost: £42-54 (33-50 weeks)</u> |
| **Living out:** | • <u>Ave rent: £49</u> | |

# BATH SPA UNIVERSITY COLLEGE
(1) Bath Spa University College, Newton St Loe, Bath, BA2 9BN.
Tel: (01225) 875875. Fax: (01225) 875444. E-mail: enquiries@bathspa.ac.uk
(2) Bath Spa University College, Sion Hill, Lansdown, Bath, BA1 5SF.
Tel: (01225) 875684. Fax: (01225) 875666.

**DEBTS:** • <u>Average debt: £900</u>
• <u>Access fund: £220,000</u> • <u>Successful applications per year: 800</u>
**Banks on campus:** NatWest cashpoint.

**EMPLOYMENT:** • <u>Unemployed after 6 months: 10%</u>
**Paid work:** The Uni has a Jobshop and there are the usual suspects in town.

**TRAVEL:** See <u>University of Bath</u>
**Local:** Buses are the best way of getting from the campus at Newton Park into Bath. There are two an hour, quite reliably, until around 2:30am. The Orange Bus runs between town, Bath Spa and Bath University and does season tickets (£7.50 for 10 journeys, £170pa). A bus also runs between Newton Park and Sion Hill.

**ENTERTAINMENTS:** • <u>Booze index: £1.78</u>

| | | |
|---|---|---|
| **Town/city:** | • <u>Pint of beer: £2</u> | • <u>Glass of wine: £1.80</u> |
| **University:** | • <u>Pint of beer: £1.50</u> | • <u>Glass of wine: £1.20</u> |

**ACCOMMODATION:**

| | | |
|---|---|---|
| **Living in:** | • <u>Self-catering: 22%</u> | • <u>Cost: £48-71 (38-40 weeks)</u> |
| **Living out:** | • <u>Ave rent: £49</u> | |

# UNIVERSITY OF BIRMINGHAM

University of Birmingham, Edgbaston, Birmingham, B15 2TT.
Tel: (0121) 414 6679. Fax: (0121) 414 3850. E-mail: schoolsliaison@bham.ac.uk

**DEBTS:** • Average debt: £1,050
• Access fund: £875,448 • Successful applications per year: 1,183
In addition to numerous scholarships and prizes there's a hardship fund administered jointly by the University and Guild of Students and special support to help student parents.
**Banks on campus:** HSBC, Halifax & Co-op.

**EMPLOYMENT:** • Unemployed after 6 months: 3.6%
**Paid work:** The Guild's the best bet for a fuller pocket, employing around 430 students on a casual basis at any one time. Check out the Job Zone (jobshop) too.

**TRAVEL:**
**National:** Trains: Being the belly button of Britain, Brum is brilliantly placed for rail links. Mainline links from London (£19.60), Manchester (£15.85), Edinburgh (£50.15) and just about every city in the country come into New Street Station. Buses: National Express to London (£11), Manchester (£8.20), Edinburgh (£26) and, well, all over the shop, really. Also West Midlands Travel and London Liner.
**Local:** Bus services run late into the night (85p from campus to town). The Guild and the University between them run a bus service between halls and campus (40p for the round trip). Overground trains run around the city – they're faster than buses, but more expensive and very unreliable. Not worth using, except by students who live in Selly Oak.

**ENTERTAINMENTS:** • Booze index: £1.62
**Town/city:** • Pint of beer: £1.90 • Glass of wine: £1.50
**University:** • Pint of beer: £1.65 • Glass of wine: £1.30

**ACCOMMODATION:**
**Living in:** • Catered: 18% • Cost: £76-106 (30-40 weeks)
• Self-catering: 19% • Cost: £44-66 (40 weeks)
**Living out:** • Ave rent: £42

# BOLTON INSTITUTE OF HIGHER EDUCATION

Bolton Institute of Higher Education, Deane Road, Bolton, BL3 5AB.
Tel: (01204) 900600. Fax: (01204) 399074. E-mail: enquiries@bolton.ac.uk

**DEBTS:** • Average debt: £1,300
• Access fund: £317,471 • Successful applications per year: 523
The access fund concentrates on child-care support.
**Banks on campus:** Coop Bank.

**EMPLOYMENT:** • Unemployed after 6 months: 36%
**Paid work:** Usual bar and shop work, etc, but not much of it. There is a jobshop run by the careers service.

**TRAVEL:**
**National:** Trains: The Institute is half a mile from Bolton mainline station with connections to Manchester (£2.15) every 15 minutes, Blackpool, Wigan, Blackburn. Via Manchester, you can go anywhere. See Manchester University.
**Local:** Students often use the buses which go from the Institute to the halls every 10 or 15 minutes until 11.30pm. A nightbus from Manchester pulls in at 1am or 2.30am on Fridays and Saturdays. There are also plans to expand Manchester's excellent Metro service to Bolton.

**ENTERTAINMENTS:** • Booze index: £1.63
**Town/city:** • Pint of beer: £1.70 • Glass of wine: £1.80
**University:** • Pint of beer: £1.20 • Glass of wine: £1.25

**ACCOMMODATION:**
Living in: • Self-catering: 23%   • Cost: £46 (40 weeks)
Living out: • Ave rent: £38

**UNUSUAL COSTS:**
All students are eligible for a Bolton Leisure Card for sports which costs £2.

---

## BOURNEMOUTH UNIVERSITY
Formerly Bournemouth Polytechnic, Dorset Institute
Bournemouth University, Fern Barrow, Poole, Dorset, BH12 5BB.
Tel: (01202) 524111. Fax: (01202) 595287. E-mail: enquries@bournemouth.ac.uk

**DEBTS:** • Average debt: £1,600
• Access fund: £384,087 • Successful applications per year: 732
The students' union runs a small emergency loan fund.
**Banks on campus:** Barclays Bank with cash-point.

**EMPLOYMENT:** • Unemployed after 6 months: 18%
**Paid work:** Tourism brings many vacancies for deckchair attendants, ice cream vendors and hotel work, but most students go home in summer. Some teach English to foreigners. There's a Work Bank and a job noticeboard.

**TRAVEL:**
**National:** Trains: From Bournemouth station, 2 miles from the campus, to London (£17.15), Brighton (£14.70) and all over. Coaches: National Express: London (£11), Brighton (£10.50).
**Local:** Buses run regularly until about 11pm. Trains stop frequently along the coast, but few students bother. The uni runs free buses between town and college in term-time.

**ENTERTAINMENTS:** • Booze index: £1.67
Town/city: • Pint of beer: £1.85   • Glass of wine: £1.60
University: • Pint of beer: £1.40   • Glass of wine: £1.30

**ACCOMMODATION:**
Living in: • Self-catering: 14%   • Cost: £60-64 (34-40 weeks)
Living out: • Ave rent: £55

Why split up your mum's precious glassware collection? Simply steal it from pubs. Especially nice are the Stella Artois pint glasses. Just remember to take a big bag or a large coat.

Liz Gayther, De Montfort University (Lincoln)

7

# UNIVERSITY OF BRADFORD

University of Bradford, Richmond Road, Bradford, West Yorkshire, BD7 1DP.
Tel: (01274) 233081. Fax: (01274) 236260. E-mail: enquiries@bradford.ac.uk

**DEBTS:** • Average debt: £2,050
• Hardship fund: £385,141 • Successful applications per year: 850
The University operates its own hardship fund and there's a £10,000 trust fund
for female students.
**Banks on campus:** NatWest with cashpoint.

**EMPLOYMENT:** • Unemployed after 6 months: 6%
Bradford's vocational training makes it popular with employers, especially in
engineering and technology sectors.
**Paid work:** The University runs a jobshop. Having plenty of local pubs and
restaurants also spells opportunity.

**TRAVEL:**
**National:** Trains: Services from Bradford Interchange to London (£39.95),
Manchester (£7.55), Birmingham (£23.90). Coaches: National Express services
to, among other places, London (£16.75) and Manchester (£6.50).
**Local:** Regular and cheap bus services from the campus to the city centre, but
everybody walks if it isn't raining. There are 3 stations around the city (including
neighbouring Shipley) which are useful for getting to Leeds (80p). A West Yorkshire
Metrocard gives unlimited travel on trains and buses – students can get one for a
bargain £29.70 a month.

**ENTERTAINMENTS:** • Booze index: £1.55
**Town/city:** • Pint of beer: £1.60 • Glass of wine: £1.80
**University:** • Pint of beer: £1.40 • Glass of wine: £1

**ACCOMMODATION:**
**Living in:** • Self-catering: 30% • Cost: £42-61 (30 weeks)
**Living out:** • Ave rent: £33

# UNIVERSITY OF BRIGHTON

University of Brighton, Mithras House, Lewes Road, Brighton, BN2 4AT.
Tel: (01273) 600900. Fax: (01273) 642825. E-mail: admissions@brighton.ac.uk

**DEBTS:** • Average debt: £1,850
• Access fund: £731,492 • Successful applications per year: 1,441
Hardship loans up to £500.

**EMPLOYMENT:** • Unemployed after 6 months: 6%
**Paid work:** Although the jobs are no different from other towns, prospects are
more hopeful, especially during the tourist season. The SU's Work Shop can find
function for fidgeting fingers.

**TRAVEL:**
**National:** Trains: Connections from Brighton station to London (£6.60), Bristol
(£23.75), Sheffield (£38.30) and elsewhere. Coaches: All over the country
including London (£10.50), Bristol (£32), Sheffield (£25).
**Local:** The local buses are reliable but take forever. Trains provide a
comprehensive local service inland and along the coast linking Brighton and
Eastbourne.

**ENTERTAINMENTS:** • Booze index: £1.63
**Town/city:** • Pint of beer: £1.95 • Glass of wine: £1.45
**University:** • Pint of beer: £1.40 • Glass of wine: £1.20

**ACCOMMODATION:**

| | | |
|---|---|---|
| **Living in:** | • Catered: 1% | • Cost: £77-81 (32 weeks) |
| | • Self-catering: 16% | • Cost: £45-62 (38-50 weeks) |
| **Living out:** | • Ave rent: £48 | |

## BRISTOL UNIVERSITY

University of Bristol, Senate House, Tyndall Avenue, Bristol, BS8 1TH.
Tel: (0117) 928 9000. Fax: (0117) 925 1424. E-mail: admissions@bris.ac.uk

**DEBTS:** • Average debt: £1,250
• Access fund: £516,355 • Successful applications per year: 548
**Banks on campus:** NatWest and Lloyds Bank cash machines.

**EMPLOYMENT:** • Unemployed after 6 months: 3%
**Paid work:** There's always go-go dancing, but otherwise just the normal limited
selection of bar work and restaurants. The SU runs a student employment office.

**TRAVEL:**
**National:** Trains: Bristol Temple Meads is one of the country's centres for mainline
routes: London (£27.15), Birmingham (£20.45) and elsewhere. Bristol Parkway for
Wales. Coaches: Bristol is similarly well served by coach services, including
National Express buses to, among other places, London (£15), Birmingham
(£12.75) and Cardiff (£6.50). Arrow and Bakers Dolphin also offer cheap return
trips to London.
**Local:** There are several British Rail stops in and around the city providing a
reliable, frequent and comprehensive service without staggering cost. Local buses
fill in where trains can't go, costing £1 from Temple Meads Station to the Union.

**ENTERTAINMENTS:** • Booze index: £1.75

| | | |
|---|---|---|
| **Town/city:** | • Pint of beer: £2 | • Glass of wine: £2 |
| **University:** | • Pint of beer: £1.15 | • Glass of wine: £1 |

**ACCOMMODATION:**

| | | |
|---|---|---|
| **Living in:** | • Catered: 16% | • Cost: £65-92 (30 weeks) |
| | • Self-catering 9% | • Cost: £35-60 (30-38 weeks) |
| **Living out:** | • Ave rent: £50 | |

## BRISTOL: UNIVERSITY OF THE WEST OF ENGLAND

University of the West of England, Frenchay Campus, Coldharbour Lane, Bristol,
BS16 1QY. Tel: (0117) 965 6261. Fax: (0117) 344 2810.
E-mail: admissions@uwe.ac.uk

**DEBTS:** • Average debt: £1,700
• Access fund: £910,535 • Successful applications per year: 1,123
**Banks on campus:** NatWest Bank (with cashpoint at Frenchay).

**EMPLOYMENT:** • Unemployed after 6 months: 5.5%

**TRAVEL:** See University of Bristol
**Local:** Bus services link the Frenchay campus to the city centre (£1.35 rtn) and
run between the sites (which isn't often necessary). Local buses have improved
with a new late night service that runs every hour from the city centre but only on
weekends. The most convenient station for Frenchay is Bristol Parkway.

**ENTERTAINMENTS:** • Booze index: £1.90

| | | |
|---|---|---|
| **Town/city:** | • Pint of beer: £2 | • Glass of wine: £2 |
| **University:** | • Pint of beer: £1.30 | • Glass of wine: £1.30 |

**ACCOMMODATION:**

| | | |
|---|---|---|
| **Living in:** | • Self-catering: 15% | • Cost: £46-51 (40-46 weeks) |
| **Living out:** | • Ave rent: £50 | |

**7**

## BRUNEL UNIVERSITY

Brunel University, Uxbridge, Middlesex, UB8 3PH. Tel: (01895) 274000.
Fax: (01895) 232806. E-mail: courses@brunel.ac.uk and admissions@brunel.ac.uk

**DEBTS:** • Access fund: £558,193 • Successful applications per year: 1,546
Welfare loans (up to £150) from the SU. Sponsorships and placement pay can
ease the financial burden for many.
**Banks on campus:** HSBC Bank cash machine.

**EMPLOYMENT:** • Unemployed after 6 months: 4%
Since so many students go on placements they have a useful mix of qualifications
and experience.
**Paid work:** Even with the placements, students find it necessary to earn an extra
buck, which is unfortunate, since local opportunities are only slightly more
common than the local amphibious giraffes.

**TRAVEL:**
**National:** Trains: West Drayton and Hayes are the BR stations nearest to the
Uxbridge site both a short bus ride away (Uxbridge tube station is closer). For
other services, the quickest route is usually via London mainline stations. For
trains to and from Egham, which is the nearest station to the Runnymede site, see
Royal Holloway College. Buses: National Express and London Country coach
services bypass both Uxbridge and Egham. The nearest stop is Heathrow Airport
(25 minutes).
**Local:** Uxbridge is still within London's bus and Tube transport network. Uxbridge
station (a mile from campus) is the last stop on the Metropolitan and Piccadilly
Lines and offers a fast but expensive service into London. The Uni runs an
insufficient bus service between Uxbridge and Runnymede.

**ENTERTAINMENTS:** • Booze index: £1.97
**Town/city:** • Pint of beer: £2.20    • Glass of wine: £2
**University:** • Pint of beer: £1.60    • Glass of wine: £1.75

**ACCOMMODATION:**
**Living in:** • Catered: 4%         • Cost: £48-60 (37-52 weeks)
              • Self-catering: 27%   • Cost: £43 (37 weeks)
**Living out:** • Ave rent: £65

## UNIVERSITY OF BUCKINGHAM

University of Buckingham, Buckingham, MK18 1EG. Tel: (01280) 814080.
Fax: (01280) 822245. E-mail: admissions@buckingham.ac.uk

**DEBTS:**
Being a private university, average debts vary beyond belief. Some students owe
nothing while others are in debt to the tune of their entire course costs. Also as a
private university, Buckingham has no Government access fund provisions.
Instead, scholarships are available and there's a limited hardship fund provides up
to £750 to students who can present a good case.

**EMPLOYMENT:** • Unemployed after 6 months: 17%
The careers service is open to the public, for a small charge, of course (all in the
best free market tradition of a private university).
**Paid work:** Nothing original here and fewer opportunities for conventional student
jobs than most places but very few UB students need fast cash or have the time
to earn it. That comes later.

**TRAVEL:**
**National:** Trains: The nearest stations are at Bicester and Milton Keynes (London
to MK £8.20 day rtn). Buses: Buses take 20 minutes to get to MK and National
Express services go from there all over the country. Hourly Stagecoach Express
goes between Oxford and Cambridge, taking in Buckingham, Bedford and MK en

route. Also 2 coaches a day to Northampton and Leicester, one a day
to Nottingham.
**Local:** A shuttle runs betwixt bus station, campus and Tesco's.

**ENTERTAINMENTS:** • Booze index: £1.19
**Town/city:** • Pint of beer: £2.10   • Glass of wine: £1.75
**University:** • Pint of beer: £1.20   • Glass of wine: £0.95

**ACCOMMODATION:**
**Living in:** • Self-catering: 87%   • Cost: £57-100 (52 weeks)
**Living out:** • Ave rent: £80

# BUCKINGHAMSHIRE CHILTERNS UNIVERSITY COLLEGE

(1) Buckinghamshire Chilterns University College, Queen Alexandra Road, High
Wycombe, Bucks, HP11 2JZ. Tel: (01494) 522141. Fax: (01494) 524392.
E-mail: marketing@buckscol.ac.uk
(2) Buckinghamshire Chilterns University College, Wellesbourne Campus, Kingshill
Road, High Wycombe, Bucks, Buckinghamshire HP13 5BB. Tel: (01494) 522141.
Fax: (01494) 465432.
(3) Buckinghamshire Chilterns University College, Chalfont Campus, Gorelands
Lane, Chalfont St Giles, Bucks, HP8 4AD. Tel: (01494) 522141.
Fax: (01494) 871954.

**DEBTS:**   • Average debt: £1,750
            • Access fund: £150,000   • Successful applications per year: 650

**EMPLOYMENT:** • Unemployed after 6 months: 8%
**Paid work:** More than half the students have jobs and there are plenty in this
home-counties suburbia if you don't mind a bit of temp work or shelf-stacking. The
Uni runs a jobshop.

**TRAVEL:**
**National:** Trains: High Wycombe station is 1 / 4 of a mile from campus. London
(£5.20) is 35 minutes by train. Coaches: One National Express service a day to
London (£2.50), Bristol (£28.50) or Heathrow (£3.30). Local buses go to Oxford,
Cambridge, Reading and all over.
**Local:** Good local buses but where are you going to go?

**ENTERTAINMENTS:** • Booze index: £1.86
**Town/city:** • Pint of beer: £2     • Glass of wine: £1.80
**University:** • Pint of beer: £1.55   • Glass of wine: £1.80

**ACCOMMODATION:**
**Living in:** • Self-catering: 20%   • Cost: £56-68 (38 weeks)
**Living out:** • Ave rent: £57

Get a friend to cut your hair —
preferably one who knows what they're
doing. Alternatively, find your
nearest hairdresser and ask if they
want any models. You'll only pay about
£5 and get just about whatever haircut
you want.

**7**

# UNIVERSITY OF CAMBRIDGE

University of Cambridge, Intercollegiate Applications Office, Kellet Lodge, Tennis Court Road, Cambridge, CB2 1QJ. Tel: (01223) 333308. Fax: (01223) 366383. E-mail: ucam-undergraduate-admissions@lists.cam.ac.uk

**DEBTS:**
Financial assistance usually comes from individual colleges, many of which have considerable bursaries and scholarships.

**EMPLOYMENT:** • Unemployed after 6 months: 4%
**Paid work:** The tourist trade provides the only opening beyond the ordinary.

**TRAVEL:**
**National:** Trains: Cambridge Station connects to London King's Cross and Liverpool Street (£8.45), Birmingham (£30.60), Bristol (£41) and more. Incidentally, the station is some way beyond the city centre because the University authorities didn't want rough common London folk coming too close to the sensitive young undergraduates. Coaches: Plenty of competitive services, for example, Greenline, Premier Travel and National Express who offer runs to London (£7.50), Bristol (£17) and elsewhere.
**Local:** The local buses, which are regular as prunes, go round the surrounding villages, the station and the outer colleges. Cambridge is too small to need much more.

**ENTERTAINMENTS:** • Booze index: £1.34
**Town/city:** • Pint of beer: £2.30 • Glass of wine: £1.70
**University:** • Pint of beer: £1.30 • Glass of wine: £1.20

**ACCOMMODATION:**
**Living in:** • Catered: 95%
**Living out:** • Ave rent: £55

# CARDIFF UNIVERSITY

Cardiff University, PO Box 921, Cardiff, CF10 3XQ. Tel: (029) 20 874839. Fax: (029) 20 874457. E-mail: prospectus@cardiff.ac.uk

**DEBTS:** • Access fund: £612,492 • Successful applications per year: 701
The Oldfield Davies Trust can help women with health problems and there are also short-term loans up to £100 and small grants, usually limited to finalists.

**EMPLOYMENT:** • Unemployed after 6 months: 5%
**Paid work:** Cardiff, particularly during the tourist season, has lots of opportunities for casual cash and the SU runs a Jobshop. Unfortunately, there are truckloads of students going for jobs. The Union employs 700 students every year.

**TRAVEL:**
**National:** Trains: Direct trains from Cardiff Central: London (£17.15); Birmingham (£13.20); Manchester (£25.10) and so on. Coaches: National Express to most places: London (£18), Birmingham (£14.50) and all over.
**Local:** Local bus services run every 20–30 mins all round town. They're reliable with an average trip costing 50p.

**ENTERTAINMENTS:** • Booze index: £1.62
**Town/city:** • Pint of beer: £1.90 • Glass of wine: £1.40
**University:** • Pint of beer: £1.60 • Glass of wine: £1.50

**ACCOMMODATION:**
**Living in:** • Catered: 4% • Cost: £55-67 (39 weeks)
• Self-catering 31% • Cost: £39-58 (39-52 weeks)
**Living out:** • Ave rent: £46

# UNIVERSITY OF CENTRAL LANCASHIRE

Formerly Preston Polytechnic, Lancashire Polytechnic
University of Central Lancashire, Preston, PR1 2HE. Tel: (01772) 892400.
Fax: (01772) 892935. E-mail: c.enquiries@uclan.ac.uk

**DEBTS:** • <u>Average debt: £850</u>
• <u>Access fund: £710,000</u> • <u>Successful applications per year: 700</u>
There's also a Hardship Fund and postgraduate bursaries.
**Banks on campus:** HSBC Bank and cashpoint.

**EMPLOYMENT:** • <u>Unemployed after 6 months: 5%</u>
**Paid work:** Jobshop called 'The Bridge'. There's an abundance of pubs and
restaurants hungry for part-time staff.

**TRAVEL:**
**National:** Trains: Preston Station, half a mile from the campus, runs direct trains
to London (£28.40), Manchester (£6.55) and beyond. Coaches: National Express
services to, among other places, London (£18.50), Manchester (£3.40).
**Local:** Local buses keep to an exact fare system (no change given). Discounted
Rambler tickets (anywhere in town, £5.20/week) are available.

**ENTERTAINMENTS:** • <u>Booze index: £1.52</u>
**Town/city:** • <u>Pint of beer: £1.70</u> • <u>Glass of wine: £1.40</u>
**University:** • <u>Pint of beer: £1.10</u> • <u>Glass of wine: £1.50</u>

**ACCOMMODATION:**
**Living in:** • <u>Self-catering: 14%</u> • <u>Cost: £45-53 (37 weeks)</u>
**Living out:** • <u>Ave rent: £36</u>

**UNUSUAL COSTS:**
There is limited, permit-only parking (£36 per year).

# CHELTENHAM & GLOUCESTER COLLEGE OF HIGHER EDUCATION

Cheltenham & Gloucester College of Higher Education, PO Box 220, The Park,
Cheltenham, Gloucestershire, GL50 2QF. Tel: (01242) 532825.
Fax: (01242) 543334. E-mail: admissions@chelt.ac.uk

**DEBTS:** • <u>Average debt: £1,200</u>
• <u>Access fund: £382,766</u> • <u>Successful applications per year: 1,143</u>
Student Services provides small short-term emergency loans.

**EMPLOYMENT:** • <u>Unemployed after 6 months: 6%</u>
**Paid work:** UCAS, the University applications processing body, has its
headquarters locally and during the vacations it often takes on temporary clerical
help. The racecourse sometimes uses casual labour, but don't put your grant
cheque on a sure-fire tip for the 2.30. The Student Employment Centre will help
you find part-time work locally.

**TRAVEL:**
**National:** Trains: Cheltenham Spa station is 2 miles from Park Campus, offering
direct links to London (£23.10), Birmingham (£9.40), Manchester (£20.70) and
elsewhere. Coaches: National Express, Marchants and Swanbrook operate coach
services from Cheltenham; a return trip to London will cost £16.50.
**Local:** The College runs its own free bus service between all the sites. It's quite
reliable and runs until 11.30pm. Local buses take up the slack and run till
midnight, but cost 65p from Park Campus to the town centre.

**ENTERTAINMENTS:** • <u>Booze index: £1.90</u>
**Town/city:** • <u>Pint of beer: £2.20</u> • <u>Glass of wine: £1.80</u>
**University:** • <u>Pint of beer: £1.40</u> • <u>Glass of wine: £1.30</u>

**ACCOMMODATION:**
Living in: • Self-catering: 14% • Cost: £49-59 (41 weeks)
Living out: • Ave rent: £44

# CITY UNIVERSITY
City University, Northampton Square, London, EC1V 0HB.
Tel: (020) 7040 5060. Fax: (020) 7 477 8560.

**DEBTS:** • Average debt: £1,000 • Access fund: £260,000
There is a hardship fund and the SU can make short-term loans of £50.

**EMPLOYMENT:** • Unemployed after 6 months: 3.9%
The University's vocational emphasis is rewarded by a good employment record.
**Paid work:** There are more opportunities in London for part-time work than
anywhere else, but there are also more people trying to get those jobs. Students
find work quite easily in all the usual places like bars and restaurants and also in
theatres, offices and shops.

**TRAVEL:**
**National:** Trains: Liverpool Street and King's Cross mainline stations are both
within 20 minutes walk of the University.
**Local:** Underground and buses.

**ENTERTAINMENTS:** • Booze index: £2.23
Town/city: • Pint of beer: £2.20 • Glass of wine: £2.50
University: • Pint of beer: £1.60 • Glass of wine: £2

**ACCOMMODATION:**
Living in: • Catered: 7% • Cost: £90 (39 weeks)
• Self-catering: 14% • Cost: £77 (39-42 weeks)
Living out: • Ave rent: £75

# COURTAULD INSTITUTE OF ART, LONDON
• The Institute is part of University of London and students are entitled to use its
facilities.
The Courtauld Institute of Art, Somerset House, Strand, London, WC2R 0RN. Tel:
(020) 7848 2645. Fax: (020) 7848 2410. E-mail: ugadmission@courtauld.ac.uk

**DEBTS:** • Access fund: £20,000

**EMPLOYMENT:**
**Paid work:** see University of London

**TRAVEL:**
**National:** The nearest mainline BR stations are Charing Cross ($^1/_4$ mile), Waterloo
($^1/_2$ mile) and Blackfriars ($^1/_2$ mile).
**Local:** Underground and buses.

**ENTERTAINMENTS:** • Booze index: £2.35
Town/city: • Pint of beer: £2.20 • Glass of wine: £2.50
University (at King's College):
• Pint of beer: £1.55 • Glass of wine: £1.10
No bar of their own, but good access to King's College bar next door. Courtauld is
extremely well served for entertainments and culture, but this is central London
and it's an expensive place to buy a canned drink, let alone an alcoholic one.

**ACCOMMODATION:**
Living in: • Catered: 31% • Cost: £77-102 (30 weeks)
No accommodation of its own but students can apply for University of London's
intercollegiate housing
Living out: • Ave rent: £75

# COVENTRY UNIVERSITY
Coventry University, Priory Street, Coventry, CV1 5FB. Tel: (024) 7688 7688. Fax: (024) 7688 8638. E-mail: education.cor@coventry.ac.uk

**DEBTS:** • <u>Average debt: £1,450</u>
• <u>Access fund: £740,427</u> • <u>Successful applications per year: 634</u>
As well as the access fund there's a small welfare fund for the desperate, short term loans of up to £50 and arts and sports bursaries worth £500 each.

**EMPLOYMENT:** • <u>Unemployed after 6 months: 16%</u>
The Careers Office is off campus (about 5 minutes walk) and many students seem unaware of its existence.
**Paid work:** CUBE (Coventry University Bureau of Employment) is run by students to help them find part-time and vacation work, from bar work to market research.

**TRAVEL:**
**National:** Trains: The Grade II listed Coventry Station is about 1 mile from the Coventry University campus and on the main London (£11.80) to Birmingham (£2.30) line. Coaches: National Express, Bharat and Harry Shaw services all over the place, including London (£12), Birmingham (£4), Manchester (£11) and more.
**Local:** There are three BR train stops within the confines of Coventry, but the reliable local bus services are more useful for getting to places students haven't got the welly to walk to.

**ENTERTAINMENTS:** • <u>Booze index: £1.77</u>
**Town/city:** • <u>Pint of beer: £1.80</u>  • <u>Glass of wine: £1.90</u>
**University:** • <u>Pint of beer: £1.45</u>  • <u>Glass of wine: £1.30</u>

**ACCOMMODATION:**
**Living in:** • <u>Catered: 6%</u>       • <u>Cost: £71 (40-52 weeks)</u>
• <u>Self-catering: 10%</u>  • <u>Cost: £45-57 (40-52 weeks)</u>
**Living out:** • <u>Ave rent: £35-40</u>

# CRANFIELD UNIVERSITY
(1) Royal Military College of Science, Shrivenham, Swindon, Wiltshire, SN6 8LA. Tel: (01793) 785400. Fax: (01793) 783966.
(2) Silsoe College, Silsoe, Bedfordshire, MK45 4DT. Tel: (01525) 863319. Fax: (01525) 863316. Email for both sites: recruitment@cranfield.ac.uk

**DEBTS:** • <u>Average debt: £1,300</u>
**RMCS:** • <u>Access fund: £4,550</u> • <u>Successful applications per year: 20</u>
Many RMCS students are sponsored by the forces.
**Silsoe:** • <u>Access fund: £110,000</u> • <u>Successful applications per year: 80</u>

**EMPLOYMENT:**
Although the armed forces have been cutting back in recent years, Shrivenham graduates don't appear to have been effected.

**TRAVEL:**
At both sites non-drivers are at a distinct disadvantage. Silsoe's nearest train station is Flitwick, 3 miles away, but it's way off any beaten track, so Luton's the best bet (see <u>Luton University</u>). Local buses supposedly run every hour or so (£2.70 rtn to Luton), but don't count on it. Shrivenham is even more remote, but at least Swindon has rail and coach connections to most major cities. London is £13.85 by train, £12.75 by coach. The A420 runs near the college and local buses go from the main gate every hour.

**7**

**ENTERTAINMENTS:** • Booze index: £1.64

| | | |
|---|---|---|
| Shrivenham Village: | • Pint of beer: £1.80 | • Glass of wine: £1.20 |
| Silsoe Village: | • Pint of beer: £1.90 | • Glass of wine: £1.90 |

**University:**

| | | |
|---|---|---|
| RMCS: • Pint of beer: £1.20 | • Glass of wine: £1.10 | |
| Silsoe: • Pint of beer: £1.60 | • Glass of wine: £1.40 | |

**ACCOMMODATION:**

| | | | |
|---|---|---|---|
| **Living in:** | RMCS: | • Catered: 14% | • Cost: £81 (32 weeks) |
| | | • Self-catering: 13% | • Cost: £35-55 (52 weeks) |
| | Silsoe: | • Catered: 80% | • Cost: £60(30 weeks) |
| | | • Self-catering: 20% | • Cost: £40-67(40-50 weeks) |
| **Living out:** | • Ave rent: £50 | | |

# DE MONTFORT UNIVERSITY

Telephone hotline to all campuses: (0645) 454647. E-mail: enquiry@dmu.ac.uk
(1) De Montfort University Leicester, The Gateway, Leicester, LE1 9BH.
Tel: (0116) 255 1551. Fax: (0116) 255 0307.
(2) De Montfort University Bedford, 37 Landsdowne Road, Bedford, MK40 2BZ.
Tel: (01234) 211688. Fax: (01234) 347357.
(3) De Montfort University Lincoln, School of Agriculture and Horticulture,
Caythorpe Court, Caythorpe, Grantham, Lincolnshire, NG32 3EP.
Tel: (01400) 272521. Fax: (01400) 272722.
(4) De Montfort University Lincoln, School of Applied Art and Design, Lindum Road,
Lincoln, LN2 1NP. Tel: (01522) 512912. Fax: (01522) 895147.

**DEBTS:** • Average debt: £1,850
• Access fund: £1,500,000 • Successful applications: 1,563
Bursaries are available in science and engineering subjects. Debts are higher
overall at Leicester, maybe because there are more spending temptations in town.

**EMPLOYMENT:** • Unemployed after 6 months: 4%
The Careers Service publishes the fortnightly 'Grapevine', listing job opportunities,
which is distributed to all sites. They also arrange workshops and talks from
employers.
**Paid work:** The Workbank operates from Leicester but caters for all sites.

**TRAVEL:** See University of Leicester

**ENTERTAINMENTS:** • Booze index: £1.49

| | | |
|---|---|---|
| **Town/city:** | • Pint of beer: £2 | • Glass of wine: £1.70 |
| **University:** | • Pint of beer: £1.30 | • Glass of wine: £1.50 |

**ACCOMMODATION:**

| | | | |
|---|---|---|---|
| **Living in:** | Leicester: | • Catered: 7% | • Cost: £59 (30 weeks) |
| | | • Self-catering 8% | • Cost: £41-51 (38 weeks) |
| | Bedford: | • Catered: 21% | • Cost: £53 (35-39 weeks) |
| | | • Self-catering 1% | • Cost: £43 (35-39 weeks) |
| | Lincoln: | • Catered: 23% | • Cost: £65-79 (31-33 weeks) |
| **Living out:** | • Ave rent: £38 | | |

# UNIVERSITY OF DERBY

University of Derby, Kedleston Road, Derby, DE22 1GB. Tel: (01332) 590500.
Fax: (01332) 294861.

**DEBTS:** • Average debt: £1,050
• Access fund: £928,366 • Successful applications per year: 1,295
**Banks on campus:** Natwest Bank.

**EMPLOYMENT:** • Unemployed after 6 months: 10%
**Paid work:** There's a Student Employment Service to assist in the search for part-time work.

**TRAVEL:**
**National:** Trains: Derby BR station is 2 1 / 2 miles from Kedleston Road: London (£23.10), Sheffield (£4.75) and beyond. Coaches: National Express and other services operate to London (£15.75) and Sheffield (£5),.
**Local:** Reliable buses run every 15 minutes to the town centre from the main campus. Weekly passes are available.

**ENTERTAINMENTS:** • Booze index: £1.60
**Town/city:** • Pint of beer: £1.80 • Glass of wine: £1.40
**University:** • Pint of beer: £1.20 • Glass of wine: £2

**ACCOMMODATION:**
**Living in:** • Self-catering 29% • Cost: £51-63 (35-52 weeks)
**Living out:** • Ave rent: £40

# UNIVERSITY OF DUNDEE

University of Dundee, Dundee, DD1 4HN. Tel: (01382) 344000.
Fax: (01382) 201604. E-mail: secretary@dundee.ac.uk

**DEBTS:** • Average debt: £1,650
• Access fund: £520,000 • Successful applications per year: 903
The University doles out various bursaries and the Students' Association (SA) has its own hardship fund. There's a set of bursaries from the St Andrews Royal & Ancient Golf Club worth £1,500 each to eight students hot with a 3-iron.
**Banks on campus:** Clydesdale & Royal Bank of Scotland.

**EMPLOYMENT:** • Unemployed after 6 months: 2%
Despite lots of resources available and the Careers Office open in vacations, personal help is felt to be in short supply.
**Paid work:** Some seasonal work at the local Outdoor Pursuits Centre and tourist spots across the Tay in Fife. Local part-time work is hard to find, but the SA employs up to 200.

**TRAVEL:**
**National:** Trains: Dundee BR has services to London (£54.90), Glasgow (£14.40) and routes to most parts of Scotland and England. Coaches: National Express, Stagecoach and Citylink services including London (£32), Glasgow (£11) and Edinburgh (£10).
**Local:** There's a good bus service and it's fairly cheap (80p across town), but the last is at around 11.15pm. There's only one train stop in Dundee – one line comes along the Tay from Perth and the other crosses the Tay heading south.

**ENTERTAINMENTS:** • Booze index: £1.80
**Town/city:** • Pint of beer: £1.80 • Glass of wine: £2
**University:** • Pint of beer: £1.30 • Glass of wine: £1.50

**ACCOMMODATION:**
**Living in:** • Catered: 7% • Cost: £72 (31 weeks)
• Self-catering 14% • Cost: £37-58 (38-52 weeks)
**Living out:** • Ave rent: £45

**UNUSUAL COSTS:**
Parking permits cost £50 a year.

# UNIVERSITY OF DURHAM

(1) The University of Durham, Old Shire Hall, Old Elvet, Durham, DH1 3HP.
Tel: (0191) 374 2000. Fax: (0191) 374 7250.
(2) University of Durham Stockton Campus, University Boulevard, Thornaby,
Stockton-on-Tees, Cleveland, TS17 6BH. Tel: (01642) 335300.
Fax: (01642) 618345.

**DEBTS:** • Average debt: £850
• Access fund: £442,571 • Successful applications per year: 390
There's a hardship fund of £30,000 but a student has to be in seriously deep poo
to benefit from it. There are also scholarships, bursaries and prizes galore.

**EMPLOYMENT:** • Unemployed after 6 months: 6%
**Paid work:** Few openings, although the SU runs a jobshop. Recently, 700 sought
work through the shop and 350 of them were blessed.

**TRAVEL:**
**National:** Trains: Mainline connections to London King's X (£47.50), Newcastle
(£2.60) and more. Coaches: National Express and Blue Line services to many
destinations: London (£25.50), Newcastle (£3) and so on.
**Local:** Good buses around town and surrounds which lazy students use to get to
the hill colleges. Fares from 32p. No trains around the city but a useful service
into Newcastle.

**ENTERTAINMENTS:** • Booze index: £1.47
**Town/city:** • Pint of beer: £1.80 • Glass of wine: £1.75
**University:** • Pint of beer: £1.30 • Glass of wine: £1.20

**ACCOMMODATION:**
**Living in:** • Catered: 48% • Cost: £80 (29 weeks)
• Self-catering: 10% • Cost: £45-55 (29 weeks)
**Living out:** • Ave rent: £48

**UNUSUAL COSTS:**
The Durham Union Society (DUS) is the long-standing debating society which offers
more than just debating – often seen as a right-wing refuge for the sophisticated
Sloane – whatever, it costs £35 to join.

# UNIVERSITY OF EAST LONDON

(1) University of East London, Barking Campus, Longbridge Road, Dagenham,
Essex, RM8 2AS. Tel: (020) 8223 3000. Fax: (020) 8590 7799.
(2) University of East London, Stratford Campus, Romford Road, London, E15 4LZ.
(3) University of East London, Docklands Campus, Royal Albert Way, London,
E16 2QT. Tel (020) 8223 3000.

**DEBTS:** • Average debt: £2,000
• Access fund: £303,000 • Successful applications per year: 1,324
There are 7 scholarships for part-time unwaged students, as well as partial fee
remission schemes.
**Banks on campus:** Barclays Bank.

**EMPLOYMENT:** • Unemployed after 6 months: 6%

**TRAVEL:**
**National:** Trains: For Stratford the nearest rail station is Maryland (10 minutes from London Liverpool St). Barking Station is 13 minutes from London Fenchurch St Station.
**Local:** Tubes, busesand the Docklands Light Railway which runs services into the City, Docklands and is being extended into South London. The Docklands campus has its very own DLR station which runs directly to the campus at Stratford. Beware the service is patchy during the day and even worse at night.

**ENTERTAINMENTS:** • Booze index: £1.96
**Town/city:** • Pint of beer: £1.90 • Glass of wine: £2.20
**University:** • Pint of beer: £1.50 • Glass of wine: £1.50

**ACCOMMODATION:**
**Living in:** • Self-catering: 18% • Cost: £40-66 (52 weeks)

# UNIVERSITY OF EDINBURGH
The University of Edinburgh, Old College, South Bridge, Edinburgh, EH8 9YL. Tel: (0131) 650 1000. Fax: (0131) 650 2147.

**DEBTS:** • Average debt: £800
• Access fund: £997,940 • Successful applications per year: 995
EUSA can offer a small crisis loan (up to £100) on a 6-month repayment scheme and limited grants are available from the University Common Bursaries Fund. There are also 50 bursaries of £1,000 each per year as well as 25 open bursaries.
**Banks on campus:** NatWest and Bank of Scotland cashpoints.

**EMPLOYMENT:** • Unemployed after 6 months: 4.2%
**Paid work:** The Uni/Union-run Student Employment Service helps with part-time and vacation work with students making up many of the union employees and there's always plenty of work around the Festivals for those who get in early enough.

**TRAVEL:**
**National:** Trains: Edinburgh Waverley Station is the most central in Edinburgh with a direct line to Glasgow (£4.95) and others to the north and the south (via Newcastle and York) to London (£50.80). Connections also to Birmingham and Bristol. Coaches: National Express, Stagecoach and Citylink services to London (£27.25), Glasgow (£5) and so on.
**Local:** Bus services are good all round the city and quite cheap (from 50p). They run less frequently between 7pm and midnight.

**ENTERTAINMENTS:** • Booze index: £1.92
**Town/city:** • Pint of beer: £2.40 • Glass of wine: £2
**University:** • Pint of beer: £1.55

**ACCOMMODATION:**
**Living in:** • Catered: 15% • Cost: £84-97 (30 weeks)
• Self-catering: 28% • Cost: £52-67 (30-50 weeks)
**Living out:** • Ave rent: £55

# UNIVERSITY OF ESSEX
University of Essex, Wivenhoe Park, Colchester, CO4 3SQ. Tel: (01206) 873666. Fax: (01206) 873423. E-mail: admit@essex.ac.uk

**DEBTS:** • Average debt: £1,700
Hardship funds available from the Student Support Office and loans from the SU.
**Banks on campus:** Lloyds/NatWest cashpoint.

**EMPLOYMENT:** • Unemployed after 6 months: 3%
**Paid work:** The SU has a policy of giving students paid work in shops and bars.

**TRAVEL:**
**National:** Trains: The nearest mainline station to the campus is Colchester, 3 miles away (there are 2 other stations in town). Direct services run into London Liverpool Street (£8.70). Connections via London are possible all over the country including Birmingham, Bristol and Edinburgh. Coaches: National Express services to London (£6.75), Birmingham (£16.75) and more.
**Local:** Buses are expensive (£1 return to the town centre), but they are reliable and they tour the local villages which is useful for those living there.

**ENTERTAINMENTS:** • Booze index: £1.33
**Town/city:** • Pint of beer: £1.90 • Glass of wine: £1.40
**University:** • Pint of beer: £1.25 • Glass of wine: £1

**ACCOMMODATION:**
**Living in:** • Self-catering: 65% • Cost: £36-57 (39 weeks)
**Living out:** • Ave rent: £40

# UNIVERSITY OF EXETER

(1) University of Exeter, Northcote House, The Queen's Drive, Exeter, EX4 4QJ.
Tel: (01392) 263263. Fax: (01392) 263108. E-mail: registry@exeter.ac.uk
(2) Camborne School of Mines, Pool, Redruth, Cornwall, TR15 3SE.
Tel: (01209) 714866. Fax: (01209) 716977.

**DEBTS:** • Average debt: £1,650
• Access fund: £295,000 • Successful applications per year: 990
There are sports scholarships and bursaries of £1,000 for some education courses.

**EMPLOYMENT:** • Unemployed after 6 months: 3%
**Paid work:** A few local jobs for students in the tourist trade and some bar and clerical work in the Guild. Also an on-line bulletin board has just been set up and is available at www.ex.ac.uk/jobsurfing

**TRAVEL:**
**National:** Trains: Exeter St Davids Station is half a mile from the University. There are direct lines to London (£26.40), Bristol (£10.90), Birmingham (£30.35) and connections all over. Buses: National Express services all over the country, include London (£22), Birmingham (£22.50) and more.
**Local:** Local buses are reliable and quite comprehensive, but not cheap. The same can be said of local trains – there are four stations around the city, but they're not very usefully placed.

**ENTERTAINMENTS:** • Booze index: £1.49
**Town/city:** • Pint of beer: £1.70 • Glass of wine: £1.80
**University:** • Pint of beer: £1.30 • Glass of wine: £1.40

**ACCOMMODATION:**
**Living in:** • Catered: 26% • Cost: £82.50-99.80 (31 weeks)
• Self-catering: 30% • Cost: £42.90-77.60 (34-50 weeks)
**Living out:** • Ave rent: £47

# UNIVERSITY OF GLAMORGAN

University of Glamorgan, Treforest, Pontypridd, Mid Glamorgan, CF37 1DL.
Tel: 0800 716 925. Fax: (01443) 480558. E-mail: enquiries@glam.ac.uk

**DEBTS:** • Average debt: £1,100
• Access fund: £753,511 • Successful applications per year: 809
There's a specialist finance advisor in the Department of Student Services. Bursaries.

**EMPLOYMENT:** • Unemployed after 6 months: 7.2%
**Paid work:** A Union-run employment service finds students jobs at open days and in college bars, but that's about your lot.

**TRAVEL:**
**National:** Trains: From Treforest station, only 400 yards from the campus, trains go every 20 minutes to Cardiff (£1.60). Unfortunately the last return train is just after 10pm. London (£24.60), Swansea (£8.80), Manchester (£26.20). Coaches: National Express to London (£16.00). Cardiff is a better bet for getting elsewhere.
**Local:** There are local bus services going every 20 minutes to Ponty and every 25 minutes to Cardiff – last bus from Cardiff is at 11.30pm. A free shuttle bus within a 10-mile radius of the campus is run for students after 10.30pm.

**ENTERTAINMENTS:** • Booze index: £1.66
**Town/city:** • Pint of beer: £1.90   • Glass of wine: £1.20
**University:** • Pint of beer: £1.50   • Glass of wine: £1.10

**ACCOMMODATION:**
**Living in:**   • Catered: 1%          • Cost: £78 (37 weeks)
                 • Self-catering: 9%    • Cost: £35-55 (37 weeks)
**Living out:**  • Ave rent: £38

# GLASGOW UNIVERSITY
University of Glasgow, Glasgow, G12 8QQ.
Tel: (0141) 339 8855. Fax: (0141) 330 4808.

**DEBTS:**    • Access fund: £894,508   • Successful applications per year: 1,584
Student Hardship Fund as well as the access fund. Also, plenty of little grants and bequests.

**EMPLOYMENT:** • Unemployed after 6 months: 5%
The Careers Service holds information about part-time work as well as opportunities after graduation. It also offers a temping agency for students hunting out term-time jobs.
**Paid work:** Glasgow has been heaving itself out of the doldrums for more than a decade now and is still heaving. There is work around in bars and so on but there's others than students looking for it. There is a jobshop run by the Students Representative Council and Student Templine, a University supported temp agency.

**TRAVEL:**
**National:** Trains: Queen's Street and Central Stations are the mainline stops and run regular services to London (£41.60), Edinburgh (£9.60), Birmingham (£32) and most other major stops. Coaches: Services to London (£27.25), Birmingham (£28.75) and all over Scotland and beyond.
**Local:** Buses are frequent with cheap and comprehensive, fares from 45p to 90p to the city centre. The local trains are fast and efficient, with several stops around the city. A 10-week Zonecard covering all travel in the city costs £339.

**ENTERTAINMENTS:** • Booze index: £1.70
**Town/city:** • Pint of beer: £1.90   • Glass of wine: £1.60
**University:** • Pint of beer: £1.50   • Glass of wine: £1.35

**ACCOMMODATION:**
**Living in:**   • Catered: 5%          • Cost: £66-89 (31 weeks)
                 • Self-catering: 12%   • Cost: £45-64 (38-52wk)
**Living out:**  • Ave rent: £55

**7**

## GLASGOW CALEDONIAN UNIVERSITY

Glasgow Caledonian University, City Campus, Cowcaddens Road, Glasgow, G4 0BA.
Tel: (0141) 331 3000. Fax: (0141) 331 3005. E-mail: rhu@gcal.ac.uk

**DEBTS:** • Average debt: £700
• Access fund: £241,715 • Successful applications per year: 1,003
University Hardship Fund and Childcare Fund.

**EMPLOYMENT:** • Unemployed after 6 months: 10.5%
The service is rather under-used because it's rather under-publicised.
**Paid work:** Student job shop run by the Welfare department helps to find the odd
bit of shit-shovelling.

**TRAVEL:** See Glasgow University
**Local:** Queen Street station is 10 minutes' walk from the City Campus.

**ENTERTAINMENTS:** • Booze index: £1.72
**Town/city:** • Pint of beer: £1.90 • Glass of wine: £1.60
**University:** • Pint of beer: £1.50 • Glass of wine: £1.20

**ACCOMMODATION:**
**Living in:** • Catered: 1.3% • Cost: £64 (37 weeks)
• Self-catering: 5.1% • Cost: £38-55 (37 weeks)
**Living out:** • Ave rent: £55

## GOLDSMITHS COLLEGE, LONDON

• The College is part of University of London and students are entitled to use its
facilities.
Goldsmiths College, New Cross, London, SE14 6NW.
Tel: (020) 7919 7171. Fax: (020) 7919 7975. E-mail: admissions@gold.ac.uk

**DEBTS:** • Average debt: £1,750
• Access fund: £350,000 • Successful applications per year: 760
**Banks on campus:** NatWest Bank.

**EMPLOYMENT:** • Unemployed after 6 months: 5%

**TRAVEL:**
**Local:** Trains and buses but oddly ill-served by the Tube.

**ENTERTAINMENTS:** • Booze index: £1.65
**Town/city:** • Pint of beer: £1.90 • Glass of wine: £1.60
**University:** • Pint of beer: £1.40 • Glass of wine: £1.30

**ACCOMMODATION:**
**Living in:** • Catered: 4% • Cost: £62 (34 weeks)
• Self-catering: 20% • Cost: £60-80 (39 weeks)
**Living out:** • Ave rent: £75

## UNIVERSITY OF GREENWICH

University of Greenwich, Old Royal Naval College, Park Row, London, SE10 9LS.
Tel: 0800 005 006. Fax: (020) 8331 8145. E-mail: courseinfo@gre.ac.uk

**DEBTS:** • Average debt: £2,050
• Access fund: £1 million • Successful applications per year: 1,243

**EMPLOYMENT:** • Unemployed after 6 months: 7%
**Paid work:** see University of London

**TRAVEL:**
**Local:** Trains and buses to most sites.

**ENTERTAINMENTS:** • Booze index: £2.13
**Town/city:** • Pint of beer: £2.20 • Glass of wine: £2.50
**University:** • Pint of beer: £1.60 • Glass of wine: £1.20

**ACCOMMODATION:**
**Living in:** • Catered: 3% • Cost: £75 (34-46 weeks)
• Self-catering: 20% • Cost: £46-84 (40-50 weeks)
**Living out:** • Ave rent: £58

## HERIOT-WATT UNIVERSITY
Heriot-Watt University, Riccarton, Edinburgh, EH14 4AS.
Tel: (0131) 449 5111. Fax: (0131) 449 5153. E-mail: edu.liason@hw.ac.uk

**DEBTS:** • Average debt: £1,350
• Access fund: £301,982 • Successful applications per year: 883
The Student Association runs a crisis fund and there are sports bursaries worth
between £500 and £1,500. Also a hardship fund.

**EMPLOYMENT:** • Unemployed after 6 months: 5%

**TRAVEL:** See Edinburgh University
**Local:** Buses to the city centre cost 90p and take 25 minutes. There is a night
service until 4.30am.

**ENTERTAINMENTS:** • Booze index: £1.75
**Town/city:** • Pint of beer: £2.40 • Glass of wine: £2
**University:** • Pint of beer: £1.30 • Glass of wine: £1.15

**ACCOMMODATION:**
**Living in:** • Catered: 6% • Cost: £55 (33 weeks)
• Self-catering: 40% • Cost: £30-56 (35-50 weeks)
**Living out:** • Ave rent: £55

## UNIVERSITY OF HERTFORDSHIRE
University of Hertfordshire, College Lane, Hatfield, Hertfordshire, AL10 9AB.
Tel: (01707) 284800. Fax: (01707) 284870.

**DEBTS:** • Average debt: £2,250
• Access fund: £727,393 • Successful applications per year: 1,974
There's also a hardship fund of £500 and a fee waiver system.

**EMPLOYMENT:** • Unemployed after 6 months: 5.2%
**Paid work:** There are many local temping agencies and the local Galleria shopping
mall offers some hope for shop and café jobs but luck still plays a large part. The
SU Studentemps agency can offer part-time work within the Union and the local
area.

**TRAVEL:**
**National:** Hertford station is about half an hour from London (£8.90). No National
Express service to Hatfield or Hertford. The nearest stops are London's Victoria
Coach Station and Luton (12 miles away). London Country and Greenline buses
run services to and from London.
**Local:** Buses aren't the cheapest in the country, but are useful for quick
trips into Hatfield. The University also provides a bus service between sites, 90p
for students on all routes. Also has routes from Hatfield to St Albans, Stevenage,
Watford and Welwyn Garden City.

**7**

**ENTERTAINMENTS:** • <u>Booze index: £1.93</u>
**Town/city:** • <u>Pint of beer: £2.20</u> • <u>Glass of wine: £1.90</u>
**University:** • <u>Pint of beer: £1.60</u> • <u>Glass of wine: £1.40</u>

**ACCOMMODATION:**
**Living in:** • <u>Self-catering: 22%</u> • <u>Cost: £42-59 (38-52 weeks)</u>
**Living out:** • <u>Ave rent: £60</u>

# HEYTHROP COLLEGE, LONDON
• The College is part of University of London and students are entitled to use its facilities.
Heythrop College, Kensington Square, London, W8 5HQ.
Tel: (020) 7795 6600. Fax: (020) 7795 4200. E-mail: r.bolland@heythrop.ac.uk

**DEBTS:**
Small bursary fund for fee-paying students.

**TRAVEL:**
**National:** see <u>University of London</u>
**Local:** Tubes and buses.

**ENTERTAINMENTS:** • <u>Booze index: £2.35</u>
**Town/city:** • <u>Pint of beer: £2.20</u> • <u>Glass of wine: £2.50</u>
**University:** • <u>Pint of beer: £1.40</u> • <u>Glass of wine: £1.50</u>
No bar, but students make use of Imperial College.

**ACCOMMODATION:**
**Living in:** • <u>Catered: 31%</u> • <u>Cost: £77-102 (30 weeks)</u>
Heythrop only has catered halls for 18 people, but there is access to University of London intercollegiate halls.
**Living out:** • <u>Ave rent: £75</u>

**UNUSUAL COSTS:**
£15 membership of the JCR gets you free newspapers, tea and coffee.

# UNIVERSITY OF HUDDERSFIELD
University of Huddersfield, Queensgate, Huddersfield, HD1 3DH.
Tel: (01484) 422288. Fax: (01484) 516151.
E-mail: schools.prospectus@hud.ac.uk

**DEBTS:** • <u>Average debt: £2,100</u>
• <u>Access fund: £678,634</u> • <u>Successful applications per year: 906</u>
The Union offers emergency welfare loans of about £30/week and there's money available for disabled and overseas students.

**EMPLOYMENT:** • <u>Unemployed after 6 months: 4.9%</u>
**Paid work:** Local unemployment keeps opportunities limited, but the SU employs over 500 students and the Uni runs a professionally managed jobshop to help the rest get some readies.

**TRAVEL:**
**National:** Trains: The main site is 10 minutes walk from Huddersfield BR station which has direct lines to Leeds (£2.80) and Manchester (£5.80) every 30 mins. Trains to London (£29.60) via Wakefield. Coaches: National Express services to London (£16.75), Birmingham (£13.75) and elsewhere.
**Local:** Buses are comprehensive, charging between 60p and £1.30. A Metrocard is a worthwhile investment.

**ENTERTAINMENTS:** • <u>Booze index: £1.65</u>
**Town/city:** • <u>Pint of beer: £1.80</u> • <u>Glass of wine: £1.70</u>
**University:** • <u>Pint of beer: £1.40</u> • <u>Glass of wine: £1.20</u>

**ACCOMMODATION:**
**Living in:** • Self-catering:25%     • Cost: £38-60 (41 weeks)
**Living out:** • Ave rent: £38

# UNIVERSITY OF HULL

University of Hull, Hull, HU6 7RX. Tel: (0870) 1262000. Fax: (01482) 442290.
E-mail: admissions@admin.hull.ac.uk

**DEBTS:** • Average debt: £1,300
• Access fund: 593,822 • Successful applications per year: 1,002
The Vice Chancellor's Hardship Fund dishes out loans as does the SU in
emergencies.
**Banks on campus:** Lloyds and HSBC cash-points.

**EMPLOYMENT:** • Unemployed after 6 months: 3%
**Paid work:** Hull has got a pretty bad unemployment problem and students aren't
first in the queue, facing resentment if they try to push in, but the SU-run Job
Exchange provides details of sits vac.

**TRAVEL:**
**National:** Trains: Hull Paragon rail station runs services to London via Doncaster or
York (£19.20) and other connections to Newcastle (£20.15) and Birmingham
(£24.95). Coaches: Clipper and National Express services all over the country
including London (£22.50), Birmingham (£17.75) and Newcastle (£16.75).
**Local:** There are two fiercely competitive bus companies running until midnight-ish.
There are three train stops in Hull, two of which are useful for students, since one
is in the city centre and the other is near the campus.

**ENTERTAINMENTS:** • Booze index: £1.52
**Town/city:** • Pint of beer: £1.75     • Glass of wine: £1.60
**University:** • Pint of beer: £1.25     • Glass of wine: £1.35

**ACCOMMODATION:**
**Living in:** • Catered: 22%           • Cost: £61-79 (33 weeks)
• Self-catering: 19%     • Cost: £39-56 + fuel bills (33-50 weeks)
**Living out:** • Ave rent: £35

# IMPERIAL COLLEGE, LONDON

• Part of University of London. Students are entitled to use its facilities.
Imperial College of Science, Technology & Medicine (University of London),
London, SW7 2AZ. Tel: (020) 7594 8014. Fax: (020) 7594 8004.
E-mail: admissions@ic.ac.uk

**DEBTS:** • Average debt: £2,750
• Access fund: £452,918 • Successful applications per year: 864
Many scholarships and sponsorships are available.

**EMPLOYMENT:** • Unemployed after 6 months: 2.7%
Potential employers, particularly in scientific and technical areas, regard Imperial
as a goldmine of bright bods.
**Paid work:** Imperial students can appeal to the firms constantly vying for their
talents for vacation work or there's Imperial's UROP scheme where they help
lecturers with their research work and can expect to earn anything up to £120 a
week and many brownie points.

**TRAVEL:**
**National:** Trains: London is the centre of the network: Birmingham (£12);
Manchester (£16); Leeds (£34); Bristol (£21); Glasgow (£42.50). Coaches:
London is also the centre of the National Express system and a whole variety of
other national bus services (Green Line, Blue Line and so on): Birmingham (£13),
Manchester (£21) and so on.
**Local:** Buses and tubes.

**7**

**ENTERTAINMENTS:** • Booze index: £2.04
**Town/city:** • Pint of beer: £2.20 • Glass of wine: £2.50
**University:** • Pint of beer: £1.40 • Glass of wine: £1.50

**ACCOMMODATION:**
**Living in:** • Catered: 3% • Cost: £64-83 (34 weeks)
• Self-catering 32% • Cost: £43-95 (34-51 weeks)
**Living out:** • Ave rent: £75

# KEELE UNIVERSITY

Keele University, Keele, Staffordshire, ST5 5BG. Tel: (01782) 584005.
Fax: (01782) 632343. E-mail: aaa20@admin.keele.ac.uk

**DEBTS:** • Average debt: £1,550
• Access fund: £370,765 • Successful applications per year: 578
Help is provided by the International Loan Fund, the Lindsay Loan Fund and the
Emergency Hardship Fund. The SU and chaplains have similar arrangements.
**Banks on campus:** NatWest and Halifax cash machines.

**EMPLOYMENT:** • Unemployed after 6 months: 5.4%

**TRAVEL:**
**National:** Trains: There's no station at Keele or at Newcastle (that's the little one
nearby). Trains from Stoke-on-Trent go to London (£24.10), Manchester (£5.00),
Newcastle (that's the big one up North – £31.30) and all over. Coaches: National
Express doesn't go to Keele either, the nearest service being Stoke, from where
there are services to London (£12) and Manchester (£3.80).
**Local:** Buses run between the campus and the surrounding towns every 10
minutes and as far afield as Chester and Sheffield. The SU runs a free bus
service for off-campus students.

**ENTERTAINMENTS:** • Booze index: £1.48
**Town/city:** • Pint of beer: £2 • Glass of wine: £1.50
**University:** • Pint of beer: £1.50 • Glass of wine: £1.30
Since students usually have to venture beyond Keele itself if they want off-campus
adventure, some go the whole hog and stray as far as Birmingham and
Manchester.

**ACCOMMODATION:**
**Living in:** • Self-catering 77% • Cost: £39-64 (33-51 weeks)
**Living out:** • Ave rent: £35

# UNIVERSITY OF KENT AT CANTERBURY

The University of Kent at Canterbury, The Registry, Canterbury, Kent, CT2 7NZ.
Tel: (01227) 764000. Fax: (01227) 452196. E-mail: admissions@ukc.ac.uk

**DEBTS:** • Average debt: £400
• Access fund: £145,000 • Successful applications per year: 1,200
Sports and music bursaries are available.

**EMPLOYMENT:** • Unemployed after 6 months: 2.7%
**Paid work:** During the summer, the Garden of England offers a monumental set of
gardening tasks such as hop and fruit picking. There's a new jobshop on campus,
but even so there isn't a lot going. A foreign language is handy for touristy
Canterbury and it's also possible to find jobs teaching English as a foreign
language.

**TRAVEL:**
**National:** Trains: Although Canterbury West is closer, Canterbury East is the
station with the mainline connections to London (£14.15) and Dover and
connections to Edinburgh, Birmingham and Bristol. Coaches: National Express
services all over the country.

**Local:** Buses from town to campus every 15 minutes and student bus cards are available.

**ENTERTAINMENTS:** • Booze index: £1.63
**Town/city:** • Pint of beer: £2.20 • Glass of wine: £1.60
**University:** • Pint of beer: £1.60 • Glass of wine: £1.20

**ACCOMMODATION:**
**Living in:** • Catered: 26% • Cost: £60-77 (30 weeks)
• Self-catering 28% • Cost: £42-47 (37 weeks)
**Living out:** • Ave rent: £50-55

## KING'S COLLEGE, LONDON
• The College is part of University of London and students are entitled to use its facilities.
King's College London, University of London, The Strand, London, WC2R 2LS.
Tel: (020) 7836 5454. Fax: (020) 7836 1799.

**DEBTS:** • Average debt: £1,750
• Access fund: £636,000 • Successful applications per year: 496
Overseas Students' Hardship Fund.

**EMPLOYMENT:** • Unemployed after 6 months: 4%
**Paid work:** see University of London.

**TRAVEL:**
**Local:** Buses and trains to all sites. Underground to the main sites too.

**ENTERTAINMENTS:** • Booze index: £2.03
**Town/city:** • Pint of beer: £2.20 • Glass of wine: £2.50
**University:** • Pint of beer: £1.55 • Glass of wine: £1.10

**ACCOMMODATION:**
**Living in:** • Catered: 6% • Cost: £98-121 (30 weeks)
• Self-catering 25% • Cost: £62-68 (36-50 weeks)
**Living out:** • Ave rent: £75

## KINGSTON UNIVERSITY
Kingston University, Student Enquiry and Applicant Services, Cooper House,
40-46 Surbiton Road, Kingston Upon Thames, Surrey, KT1 2HX.
Tel: (020) 8547 2000. Fax: (020) 8547 7080
E-mail: admissions-info@kingston.ac.uk

**DEBTS:** • Average debt: £1,200
• Access fund: £570,969 • Successful applications per year: 627

**EMPLOYMENT:** • Unemployed after 6 months: 3.6%
**Paid work:** The many local fast food joints always need new blood (not literally) as does the union. There's a job centre desk in the Uni for part-time work and many students get work in a wide variety of all the regular fun-filled occupations.

**TRAVEL:** See University of London

**ENTERTAINMENTS:** • Booze index: £1.89
**Town/city:** • Pint of beer: £2.10 • Glass of wine: £1.90
**University:** • Pint of beer: £1.60 • Glass of wine: £1.30

**ACCOMMODATION:**
**Living in:**
• Self-catering 20% • Cost: £53-63 (40 weeks)
**Living out:** • Ave rent: £68

# LAMPETER, UNIVERSITY OF WALES

University of Wales, Lampeter, Ceredigion, SA48 7ED. Tel: (01570) 422351.
Fax: (01570) 423423. E-mail: admissions@lampeter.ac.uk

**DEBTS:** • Access fund: £128,500

**EMPLOYMENT:** • Unemployed after 6 months: 9.6%
Although there aren't many big employers on the doorstep the careers service
arranges trips to Cardiff for the milk round.
**Paid work:** The SU employs some student staff and there's a local organic farm,
but we're not talking major opportunities here.

**TRAVEL:**
**National:** Trains: From Carmarthen you can get mainline trains to London
(£27.70), Cardiff (£10.30) and Birmingham (£24.25). Aberystwyth station is better
for northbound journeys. Coaches: Lampeter is now on a National Express route to
London via Cardiff (£30.60), Cardiff (£12.10) and Birmingham via Swansea
(£26.15).
**Local:** The buses stick to the timetables, one every hour till about 5.30pm. It's
£3.50 return to Carmarthen with a similar service to Aberystwyth.

**ENTERTAINMENTS:** • Booze index: £1.44

| | | |
|---|---|---|
| **Town/city:** | • Pint of beer: £1.70 | • Glass of wine: £1.35 |
| **University:** | • Pint of beer: £1.50 | • Glass of wine: £1.10 |

**ACCOMMODATION:**

| | | |
|---|---|---|
| **Living in:** | • Catered: 9% | • Cost: £66 (30 weeks) |
| | • Self-catering: 29% | • Cost: £38-44 (35-36 weeks) |
| **Living out:** | • Ave rent: £38 | |

# LANCASTER UNIVERSITY

Lancaster University, University House, Lancaster, LA1 4YW. Tel: (01524) 65201.
Fax: (01524) 846243. E-mail: ugadmissions@lancaster.ac.uk

**DEBTS:** • Average debt: £2,000
• Access fund: £505,992 • Successful applications per year: 455
Each college administers its own hardship fund for loans and gifts. There's also a
good selection of scholarships and bursaries for academic merit. There are also 4
debt counsellors to provide commiseration.
**Banks on campus:** Barclays and NatWest banks.

**EMPLOYMENT:** • Unemployed after 6 months: 6.3%
**Paid work:** Nothing unusual except some tourist jobs in summer. The SU job-shop
has a minimum wage policy.

**TRAVEL:**
**National:** Trains: Lancaster station, 3 miles from the campus, has direct
connections to London (£36.35), Manchester (£8.50), Birmingham (£26.95) and
further afield. Coaches: National Express services from the campus all over the
country including London (£23.50), Manchester (7.50) and Birmingham (£16.00).
**Local:** There is a reliable double-decker bus service to campus every 10 minutes
(£1.10 return) and a minibus from campus to the station. Bus passes covering the
Lancaster area cost £120 for a year.

**ENTERTAINMENTS:** • Booze index: £1.50

| | | |
|---|---|---|
| **Town/city:** | • Pint of beer: £1.70 | • Glass of wine: £1.50 |
| **University:** | • Pint of beer: £1.30 | • Glass of wine: £1.30 |

**ACCOMMODATION:**

| | | |
|---|---|---|
| **Living in:** | • Self-catering: 52% | • Cost: £40-61 (31-38 weeks) |
| **Living out:** | • Ave rent: £40 | |

# UNIVERSITY OF LEEDS
The University of Leeds, Leeds, LS2 9JT. Tel: (0113) 243 1751.
Fax: (0113) 233 3991. E-mail: prospectus@leeds.ac.uk

**DEBTS:** • Average debt: £1,200
          • Access fund: £875,000 • Successful applications per year: 1,000
The Union offers emergency loans of up to £100, the usual bursaries and welfare
funds and there's a range of budgeting advice, debt counselling and even help with
bankruptcy.
**Banks on campus:** Lloyds Bank.

**EMPLOYMENT:** • Unemployed after 6 months: 3.5%
There's the highly efficient Careers Service.
**Paid work:** There's the usual bar work and stewarding at Union ents and a job-link
scheme run by the SU, a noticeboard and an on-line joblink.

**TRAVEL:**
**National:** Trains: Leeds station is the centre of the very efficient West Yorkshire
metro train network which serves all the local Yorkshire towns (Bradford,
Wakefield, Sheffield and York). Many direct services operate further afield to, for
example, London (£38.30), Manchester (£9.10) and more. Coaches: National
Express to London (£16.75), Manchester (£7), Edinburgh (£22.50) and other
destinations. Also served by Blueline.
**Local:** Very reliable, frequent trains and buses (the maximum off-peak fare is 80p).
A monthly student Metrocard (bus and train) is £39.50 while the Student First
travel card (£34 per month) is valid on bus routes from the uni through to the city
centre.

**ENTERTAINMENTS:** • Booze index: £1.53
**Town/city:** • Pint of beer: £2.05
**University:** • Pint of beer: £1     • Glass of wine: £0.80

**ACCOMMODATION:**
**Living in:** • Catered: 11%     • Cost: £58-109 (33 weeks)
          • Self-catering: 28%     • Cost: £27-65 (40 weeks)
**Living out:** • Ave rent: £43

# LEEDS METROPOLITAN UNIVERSITY
Leeds Metropolitan University, Calverley Street, Leeds, LS1 3HE.
Tel: (0113) 283 3113. Fax: (0113) 283 3114. E-mail: course-enquiries@lmu.ac.uk

**DEBTS:** • Average debt: £1,300
          • Access fund: £990,000 • Successful applications per year: 800
Debt counselling is available from the Budget Advisor and 2 part-timers.
Emergency fund for overseas students.
**Banks on campus:** Lloyds Bank.

**EMPLOYMENT:** • Unemployed after 6 months: 8%
The busy but welcoming Careers Service runs development workshops, offering
help with job applications and finding work experience.
**Paid work:** The excellent job shop has filled well over 2,000 vacancies.

**TRAVEL:** See University of Leeds

**ENTERTAINMENTS:** • Booze index: £1.83
**Town/city:** • Pint of beer: £2.05
**University:** • Pint of beer: £1.70     • Glass of wine: £1.25

**ACCOMMODATION:**
**Living in:** • Self-catering: 16%     • Cost: £41-63 (41-43 weeks)
**Living out:** • Ave rent: £43

## UNIVERSITY OF LEICESTER

University of Leicester, Admissions and Student Recruitment, University Road,
Leicester, LE1 7RH. Tel: (0116) 252 5281. Fax: (0116) 252 2200.
E-mail: admissions@le.ac.uk

**DEBTS:** • Average debt: £1,650
         • Access fund: £532,472 • Successful applications per year: 1,500
Numerous hardship funds exist, some for specific groups (mature students,
overseas students, etc), scholarships for physics, engineering and sports
bursaries. The SU gives hardship loans up to £100 and special needs students
are given priority.
**Banks on campus:** Two banks with cashpoints.

**EMPLOYMENT:** • Unemployed after 6 months: 6%
Jobshop, workshops and help from advisors.
**Paid work:** The Union-run jobshop sorts out the students with casual work and,
failing that, there's always the Walkers Crisps factory. There is also a Student
Employment Centre and you can even look it up on the web: www.susec@le.ac.uk

**TRAVEL:**
**National:** Trains: Leicester Station operates many services direct all over the
Midlands and the rest of the country, including London (£23.45), Sheffield
(£19.80), Edinburgh (£53.60), Leeds and beyond. Coaches: National Express and
other services to London (£13.25), Sheffield (£8.50), Edinburgh (£32.75) and
elsewhere.
**Local:** Buses are reliable, cheap (60p from campus to town), well used and run
until 11pm.

**ENTERTAINMENTS:** • Booze index: £1.56
**Town/city:** • Pint of beer: £2     • Glass of wine: £1.70
**University:** • Pint of beer: £1     • Glass of wine: £1.50

**ACCOMMODATION:**
**Living in:** • Catered: 27%       • Cost: £60-95 (30 weeks)
            • Self-catering: 22%   • Cost: £45-53 (39-52 weeks)
**Living out:** • Ave rent: £38

## UNIVERSITY OF LINCOLNSHIRE AND HUMBERSIDE

Formerly Humberside Polytechnic, University of Humberside
(1) Humberside Campus, Cottingham Road, Kingston-upon-Hull, HU6 7RT.
Tel: (01482) 440550. Fax: (01482) 463310. E-mail: marketing@humber.ac.uk
(2) Lincoln University, Marketing Department, Brayford Pool, Lincoln, LN6 7TS.
Tel: (01522) 882000. Fax: (01522) 882088. E-mail: marketing@lincoln.ac.uk

**DEBTS:** • Average debt: £1,750
         • Access fund: £500,000 • Successful applications per year: 1,500
The University waives fees for part-time undergraduates on income support. The
cost of living in Hull is low.

**EMPLOYMENT:** • Unemployed after 6 months: 11.8%
**Paid work:** see University of Hull

**TRAVEL:** For Hull, see University of Hull
**Lincoln:** Trains: The station, a few minutes walk from the campus, has services to
London (£27.70), Birmingham (£16.65), Edinburgh (£51.30) and more.

**ENTERTAINMENTS:** • Booze index: £1.57
**Town/city:** • Pint of beer: £1.80     • Glass of wine: £1.40
**University:** • Pint of beer: £1.50     • Glass of wine: £1.40

**ACCOMMODATION:**
**Living in:**  • Catered: 2%          • Cost: £60-65 (38 weeks)
              • Self-catering: 15%    • Cost: £53 (38 weeks)
**Living out:**  • Ave rent: £35

---

# UNIVERSITY OF LIVERPOOL
The University of Liverpool, Liverpool, L69 3GD. Tel: (0151) 794 2000.
Fax: (0151) 794 5602. E-mail: ugrecruitment@liv.ac.uk

**DEBTS:**  • Average debt: £2,000
           • Access fund: £690,000  • Successful applications per year: 938
Also Vice Chancellor's Hardship Fund (mainly for overseas students); Hillsborough
Trust Memorial Bursaries (£500, must come from Merseyside); John Lennon Fund
(£1,000, for environmental interests); Clare Hansen fund (vets).

**EMPLOYMENT:**  • Unemployed after 6 months: 5%
**Paid work:** There is high unemployment in Liverpool, so there's lots of competition
for the few places in bakeries, shops and bars. The Business Bridge scheme helps
students find local placements.

**TRAVEL:**
**National:** Trains: Mainline links with many destinations including London Euston
(£31.80), Manchester (£6.10) and Birmingham (£15.85). Coaches: National
Express to most destinations including London (£17) and Manchester (£5).
**Local:** Efficient bus services. Student fares are 60p, but it works out cheaper to
get a term bus pass. A University bus service runs between halls all day (£1).
Merseyrail for those who prefer trains.

**ENTERTAINMENTS:**  • Booze index: £1.50
**Town/city:**  • Pint of beer: £1.80   • Glass of wine: £1.40
**University:**  • Pint of beer: £1      • Glass of wine: £1.25

**ACCOMMODATION:**
**Living in:**  • Catered: 20%          • Cost: £78 (32 weeks)
              • Self-catering: 9%      • Cost: £48-54 (40-52 weeks)
**Living out:**  • Ave rent: £38

---

# LIVERPOOL JOHN MOORES UNIVERSITY
Liverpool John Moores University, Enquiry Management Team, Roscoe Court,
4 Rodney Street, Liverpool, L1 2TZ.
Tel: (0151) 231 5090. Fax: (0151) 231 3194. E-mail: recruitment@livjm.ac.uk

**DEBTS:**  • Average debt: £2,050
           • Access fund: £847,622  • Successful applications per year:2,272
Various bursaries, scholarships, a hardship fund and emergency loans. The SU
Hillsborough Fund offers help to disadvantaged students.
**Banks on campus:** Barclays Bank and cash machine.

**EMPLOYMENT:**  • Unemployed after 6 months: 6.1%
**Paid work:** There is high unemployment in Liverpool, so there's lots of competition
for the few places in bakeries, shops and bars.

**TRAVEL:** See University of Liverpool

**ENTERTAINMENTS:**  • Booze index: £1.58
**Town/city:**  • Pint of beer: £1.80   • Glass of wine: £1.40
**University:**  • Pint of beer: £1.45   • Glass of wine: £1.25

**ACCOMMODATION:**
**Living in:**  • Self-catering: 10%    • Cost: £44-59 (40 weeks)
**Living out:**  • Ave rent: £38

**7**

# UNIVERSITY OF LONDON

The University of London, Senate House, Malet Street, London, WC1E 7HU.
Tel: (020) 7862 8000. Fax: (020) 7862 8358.

**DEBTS:**
Financial assistance is provided by individual colleges, see <u>Birkbeck College</u>,
<u>Courtauld Institute of Art</u>, <u>Goldsmiths College</u>, <u>Heythrop College</u>, <u>Imperial College</u>,
<u>King's College</u>, <u>LSE</u>, <u>Queen Mary</u>, <u>Royal Academy of Music</u>, <u>Royal College of
Music</u>, <u>Royal Holloway</u>, <u>Royal Veterinary</u>, <u>St George's Hospital</u>, <u>SOAS</u>, <u>School of
Pharmacy</u> and <u>UCL.</u>
**Banks on campus:** Barclays and Halifax banks with cashpoints at the University of
London Union in Bloomsbury.

**EMPLOYMENT:**
The University Careers Service is very large and well used and even offers job
lists, careers fairs etc to non-London students for a small fee.
**Paid work:** Vacancy lists are posted up in the Union which usually has vacancies
of its own to fill. There are more opportunities in London for part-time work than
anywhere else, but there are also more people trying to get those jobs. Students
find work quite easily in all the usual places like bars and restaurants and also in
theatres, offices and shops.

**TRAVEL:**
**National:** Trains: London is the centre of the network: Birmingham (£12);
Manchester (£16); Leeds (£34); Bristol (£21); Glasgow (£42.50). Coaches:
London is also the centre of the National Express system and a whole variety of
other national bus services (Green Line, Blue Line and so on) letting you ride to
Birmingham (£13), Manchester (£21) and so on.
**Local:** The Tube and bus network pretty much cover everywhere in the centre of
London but are a bit more patchy as you get further out, where overground trains
play a greater role. Night buses run regularly to most parts – they take forever, but
at least you can get home. All London students now get 30% off all Tube and bus
fares. London transport is expensive, particularly if you don't get a Travelcard,
which can be used on all London buses, tubes and trains. See Chapter 11 for
more details.

**ENTERTAINMENTS:** • <u>Booze index: £2.16</u>
**Town/city:** • <u>Pint of beer: £2.20</u>    • <u>Glass of wine: £2.50</u>
**University:** • <u>Pint of beer: £1.50</u>    • <u>Glass of wine: £2</u>

**ACCOMMODATION:**
**Living in:** • <u>Catered: 31%</u>    • <u>Cost: £77-102 (30wks)</u>
**Living out:** • <u>Ave rent: £75</u>

# LONDON GUILDHALL UNIVERSITY

London Guildhall University, 31 Jewry Street, London, EC3N 2EY.
Tel: (020) 7320 1000. Fax: (020) 7320 1163. E-mail: enqs@lgu.ac.uk

**DEBTS:** • <u>Average debt: £1,400</u>
       • <u>Access fund: £900,000</u>   • <u>Successful applications per year: 1,080</u>
The University targets the access fund at students with special needs (ie. self-
funding students and those with children or disabilities). Other bursaries and
scholarships are available.

**EMPLOYMENT:** • <u>Unemployed after 6 months: 9%</u>
**Paid work:** see <u>University of London</u>

**TRAVEL:**
**National:** Trains: Liverpool St and Fenchurch St mainline stations are both within
10 minutes walk of almost all the University's sites.
**Local:** Buses: 70p or £1 for a single.

**ENTERTAINMENTS:** • <u>Booze index: £1.74</u>
**Town/city:** • <u>Pint of beer: £2.20</u> • <u>Glass of wine: £2.50</u>
**University:** • <u>Pint of beer: £1.50</u> • <u>Glass of wine: £1.15</u>

**ACCOMMODATION:**
**Living in:** • <u>Self-catering: 6%</u> • <u>Cost: £58-75 (38 weeks)</u>
**Living out:** • <u>Ave rent: £75</u>

## THE LONDON INSTITUTE

(1) The London Institute, 65 Davies Street, London, W1Y 2DA.
Tel: (020) 7514 6127. Fax: (020) 7514 6131. E-mail: marcom@linst.ac.uk
(2) Camberwell College of Arts, Peckham Road, London, SE5 8UF.
(3) Central Saint Martin's College of Art and Design, Southampton Row, London, WC1B 4AP.
(4) Chelsea College of Art and Design, Manresa Road, London, SW3 6LS.
(5) London College of Fashion, 20 John Princes Street, London, W1M 0BJ.
(6) London College of Printing & Distributive Trades, Elephant & Castle, London, SE1 6SB.

**DEBTS:** • <u>Average debt: £1,350</u>
Finalists at Camberwell, Central St. Martin's or Chelsea can apply to the Nancy Baker Fund.

**EMPLOYMENT:** • <u>Unemployed after 6 months: 12.5%</u>
**Paid work:** see <u>University of London</u>

**TRAVEL:** See <u>University of London</u>

**ENTERTAINMENTS:** • <u>Booze index: £2.22</u>
**Town/city:** • <u>Pint of beer: £2.20</u> • <u>Glass of wine: £2.50</u>
**University:** • <u>Pint of beer: £1.70</u> • <u>Glass of wine: £1</u>

**ACCOMMODATION:**
**Living in:** • <u>Catered: 3%</u> • <u>Cost: £102-106 (39-52 weeks)</u>
 • <u>Self-catering: 10%</u> • <u>Cost: £55-106 (39-52 weeks)</u>
**Living out:** • <u>Ave rent: £75</u>

## LOUGHBOROUGH UNIVERSITY

Loughborough University, Loughborough, Leicestershire, LE11 3TU.
Tel: (01509) 263171. Fax: (01509) 223905. E-mail: admissions@lboro.ac.uk

**DEBTS:** • <u>Average debt: £1,900</u>
 • <u>Access fund: £500,000</u> • <u>Successful applications per year: 1,300</u>
There is a hardship fund and over 200 scholarships and bursaries, 70 of which are sports-related.

**EMPLOYMENT:** • <u>Unemployed after 6 months: 4%</u>
**Paid work:** There's a very successful employment agency with a job database for students.

**TRAVEL:**
**National:** Trains: Loughborough station, 2 miles from the campus on the mainline north from London St Pancras (£25.10) to Edinburgh (£58.30). Coaches: Served by local coach company Paul Winson and National Express – London (£13.25), student special – Nottingham (£2).
**Local:** Local buses run between campus and town. For 65p students can get across town to the station.

**ENTERTAINMENTS:** • <u>Booze index: £1.56</u>
**Town/city:** • <u>Pint of beer: £1.80</u> • <u>Glass of wine: £1.60</u>
**University:** • <u>Pint of beer: £1.50</u> • <u>Glass of wine: £1.40</u>

**7**

**ACCOMMODATION:**
**Living in:** • Catered: 37%     • Cost: £56-88 (31-38 weeks)
              • Self-catering: 21%   • Cost: £39-54 (35-50 weeks)
**Living out:** • Ave rent: £40

# LSE

• The School is part of University of London and students are entitled to use its facilities.
The London School of Economics & Political Science, Houghton Street, London, WC2A 2AE. Tel: (020) 7955 7124/5. Fax: (020) 7955 6001. E-mail: ug-admissions@lse.ac.uk

**DEBTS:** • Average debt: £2,050
          • Access fund: £157,500 • Successful applications per year: 167
Generous hardship funds and scholarships ease the way more than a little. Maybe the economists help everyone to budget more successfully than at other colleges. Maybe not.

**EMPLOYMENT:** • Unemployed after 6 months: 7%
A high proportion of students go on to further training or higher degrees.
**Paid work:** see University of London

**TRAVEL:** See University of London

**ENTERTAINMENTS:** • Booze index: £2.01
**Town/city:** • Pint of beer: £2.20   • Glass of wine: £2.50
**University:** • Pint of beer: £1.50   • Glass of wine: £1.25

**ACCOMMODATION:**
**Living in:** • Catered: 23%     • Cost: £48-108 (31-52 weeks)
              • Self-catering: 11%   • Cost: £76-110 (40-52 weeks)
**Living out:** • Ave rent: £75

# UNIVERSITY OF LUTON

University of Luton, Park Square, Luton, Bedfordshire, LU1 3JU.
Tel: (01582) 734111. Fax: (01582) 743400. E-mail: admissions@luton.ac.uk

**DEBTS:** • Access fund: £636,000 • Successful applications per year: 83%
There are several bursaries, scholarships and trust funds. Funds are also available for members of specific groups, eg. ethnic minorities, mature students, local students.

**EMPLOYMENT:**
**Paid work:** The airport sometimes needs part-time staff. The Brook Street employment agency is on campus.

**TRAVEL:**
**National:** Trains: Luton is the nearest station, 5 minutes walk from the University with trains to, among other places, London King's Cross (£21.00), Bedford, Milton Keynes and east coast mainline services all the way to Edinburgh (£58.90). Coaches: Green Line and National Express services, (London £8, Birmingham £12).
**Local:** Little 'hopper' buses scuttle round the town reliably although not particularly cheaply and not late. No local trains around the town, but an excellent link into London which students often use for a day trip. However, the last train's all too early and easy to miss.

**ENTERTAINMENTS:** • Booze index: £1.67
**Town/city:** • Pint of beer: £2   • Glass of wine: £1.60
**University:** • Pint of beer: £1.50   • Glass of wine: £1

**ACCOMMODATION:**
**Living in:** • Self-catering: 23%   • Cost: £55-59 (40 weeks)
**Living out:** • Ave rent: £50

# UNIVERSITY OF MANCHESTER

University of Manchester, Oxford Road, Manchester, M13 9PL.
Tel: (0161) 275 2000.

**DEBTS:** • Average debt: £800
• Access fund: £902,642 • Successful applications per year: 1,498
In future the University will distribute the access fund by giving smaller amounts to a larger number of applicants. The Union lends up to £100 (interest-free) in emergency cases. They say that no one will be turned away. The Uni also gives short-term loans to students with cash-flow problems (everybody then?) repayable after six to eight weeks, with no interest.
**Banks on campus:** Barclays and Halifax cashpoints.

**EMPLOYMENT:** • Unemployed after 6 months: 3%
The careers service operates jointly with UMIST and is open office hours all year round.
**Paid work:** Because Manchester's such a big centre for entertainment there are lots of part-time jobs in bars, clubs and restaurants – but, of course, there are lots of people chasing them. Still, the situation's better than in some other parts of the North-West. The Careers Service advertises temporary vacancies.

**TRAVEL:**
**National:** Trains: Two mainline stations, Manchester Piccadilly for London and the South, and Manchester Victoria for just about everywhere else. London (£29.70), Birmingham (£14.90), Edinburgh (£36.65) and more. Coaches: All sorts of coach services to, among most other places, London (£15.75), Birmingham (£8), Edinburgh (£15) and beyond.
**Local:** Manchester has a major bus network, running all over town, especially up and down Oxford Road. Trains are a quicker alternative, especially for the outskirts. The Metrolink tram service trundles around helpfully.

**ENTERTAINMENTS:** • Booze index: £1.32
**Town/city:** • Pint of beer: £1.50   • Glass of wine: £1.30
**University:** • Pint of beer: £1.35   • Glass of wine: £1.05

**ACCOMMODATION:**
**Living in:** • Catered: 17%   • Cost: £60-105 (31-51 weeks)
• Self-catering 23%   • Cost: £46-69 (31-52 weeks)
**Living out:** • Ave rent: £38

# MANCHESTER METROPOLITAN UNIVERSITY

Manchester Metropolitan University, All Saints, Oxford Road, Manchester, M15 6BH. Tel: (0161) 247 2000. Fax: (0161) 247 6390.
E-mail: prospectus@mmu.ac.uk

**DEBTS:** • Average debt: £800
• Access fund: £1,076,881 • Successful applications: 1,428
The SU can give loans of up to £75 (or higher in exceptional circumstances), but they want the money back by the end of the year, thank you.
**Banks on campus:** Barclays and Link cash machines.

**EMPLOYMENT:** • Unemployed after 6 months: 5%
**Paid work:** see University of Manchester. The student jobshop 'Steam' has close links with local job networks.

**TRAVEL:** See University of Manchester

**7**

**ENTERTAINMENTS:** • Booze index: £1.37
**Town/city:** • Pint of beer: £1.50  • Glass of wine: £1.30
**University:** • Pint of beer: £1  • Glass of wine: £1.30

**ACCOMMODATION:**
**Living in:** • Catered: 4%  • Cost: £70-73 (34 weeks)
• Self-catering 10%  • Cost: £45-60 (40-44 weeks)
**Living out:** • Ave rent: £38

# MIDDLESEX UNIVERSITY

Middlesex University, White Hart Lane, London, N17 8HR.
Tel: (020) 8411 5000. Fax: (020) 8411 5649. E-mail: admissions@mdx.ac.uk

**DEBTS:** • Average debt: £1,750
• Access fund: £1,113,787 • Successful applications per year: 1,114
Scholarships, loans and part-time fee remission.

**EMPLOYMENT:** • Unemployed after 6 months: 7%
Careers advisors travel between sites.
**Paid work:** Apart from bar and ents work, the SU has work for about 100
students, including decorating and so on during the holidays. The national
headquarters of the Small Press Association are at the Tottenham campus. There
are about 5,000 members and work placements often come up for students.

**TRAVEL:** See University of London

**ENTERTAINMENTS:** • Booze index: £1.77
**Town/city:** • Pint of beer: £2.20  • Glass of wine: £2.50
**University:** • Pint of beer: £1.70  • Glass of wine: £1.35

**ACCOMMODATION:**
**Living in:** • Self-catering 10%  • Cost: £58-69 (40 weeks)
**Living out:** • Ave rent: £75

# NAPIER UNIVERSITY

Napier University, Craiglockhart Campus, 219 Colinton Road, Edinburgh,
EH14 1DJ. Tel: 0500 353570. Fax: (0131) 455 6333. E-mail: info@napier.ac.uk

**DEBTS:** • Access fund: £500,000 • Successful applications per year: 1,200
The Students' Association has a hardship fund of £3,000 (or 50p per undergrad),
which it dishes out as £30 loans to the desperate. £15,000 nursery relief fund.

**EMPLOYMENT:** • Unemployed after 6 months: 6%
**Paid work:** The SA runs a job-shop, which has policies of minimum wages. There's
also a net-based job-bank. See University of Edinburgh.

**TRAVEL:**
**National:** see University of Edinburgh
**Local:** Trains: The closest stations to each site are: Haymarket for Merchiston,
Redwood House; Waverley for Marchmont; Slateford for Craiglockhart; Wester
Hailes or South Gyle for Sighthill. Buses: Public buses offer good services
between the sites and into the city centre from 50p upwards. The inter-site buses
are too small, too infrequent and their drivers are best described as 'relaxed'.

**ENTERTAINMENTS:** • Booze index: £2.11
**Town/city:** • Pint of beer: £2.40  • Glass of wine: £2
**University:** • Pint of beer: £1.50  • Glass of wine: £1.60

**ACCOMMODATION:**
**Living in:** • Self-catering: 14%  • Cost: £34-57 (33-39 weeks)
**Living out:** • Ave rent: £55

# UNIVERSITY OF NEWCASTLE

University of Newcastle, 6 Kensington Terrace, Newcastle upon Tyne, NE1 7RU.
Tel: (0191) 222 6000. Fax: (0191) 222 6139.
E-mail: admissions-enquiries@ncl.ac.uk

**DEBTS:**
- Average debt: £1,000
- Access fund: £598,166 • Successful applications per year: 1,505

Debt is still a problem but the relatively low cost of living takes a few ounces of pressure off. Plus the usual dept bursaries and a part-time fee waiver fund

**EMPLOYMENT:** • Unemployed after 6 months: 2.9%

Supposedly, international employers are looking to recruit from Newcastle as an alternative to Oxford and Cambridge. Yeah, right.
**Paid work:** The Union runs a jobshop, upon registering students receive an induction on job-related issues, and it continually monitors conditions and pay. There are opportunities to augment coffers in bars, the theatres and tedious work at the Metro Centre.

**TRAVEL:**
**National:** Trains: The station's about 10 mins walk from the city centre, or 2 minutes by Metro. Direct lines to London (£37.60), Sheffield (£17.80), Edinburgh (£17.30) and all over the country. Coaches: Several coach companies, including Clipper, Blue Line and National Express, offer services to many other destinations, for example London (£26), Sheffield (£17.75), Edinburgh (£15.25) and so on.
**Local:** Bus routes through the city are regular, reliable and cheap.

**ENTERTAINMENTS:** • Booze index: £1.67

| | | |
|---|---|---|
| **Town/city:** | • Pint of beer: £1.95 | • Glass of wine: £1.70 |
| **University:** | • Pint of beer: £1.50 | • Glass of wine: £1.20 |

**ACCOMMODATION:**

| | | |
|---|---|---|
| **Living in:** | • Catered: 15% | • Cost: £62-84 (up to 52 weeks) |
| | • Self-catering: 18% | • Cost: £39-63 (up to 52 weeks) |
| **Living out:** | • Ave rent: £45 | |

# UNIVERSITY OF NORTH LONDON

University of North London, 166-220 Holloway Road, London N7 8DB.
Tel: (020) 7753 3355. Fax: (020) 7753 3271. E-mail: admissions@unl.ac.uk

**DEBTS:**
- Average debt: £2,000
- Access fund: £872,810 • Successful applications per year: 1,600

The Student Hardship Fund provides small emergency loans. There are limited amounts for postgrads and mature students and a bursary fund is being set up.

**EMPLOYMENT:** • Unemployed after 6 months: 12.1%
**Paid work:** see University of London. An internet-based job-shop can e-mail student vacancies.

**TRAVEL:**
**National:** see University of London
**Local:** Buses and Tubes.

**ENTERTAINMENTS:** • Booze index: £2.23

| | | |
|---|---|---|
| **Town/city:** | • Pint of beer: £2.20 | • Glass of wine: £2.50 |
| **University:** | • Pint of beer: £1.50 | • Glass of wine: £1.10 |

**ACCOMMODATION:**

| | | |
|---|---|---|
| **Living in:** | • Catered: 3% | • Cost: £80 (39-50 weeks) |
| | • Self-catering: 8% | • Cost: £68 (39-50 weeks) |
| **Living out:** | • Ave rent: £75 | |

**7**

# UNIVERSITY COLLEGE NORTHAMPTON

(1) University College Northampton, Park Campus, Boughton Green Road, Northampton, NN2 7AL. Tel: (01604) 735500. Fax: (01604) 722083.
E-mail: admissions@northampton.ac.uk
(2) University College Northampton, Avenue Campus, St George's Avenue, Northampton, NN2 6JD. Tel: (01604) 735500.

**DEBTS:** • Average debt: £1,750
• Access fund: £486,555 • Successful applications per year: 660
Short-term loans of up to £100 are available from the Extreme Hardship Fund. Bursaries for student nurses and a childcare fund.

**EMPLOYMENT:** • Unemployed after 6 months: 5%
**Paid work:** The SU and the University's Student Services unit between them run Jobs Junction which links up with local employers.

**TRAVEL:**
**National:** Trains: Northampton station is about 4 miles from the Park Campus, offering mainline services to London (£23.15), Birmingham (£8.05), Manchester (£23.95) and beyond. Coaches: Midland Fox and National Express services to, among others, London (£9) and Birmingham (£4).
**Local:** Buses are reliable, running every 15 minutes between the Park campus and the town (90p one way). There's also a free (but unreliable) bus between the 2 UCN campuses.

**ENTERTAINMENTS:** • Booze index: £1.92
**Town/city:** • Pint of beer: £2.20 • Glass of wine: £2
**University:** • Pint of beer: £1.60 • Glass of wine: £1

**ACCOMMODATION:**
**Living in:** • Self-catering: 23% • Cost: £30-57 (40 weeks)
**Living out:** • Ave rent: £40

# UNIVERSITY OF NORTHUMBRIA AT NEWCASTLE

(1) University of Northumbria at Newcastle, Ellison Place, Newcastle-upon-Tyne, NE1 8ST. Tel: (0191) 2326002. Fax: (0191) 2274017.
(2) University of Northumbria, Longhirst Campus, Longhirst Hall, Longhirst, Morpeth, Northumberland, NE61 3LL.
Tel: (01670) 795000. Fax: (01670) 795021.
(3) University of Northumbria, Carlisle Campus, 45 Paternoster Row, Carlisle, Cumbria, CA3 8TB. Tel: (0191) 227 4550. Fax: (0191) 227 4820.
E-mail: carlisle.admin@unn.ac.uk

**DEBTS:** • Average debt: £1,850
• Access fund: £220,000 • Successful applications per year: 709
Assistance with part-time fees is available and there are also specialist bursaries.

**EMPLOYMENT:** • Unemployed after 6 months: 5%
**Paid work:** see University of Newcastle

**TRAVEL:**
**National:** see University of Newcastle

**ENTERTAINMENTS:** • Booze index: £1.77
**Town/city:** • Pint of beer: £1.95 • Glass of wine: £1.70
**University:** • Pint of beer: £1.35 • Glass of wine: £1.70

**ACCOMMODATION:**
**Living in:** • Catered: 5% • Cost: £76-81 (33-35 weeks)
• Self-catering: 13% • Cost: £48-54 (43 weeks)
**Living out:** • Ave rent: £45

# UNIVERSITY OF NOTTINGHAM
(1) University of Nottingham, University Park, Nottingham, NG7 2RD.
Tel: (0115) 951 5151. Fax: (0115) 951 3666.
E-mail: undergraduate-enquiries@nottingham.ac.uk
(2) University of Nottingham, School of Biological Science, Sutton Bonington,
Nr Loughborough, Leicestershire, LE12 5RD. Tel: (0115) 951 5151.

**DEBTS:** • Average debt: £1,200
           • Access fund: £278,234 • Successful applications per year: 807
The Registrar's Necessitous Student Fund can offer limited assistance to anyone
who can say 'necessitous' and the University gives £50 loans when needed.
**Banks on campus:** NatWest and HSBC Banks with cashpoints.

**EMPLOYMENT:** • Unemployed after 6 months: 3.7%
**Paid work:** The Union runs a job agency, 'Nucleus'. Apart from the usual money
scrambles, students have been known to sell themselves as guinea pigs at the
medical school (£120 for 3 days).

**TRAVEL:**
**National:** Trains: Nottingham Station offers services all round the country (north
and south are simpler than east and west), including London (£28.05),
Birmingham (£9.85), Manchester (£18.15) and Edinburgh (£51.90). Coaches:
National Express services to, among other places, London (£15.75), Birmingham
(£5.75) and Glasgow (£31.25).
**Local:** Buses run every 15 minutes from the campus into the city centre until 9pm
and cost around 75p.

**ENTERTAINMENTS:** • Booze index: £1.85
**Town/city:** • Pint of beer: £2.20    • Glass of wine: £2
**University:** • Pint of beer: £1.35    • Glass of wine: £1

**ACCOMMODATION:**
**Living in:** • Catered: 22%           • Cost: £80-93 (31 weeks)
           • Self-catering: 5%     • Cost: £40-93 (44 weeks)
**Living out:** • Ave rent: £42

# NOTTINGHAM TRENT UNIVERSITY
The Nottingham Trent University, Burton Street, Nottingham, NG1 4BU.
Tel: (0115) 941 8418. Fax: (0115) 848 6503. E-mail: marketing@ntu.ac.uk

**DEBTS:** • Average debt: £1,850
           • Access fund: £1,013,556 • Successful applications per year: 992
There's an Emergency Hardship Fund to which students can appeal and the
Hillsborough Memorial Bursary is for part-time students.

**EMPLOYMENT:** • Unemployed after 6 months: 3.7%
**Paid work:** see University of Nottingham. The Employment Store can help to find
work with a registration scheme which matching skills to jobs.

**TRAVEL:**
**National:** see University of Nottingham
**Local:** Nottingham Station is 1 mile from the City site. Buses cost between 50p
and 80p (£1 return) from the City site to Clifton, with several companies running
regular services. There's also a new inter-campus bus service which also covers
late-night cavorting.

**ENTERTAINMENTS:** • Booze index: £2.01
**Town/city:** • Pint of beer: £2.20    • Glass of wine: £2
**University:** • Pint of beer: £1.50    • Glass of wine: £1.45

**ACCOMMODATION:**
Living in: • Self-catering: 15%   • Cost: £50-57 (39 weeks)
Living out: • Ave rent: £42

# UNIVERSITY OF OXFORD

University of Oxford, University Offices, Wellington Square, Oxford, OX1 2JD.
Tel: (01865) 270207. Fax: (01865) 270208.
E-mail: undergraduate.admissions@admin.ox.ac.uk

**DEBTS:** • Average debt: £1,350
• Access fund: £625,931 • Successful applications per year: 78%
The University operates the central Access Fund, while other hardship funds are run by the University's colleges. Some of them are very well off and can provide support in the form of loans, grants, bursaries or prizes to a pocket-popping extent.

**EMPLOYMENT:** • Unemployed after 6 months: 3%
**Paid work:** With nearly 25,000 students (including Oxford Brookes University) competition could be an issue. Also the University doesn't really like students spending too much time on paid work.

**TRAVEL:**
**National:** Trains: Trains draw up at Oxford Station, close to the steps of the city's most central colleges. Mainline services to London (£11.20), Bristol (£17.80), etc. Coaches: As well as National Express serving London (£7), Bristol (£12) and all points beyond, there are other coach companies (Oxford Express) serving London only, with City Link also going to and from Heathrow and Gatwick. For London, the bus is much cheaper than the train and not much slower.
**Local:** Several local bus companies with frequent and cheap services (40p to get as far as digs in Jericho), but they're not really worth it for shorter trips.

**ENTERTAINMENTS:** • Booze index: £1.34
Town/city: • Pint of beer: £2.50   • Glass of wine: £2.10
University: • Pint of beer: £1.20   • Glass of wine: £1.20

**ACCOMMODATION:**
Living in: • Catered: 87%
Living out: • Ave rent: £55

# OXFORD BROOKES UNIVERSITY

Oxford Brookes University, Gipsy Lane, Headington, Oxford, OX3 0BP.
Tel: (01865) 484848. Fax: (01865) 483616. E-mail: query@brookes.ac.uk

**DEBTS:** • Average debt: £1,100
• Access fund: £255,000 • Successful applications per year: 445
A small hardship fund is set aside, used mainly for those disadvantaged minorities (in particular, part-time and overseas students). There's also a debt counsellor and child care grants.

**EMPLOYMENT:** • Unemployed after 6 months: 2.3%
Those students who know the careers service exists are quite happy with it and employment rates are excellent.
**Paid work:** The SU runs a jobshop with specialist staff filling over 1,500 vacancies a year.

**TRAVEL:**
**National:** see University of Oxford
**Local:** The University provides free buses between the Gipsy Lane, Harcourt and Wheatley sites, and the Cowley Centre and the John Radcliffe Hospital, every half hour, both of which take about 15 to 25 minutes. The modular course structure means that some students have academic commitments on more than one site.

**ENTERTAINMENTS:** • <u>Booze index: £2.03</u>
| | | |
|---|---|---|
| **Town/city:** | • <u>Pint of beer: £2.20</u> | • <u>Glass of wine: £2.10</u> |
| **University:** | • <u>Pint of beer: £1.40</u> | • <u>Glass of wine: £1.20</u> |

**ACCOMMODATION:**
| | | |
|---|---|---|
| **Living in:** | • <u>Catered: 11%</u> | • <u>Cost: £85 (42 weeks)</u> |
| | • <u>Self-catering 19%</u> | • <u>Cost: £36-66 (42 weeks)</u> |
| **Living out:** | • <u>Ave rent: £42</u> | |

# UNIVERSITY OF PAISLEY
(1) University of Paisley, Paisley, PA1 2BE.
Tel: 0800 027 1000. Fax: (0141) 848 3000. E-mail: uni-direct@paisley.ac.uk
(2) University of Paisley, Ayr Campus, Beech Grove, Ayr, KA8 0SR.
Tel: (01292) 260321. Fax: (01292) 611705.

**DEBTS:** • <u>Average debt: £1,100</u>
• <u>Access fund: £123,000</u> • <u>Successful applications per year: 1,468</u>
Bursary system and hardship fund (£10,000) from Student Welfare for those who
wouldn't get other help. Loans (but not grants) from the access fund available in
as little as 48 hours.
**Banks on campus:** Bank of Scotland cashpoint.

**EMPLOYMENT:** • <u>Unemployed after 6 months: 12%</u>
**Paid work:** The Student Advisory Service lists vacation vacancies and term-time
tasks, but the openings aren't out of the ordinary.

**TRAVEL:**
**National:** Trains: The nearest mainline station is 5 minutes' walk from Gilmour St.
Regular direct services to Glasgow (£1.65 return) with the last train at night at
11.46pm. London (£50.80). Coaches: Served nationally by Scottish Citylink, via
Glasgow. London (£27); Glasgow (£1.70).
**Local:** Buses allow easy short hops: at 85p, a single fare to Glasgow is cheaper
than the train and is available till 3am.

**ENTERTAINMENTS:** • <u>Booze index: £1.65</u>
| | | |
|---|---|---|
| **Town/city:** | • <u>Pint of beer: £1.80</u> | • <u>Glass of wine: £1.50</u> |
| **University:** | • <u>Pint of beer: £1.60</u> | • <u>Glass of wine: £1.70</u> |

**ACCOMMODATION:**
| | | |
|---|---|---|
| **Living in:** | • <u>Self-catering: 15%</u> | • <u>Cost: £32-40 (31 weeks)</u> |
| **Living out:** | • <u>Ave rent: £35</u> | |

# UNIVERSITY OF PLYMOUTH
(1) University of Plymouth, Drake Circus, Plymouth, PL4 8AA. Tel: (01752) 232232.
Fax: (01752) 232141. E-mail: admissions@plymouth.ac.uk
(2) Faculty of Arts & Education, University of Plymouth, Earl Richards Road North,
Exeter, EX2 6AS. Tel: (01392) 475022. Fax: (01392) 475012.
E-mail: fae-admissions@plym.ac.uk
(3) Faculty of Arts & Education, University of Plymouth, Douglas Avenue, Exmouth,
EX8 2AT. Tel: (01395) 255309. Fax: (01395) 255303.
(4) Seale-Hayne Faculty of Agriculture, Food & Land Use, University of Plymouth,
Newton Abbot, Devon, TQ12 6NQ. Tel: (01626) 325606/7. Fax: (01626) 325605.

**DEBTS:** • <u>Average debt: £1,150</u>
• <u>Access fund: £845,387</u> • <u>Successful applications per year: 730</u>
Small loans and vacation funds are available.

**EMPLOYMENT:** • <u>Unemployed after 6 months: 6.3%</u>
**Paid work:** Apart from the usual bar work and all that, there are a few tourist and
maritime based jobs in Plymouth. The SU's employment register can be fruitful, as
can hopping over the Tamar to Cornwall in the summer.

**TRAVEL:**
**National:** Trains: Plymouth station is about 5 minutes away or, if crawling, a tad longer. Services to London (£29.70), Bristol (£21.10) etc. Most stop at Newton Abbot and Exeter (on the same line). Coaches: National Express and Western National services from Plymouth to London (£26.75) and beyond.

**ENTERTAINMENTS:** • Booze index: £1.71
**Town/city:** • Pint of beer: £2.10 • Glass of wine: £1.45
**University:** • Pint of beer: £1.45 • Glass of wine: £1.15

**ACCOMMODATION:**
**Living in:** • Self-catering: 14% • Cost: £40-92 (39 weeks)
**Living out:** • Ave rent: £40

# UNIVERSITY OF PORTSMOUTH
University of Portsmouth, Winston Churchill Avenue, Portsmouth, PO1 2UP.
Tel: (023) 9284 8484. Fax: (023) 9284 2733. E-mail: info.centre@port.ac.uk

**DEBTS:** • Average debt: £2,400
• Access fund: £907,968 • Successful applications per year: 1,300
Short-term loans (£1,000 max) are available and financial workshops and debt counselling are organised.

**EMPLOYMENT:** • Unemployed after 6 months: 4%
Efficient, effective but underused service at Guildford Walk on the Guildhall campus and an information room in Milton.
**Paid work:** What with the ferries, the bars, Southsea being a holiday resort and all, there's a better than average chance of finding something to line students' pockets during vacations. A jobshop at Alex House puts students in touch with temp employers.

**TRAVEL:**
**National:** Trains: Mainline connections to, among other places, London Waterloo (£13.35), Southampton (£4.30) and Liverpool (£42.75). Coaches: National Express services to many destinations including London (£13), Southampton (£3.50) and Liverpool (£33).
**Local:** Buses are decent, but most distances are walkable.

**ENTERTAINMENTS:** • Booze index: £1.60
**Town/city:** • Pint of beer: £1.80 • Glass of wine: £1.50
**University:** • Pint of beer: £1.60 • Glass of wine: £1.10

**ACCOMMODATION:**
**Living in:** • Catered: 6% • Cost: £64-78 (38-52 weeks)
• Self-catering: 12% • Cost: £38-44 (38 weeks)
**Living out:** • Ave rent: £42

Be on the look-out for special student nights at clubs, pubs, cinemas etc. Carry your NUS card with you everywhere — it can get you so many discounts it could be your most valuable bit of plastic.

# QUEEN MARGARET UNIVERSITY COLLEGE, EDINBURGH

(1) Queen Margaret University College, Corstorphine Campus, Edinburgh,
EH12 8TS. Tel: (0131) 317 3000. Fax: (0131) 317 3248.
E-mail: admissions@mail.qmuc.ac.uk
(2) Queen Margaret University College, Leith Campus, Duke Street, Leith,
Edinburgh, EH6 8HF.
(3) Queen Margaret University College, Gateway Theatre, Leith Walk, Edinburgh.

**DEBTS:** • Average debt: £1,250
• Access fund: £150,000 • Successful applications per year: 300
Some bursaries and emergency loans from the Union.
**Banks on campus:** Royal Bank of Scotland.

**EMPLOYMENT:** • Unemployed after 6 months: 5.9%
This must be the only institution where the Careers Advisor is described (by
students) as 'lovely', 'brilliant' and 'everyone's mum'.
**Paid work:** see University of Edinburgh

**TRAVEL:** See University of Edinburgh

**ENTERTAINMENTS:** • Booze index: £2.04
**Town/city:** • Pint of beer: £2.40 • Glass of wine: £2
**University:** • Pint of beer: £1.50 • Glass of wine: £1.30

**ACCOMMODATION:**
**Living in:** • Catered: 6% • Cost: £67 (31 weeks)
• Self-catering: 14% • Cost: £42-51 (38 weeks)
**Living out:** • Ave rent: £55

# QUEEN MARY, UNIVERSITY OF LONDON

• The College is part of University of London and students are entitled to use its
facilities.
(1) Queen Mary, University of London, Mile End Road, London, E1 4NS.
Tel: (020) 7882 5555. Fax: (020) 7975 5500.
(2) Barts and the London Queen Mary University, University of London, Biomedical
sciences, Mile End Road, London, E1 4NS.
Tel: (020) 7882 5555. Fax: (020) 7882 5500

**DEBTS:** • Average debt: £850
• Access fund: £260,000 • Successful applications per year: 641
There are undergraduate bursaries of £1,500 pa for the lucky few.

**EMPLOYMENT:** • Unemployed after 6 months: 4%
There is now a careers reference library, which is handy in a careers office.
**Paid work:** see University of London

**TRAVEL:**
**National:** see University of London
**Local:** Nearest tubes are Mile End (Central, District, Jubilee, Hammersmith & City
Lines) and Stepney Green (District, Hammersmith & City peak times only).

**ENTERTAINMENTS:** • Booze index: £1.99
**Town/city:** • Pint of beer: £2.20 • Glass of wine: £2.50
**University:** • Pint of beer: £1.60 • Glass of wine: £0.90

**ACCOMMODATION:**
**Living in:** • Catered: 15% • Cost: £80-95 (31 weeks)
• Self-catering: 18% • Cost: £69-83 (38 weeks)
**Living out:** • Ave rent: £75

**7**

# THE QUEEN'S UNIVERSITY OF BELFAST

(1) The Queen's University of Belfast, University Road, Belfast, BT7 1PE.
Tel: (028) 9024 5133. Fax: (028) 9024 7895.
(2) The Queen's University at Armagh, 39 Abbey Street, Armagh, BT61 7EB.
Tel: (028) 3751 0678. Fax: (028) 3751 0679.

**DEBTS:** • Average debt: £1,200
           • Access fund: £762,250 • Successful applications per year: 901
There are several scholarships including 15 Guinness sports bursaries.
**Banks on campus:** Bank of Ireland.

**EMPLOYMENT:** • Unemployed after 6 months: 3.5%
**Paid work:** The new jobshop helps to place over 200 registered students in on/off-campus work.

**TRAVEL:**
**National:** Trains: All of Ireland's main cities and towns, north and south, are just a Northern Ireland Railways' journey away, including (London)Derry (£7.20) and Coleraine. A fast train, the Enterprise, goes to Dublin (£21). Coaches: Translink serves most destinations in Northern Ireland and the Republic, but it's somewhat difficult to catch a bus direct from Britain what with the Irish Sea and all. National Express runs a service to London (£60).
**Local:** Frequent local buses provide a 10-minute ride into the city centre for 50p.

**ENTERTAINMENTS:** • Booze index: £1.80
**Town/city:** • Pint of beer: £1.80 • Glass of wine: £1.80
**University:** • Pint of beer: £1.60 • Glass of wine: £2

**ACCOMMODATION:**
**Living in:** • Catered: 7% • Cost: £54-62 (32 weeks)
           • Self-catering 13% • Cost: £39-50 (38-50 weeks)
**Living out:** • Ave rent: £40

# UNIVERSITY OF READING

University of Reading, Whiteknights, PO Box 217, Reading, Berks RG6 6AH.
Tel: (0118) 931 6586. Fax: (0118) 931 8924.
E-mail: Schools.liason@reading.ac.uk

**DEBTS:** • Average debt: £900
           • Access fund: £350,188 • Successful applications per year: 571
Emergency loans fund, scholarships and various departmental prizes.

**EMPLOYMENT:** • Unemployed after 6 months: 11%
**Paid work:** The jobshop is run by the Union and sponsored by Barclays Bank (that's one way of making sure they get overdrafts paid back). All jobs have to offer the minimum wage to be included.

**TRAVEL:**
**National:** Trains: Reading station, about 1 ½ miles from campus, offers direct services to London Paddington and Waterloo (£6.40) and most points west. Coaches: National Express services all over the country. There are also the Reading-London Link (Reading Transport, £7) and Bee-Line Coaches.
**Local:** Buses between the University and town are reasonable (£1 rtn).

**ENTERTAINMENTS:** • Booze index: £1.84
**Town/city:** • Pint of beer: £2.30 • Glass of wine: £2
**University:** • Pint of beer: £1.50 • Glass of wine: £1.30

**ACCOMMODATION:**
**Living in:** • Catered: 30% • Cost: £74-93 (30 weeks)
• Self-catering: 16% • Cost: £41-60 (30 weeks)
**Living out:** • Ave rent: £55

# THE ROBERT GORDON UNIVERSITY

The Robert Gordon University, Schoolhill, Aberdeen, AB10 1FR.
Tel: (01224) 262180. Fax: (01224) 262185. E-mail: i.centre@rgu.ac.uk

**DEBTS:** • Average debt: £2,200
• Access fund: £175,000 • Successful applications per year: 336
The hardship fund offers small short-term loans and there are a few scholarships
and trust funds.
**Banks on campus:** Clydesdale cashpoint.

**EMPLOYMENT:** • Unemployed after 6 months: 2%
Vocational degrees make for excellent job prospects, as do industrial placements
and careers advice within courses.
**Paid work:** see University of Aberdeen

**TRAVEL:**
**National:** see University of Aberdeen
**Local:** Aberdeen Station is a mile south of Schoolhill. Buses run every 20 minutes
to most sites, but feet are the most effective way of getting around.

**ENTERTAINMENTS:** • Booze index: £1.74
**Town/city:** • Pint of beer: £1.90 • Glass of wine: £1.80
**University:** • Pint of beer: £1.35 • Glass of wine: £0.85

**ACCOMMODATION:**
**Living in:** • Self-catering: 15% • Cost: £49-63 (36 weeks)
**Living out:** • Ave rent: £50

**UNUSUAL COSTS:**
Parking is available but costs £6 per week.

# ROYAL ACADEMY OF MUSIC

• The Academy is part of University of London and students are entitled to use its
facilities.
Royal Academy of Music, Marylebone Road, London, NW1 5HT.
Tel: (020) 7873 7373. Fax: (020) 7873 7374. E-mail: registry@ram.ac.uk

**DEBTS:** • Average debt: £700
• Access fund: £47,000 • Successful applications per year: 56

**TRAVEL:**
**National:** see University of London
**Local:** Tubes and buses.

**ENTERTAINMENTS:** • Booze index: £2.35
**Town/city:** • Pint of beer: £2.20 • Glass of wine: £2.50
**University:** • Pint of beer: £1.60 • Glass of wine: £1.40

**ACCOMMODATION:**
**Living in:** • No accommodation of its own
**Living out:** • Ave rent: £75

7

# ROYAL COLLEGE OF MUSIC

Royal College of Music, Prince Consort Road, London, SW7 2BS.
Tel: (020) 7589 3643. Fax: (020) 7589 7740. E-mail: admissions@rcm.ac.uk

**DEBTS:**  • Average debt: £1,500
• Access fund: £46,979  • Successful applications per year: 86

**TRAVEL:**
**National:** see University of London
**Local:** Nearest tubes are South Kensington, Gloucester Road and Knightsbridge.

**ENTERTAINMENTS:** • Booze index: £1.95
**Town/city:**  • Pint of beer: £2.20  • Glass of wine: £2.50
**University:**  • Pint of beer: £1.60  • Glass of wine: £1.40

**ACCOMMODATION:**
**Living in:**  • Self-catering: 47%  • Cost: £48-79 (43 weeks)
**Living out:**  • Ave rent: £75

# ROYAL HOLLOWAY, LONDON

• The College is part of University of London and students are entitled to use its
facilities.
Royal Holloway, Egham, Surrey, TW20 0EX.
Tel: (01784) 434455. Fax: (01784) 471381. E-mail: liaison-office@rhul.ac.uk

**DEBTS:**  • Average debt: £1,600
• Access fund: £190,813  • Successful applications per year: 215
Loans from the Principal's Hardship Fund have to be repaid before students are
allowed to graduate. Also scholarships and bursaries for travel, instrumental
students and sports.
**Banks on campus:** NatWest Bank.

**EMPLOYMENT:** • Unemployed after 6 months: 5%
**Paid work:** The SU has vacancies for 350 students and provides a job training
scheme with vocational certificates. The University administration employs casual
envelope stuffers and the careers office helps temp job-seekers.

**TRAVEL:**
**National:** see University of London
**Local:** Trains: Trains to Waterloo from Egham every 1 / 4 hour (£3.65). Buses:
They are infrequent and dear – 90p single for a 5-minute journey to the station –
but there's a College service every 15 minutes or so (35p for the same trip) and
the SU bus is 50p to livers-out after 10pm. Coaches: Egham's just a hop from
Heathrow (useful if you want to catch a plane). Coaches cost £2.50 to the airport
and from there they go anywhere in the UK.

**ENTERTAINMENTS:** • Booze index: £1.67
**Town/city:**  • Pint of beer: £2.20  • Glass of wine: £1.50
**University:**  • Pint of beer: £1.70  • Glass of wine: £1.20

**ACCOMMODATION:**
**Living in:**  • Catered: 40%  • Cost: £45-80 (30-38 weeks)
• Self-catering: 4%  • Cost: £65-70 (38-50 weeks)
**Living out:**  • Ave rent: £55-70

## ROYAL VETERINARY COLLEGE, LONDON
• The College is part of University of London and students are entitled to use its facilities.
The Royal Veterinary College, Royal College Street, London, NW1 0TU.
Tel: (020) 7468 5000. Fax: (020) 7388 2342.

**DEBTS:** • Average debt: £2,150
• Access fund: £24,000 • Successful applications per year: 20

**TRAVEL:**
**National:** see University of London
**Local:** At the Camden site, there are trains, buses and Tubes. Two trains every hour between King's Cross and Potter's Bar (£4) for the Hawkshead site. Taxis from the station to Hawkshead cost £3.50, otherwise it's a long hike.

**ENTERTAINMENTS:** • Booze index: £2.17
**Town/city:** • Pint of beer: £2.20 • Glass of wine: £2.50
**University:** • Pint of beer: £1.30

**ACCOMMODATION:**
**Living in:** • Catered: 11% • Cost: £73 (45 weeks)
• Self-catering 6% • Cost: £53 (32-45 weeks)
**Living out:** • Ave rent: £75

## UNIVERSITY OF SALFORD
University of Salford, Salford, M5 4WT. Tel: (0161) 295 5000.
Fax: (0161) 295 5999. E-mail: ug.prospectus@salford.ac.uk

**DEBTS:** • Average debt: £1,550
• Hardship fund: £873,468 • Successful applications per year: 577
**Banks on campus:** HSBC Bank.

**EMPLOYMENT:** • Unemployed after 6 months: 9%
**Paid work:** see University of Manchester. The jobshop has part-time and casual vacancies within the University as well as Salford and Manchester.

**TRAVEL:**
**National:** see University of Manchester
**Local:** Salford is covered by Manchester's bus and train networks which are reliable, comprehensive and generally cheap. Salford Crescent station is actually on the campus, although for national services it may be necessary to change at one of Manchester's stations (trains every 15 mins). Buses go to Manchester city centre every 3 minutes.

**ENTERTAINMENTS:** • Booze index: £1.55
**Town/city:** • Pint of beer: £1.70 • Glass of wine: £1.50
**University:** • Pint of beer: £1.55 • Glass of wine: £1.20

**ACCOMMODATION:**
**Living in:** • Catered: 2% • Cost: £71-81 (33 weeks)
• Self-catering: 22% • Cost: £39-51 (39-50 weeks)
**Living out:** • Ave rent: £38

**7**

Give your money to me and I'll look after it for you.

Kate Berry, South Tyneside College

## SCHOOL OF PHARMACY, LONDON

• The College is part of University of London and students are entitled to use its facilities.

The School of Pharmacy, 29 Brunswick Square, London, WC1N 1AX.

Tel: (020) 7753 5831. Fax: (020) 7753 5827. E-mail: registry@ulsop.ac.uk

**DEBTS:** • Access fund: £29,500 • Successful applications per year: 78
Some postgraduate scholarships available.

**EMPLOYMENT:** • Unemployed after 6 months: 1%
**Paid work:** see University of London

**TRAVEL:**
**National:** see University of London
**Local:** The nearest tube station is Russell Square (Piccadilly line) and Euston, King's Cross & St Pancras stations are all pretty close.

**ENTERTAINMENTS:** • Booze index: £2.35
**Town/city:** • Pint of beer: £2.20 • Glass of wine: £2.50
**University:** • Pint of beer: £1.50 • Glass of wine: £2

**ACCOMMODATION:**
**Living in:** • No accommodation of its own
**Living out:** • Ave rent: £75

## UNIVERSITY OF SHEFFIELD

The University of Sheffield, 14 Favell Road, Sheffield, S3 7QX.
Tel: (0114) 222 2000. Fax: (0114) 222 8032.
E-mail: ug.admissions@sheffield.ac.uk

**DEBTS:** • Average debt: £1,450
• Access fund: £644,000 • Successful applications per year: 263
Short term loan scheme and trust funds. Hardship funds are available without too much difficulty and instalment payment schemes can be arranged for hall fees.
**Banks on campus:** NatWest and Co-op; 5 cash machines.

**EMPLOYMENT:** • Unemployed after 6 months: 5.1%
**Paid work:** Sheffield may offer a lot of things to students, but employment is often hard to come by. The university jobshop does its best finding vacancies in bars, shops and restaurants.

**TRAVEL:**
**National:** Trains: Sheffield Station offers services to London (£27.70), Birmingham (£15.65), Edinburgh (£43.55) and more. Coaches: Sheffield is served by South Yorkshire Transport as well as National Express, whose services go to London (£14.50), Birmingham (£11.50) and other destinations.
**Local:** Local buses run all day and all night and are frequent, reliable and quite cheap. The local minibuses are even better because they go everywhere. The Supertram is best of all, though, 'cos it's fun and cheap (£1.90 all-day pass, Megarider seven-day pass £6.30) and the University is on the tram route.

**ENTERTAINMENTS:** • Booze index: £1.72
**Town/city:** • Pint of beer: £1.75 • Glass of wine: £1.85
**University:** • Pint of beer: £1.40 • Glass of wine: £1.75

**ACCOMMODATION:**
**Living in:** • Catered: 21% • Cost: £74-95 (31 weeks)
• Self-catering: 14% • Cost: £45-58 (38 weeks)
**Living out:** • Ave rent: £40

## SHEFFIELD HALLAM UNIVERSITY
Sheffield Hallam University, City Campus, Howard Street, Sheffield, S1 1WB.
Tel: (0114) 225 5555. Fax: (0114) 225 2159.

**DEBTS:** • Average debt: £1,300
• Access fund: n/a • Successful applications per year: 1,691
Hillsborough Trust memorial bursaries, international prize, scholarships and
hardship funds. Also a loan of £50 cash or food vouchers is available in extreme
emergencies to be repaid as soon as possible.

**EMPLOYMENT:** • Unemployed after 6 months: 7%
**Paid work:** see University of Sheffield. There is a Network-Student Employment
Service at the City Campus.

**TRAVEL:**
**National:** see University of Sheffield
**Local:** Campuses are close enough to walk between but there is also well served
public transport between most of them.

**ENTERTAINMENTS:** • Booze index: £1.74
**Town/city:** • Pint of beer: £1.75 • Glass of wine: £1.85
**University:** • Pint of beer: £1.20

**ACCOMMODATION:**
**Living in:** • Catered: 7% • Cost: £60-77 (33 weeks)
• Self-catering: 13% • Cost: £60-77 (39 weeks)
**Living out:** • Ave rent: £40

## SOAS
• The College is part of University of London and students are entitled to use its
facilities.
School of Oriental & African Studies, Thornhaugh Street, Russell Square, London,
WC1H 0XG. Tel: (020) 7637 2388. Fax: (020) 7436 3844.
E-mail: registrar@soas.ac.uk

**EMPLOYMENT:** see University of London

**TRAVEL:** see University of London

**ENTERTAINMENTS:** • Booze index: £2.15
**Town/city:** • Pint of beer: £2.20 • Glass of wine: £2.50
**University:** • Pint of beer: £1.70

**ACCOMMODATION:**
**Living in:** • Self-catering: 23% • Cost: £85 (30 weeks)
**Living out:** • Ave rent: £75

## SOUTH BANK UNIVERSITY
South Bank University, 103 Borough Road, Elephant & Castle, London, SE1 0AA.
Tel: (020) 7815 8158. Fax: (020) 7815 8273. E-mail: registry@sbu.ac.uk

**DEBTS:** • Average debt: £2,250
• Access fund: £750,000 • Successful applications per year: 1,500
The University distributes a charitable fund of £12,000, mainly to those who
wouldn't otherwise get financial assistance, such as part-time and overseas
students, but that kind of amount doesn't go very far. The Access fund offers
£100 awards. Student Services also provides a Money Management Guide and
gives out £50,000 in Fee Remissions so that those who pay their own tuition
costs can finish their courses.
**Banks on campus:** HSBC Bank.

**EMPLOYMENT:** • <u>Unemployed after 6 months: 15%</u>
**Paid work:** see University of London

**TRAVEL:**
**National:** see <u>University of London</u>
**Local:** Trains (including Thameslink), tubes and buses.

**ENTERTAINMENTS:** • <u>Booze index: £2.17</u>
**Town/city:** • <u>Pint of beer: £2.20</u>   • <u>Glass of wine: £2.50</u>
**University:** • <u>Pint of beer: £1.50</u>   • <u>Glass of wine: £1</u>

**ACCOMMODATION:**
**Living in:** • <u>Self-catering: 16%</u>   • <u>Cost: £64-78 (42 weeks)</u>
**Living out:** • <u>Ave rent: £75</u>

# UNIVERSITY OF SOUTHAMPTON

University of Southampton, Southampton, SO17 1BJ.
Tel: (023) 8059 5000. Fax: (023) 8059 3037. E-mail: prospenq@soton.ac.uk

**DEBTS:** • <u>Average debt: £2,000</u>
• <u>Access fund: £672,000</u> • <u>Successful applications per year: 1,458</u>
In addition to the access fund, the University runs a hardship fund for people
whose circumstances change mid-course. The Students' Union also gives short-
term emergency loans.
**Banks on campus:** Lloyds Bank with cashpoint.

**EMPLOYMENT:** • <u>Unemployed after 6 months: 7.6%</u>
**Paid work:** The University-run job shop 'Openings' places students with part-time
and temporary work. The boat show in summer offers some opportunities not
available elsewhere.

**TRAVEL:**
**National:** Trains: Southampton Central offers services to London (£15.45), Bristol
(£19.80), Manchester (£38.60) and others. Buses: National Express services all
over the country, including London (£9.50), Manchester (£26.50) and all points
beyond.
**Local:** Buses are cheap and reliable, but infrequent. Local trains are regular with
connections all over Hampshire and there are 7 stations around the city, but it's
not the cheapest or most practical way of getting around. The University has its
own bus service, 'uni-link', linking the city and the campuses.

**ENTERTAINMENTS:** • <u>Booze index: £1.49</u>
**Town/city:** • <u>Pint of beer: £1.80</u>   • <u>Glass of wine: £1.30</u>
**University:** • <u>Pint of beer: £1.32</u>   • <u>Glass of wine: £0.70</u>

**ACCOMMODATION:**
**Living in:** • <u>Catered: 9%</u>   • <u>Cost: £74-93 (39-50 weeks)</u>
• <u>Self-catering: 31%</u>   • <u>Cost: £39-61 (30-50 weeks)</u>
**Living out:** • <u>Ave rent: £40</u>

Economise right from the off. If you blow
big bucks at the beginning of term your
fast and loose spending will only leave you
miserable and bored by the end.

## SOUTHAMPTON INSTITUTE OF HIGHER EDUCATION
Southampton Institute, East Park Terrace, Southampton, SO14 0YN.
Tel: (023) 8031 9000. Fax: (023) 8022 2259. E-mail: er@solent.ac.uk

**DEBTS:** • Average debt: £1,800
The SU provides hardship loans up to £30 and the Principal's Discretionary Fund
(£10,000) lends £150 to students waiting for their loans to arrive.
**Banks on campus:** Barclays and NatWest cash machines.

**EMPLOYMENT:** • Unemployed after 6 months: 5%
**Paid work:** There's the usual jobs offered by the SU such as bar work and
stewarding, plus a jobshop on campus. Also see University of Southampton.

**TRAVEL:** see University of Southampton

**ENTERTAINMENTS:** • Booze index: £1.54
**Town/city:** • Pint of beer: £1.80      • Glass of wine: £1.30
**University:** • Pint of beer: £1.50      • Glass of wine: £1.50

**ACCOMMODATION:**
**Living in:**   • Self-catering: 29%      • Cost: £40-77 (39-48 weeks)
**Living out:**  • Ave rent: £40

## UNIVERSITY OF ST ANDREWS
University of St Andrews, Admissions Office, 79 North Street, St Andrews, Fife,
KY16 9AJ. Tel: (01334) 462150. Fax: (01334) 463388.
E-mail: admissions@st-andrews.ac.uk

**DEBTS:**          • Average debt: £1,300
                    • Access fund: £280,694  • Successful applications per year: 658
In addition to the access fund, bursaries and scholarships, the University can
provide interest-free loans in extreme cases through the Director of Student
Support Services.
**Banks on campus:** Clydesdale cashpoint.

**EMPLOYMENT:** • Unemployed after 6 months: 3.4%
**Paid work:** A University-organised jobs databank is available and the Student
Support Service has a job club. Most vacancies are in the local tourist and golfing
trade – hotels, golf bars and so on. Caddying isn't as easy as you'd think, though.

**TRAVEL:**
**National:** Trains: Leuchars station is 5 miles from the main group of the University
buildings with direct lines to London (£53.45), Dundee and Edinburgh. For other
services, change at Edinburgh or Dundee. Coaches: National Express coaches run
from Dundee, 13 miles away, to London (£32), Glasgow (£11) and beyond.
**Local:** Buses every half hour but rarer at night, although they're quite cheap
(£1.40). In general, St Andrews is small enough to walk around.

**ENTERTAINMENTS:** • Booze index: £1.57
**Town/city:** • Pint of beer: £1.90      • Glass of wine: £1.60
**University:** • Pint of beer: £1.50      • Glass of wine: £1.35

**ACCOMMODATION:**
**Living in:**   • Catered: 38%            • Cost: £67-89 (31-50 weeks)
                 • Self-catering: 17%      • Cost: £32-55 (36-50 weeks)
**Living out:**  • Ave rent: £55

7

## ST GEORGE'S HOSPITAL MEDICAL SCHOOL, LONDON

• The Medical School is part of University of London and students are entitled to use its facilities.
St George's Hospital Medical School, Cranmer Terrace, Tooting,
London, SW17 ORE. Tel: (020) 8672 9944. Fax: (020) 8725 5919.
E-mail: adm-med@sgnms.ac.uk

**DEBTS:** • Average debt: £2,350
• Access fund: £46,880 • Successful applications per year: 51
Bursaries, grants and prizes all over the place.

**EMPLOYMENT:** see University of London

**TRAVEL:**
**National:** see University of London
**Local:** Tooting Broadway is the local underground (Northern Line).

**ENTERTAINMENTS:** • Booze index: £2.01
**Town/city:** • Pint of beer: £2.20 • Glass of wine: £2.50
**University:** • Pint of beer: £1.25 • Glass of wine: £0.70

**ACCOMMODATION:**
**Living in:** • Self-catering: 25% • Cost: £60 (30-50 weeks)
**Living out:** • Ave rent: £75

## STAFFORDSHIRE UNIVERSITY

(1) Staffordshire University, College Road, Stoke-on-Trent, ST4 2DE.
Tel: (01782) 294000. Fax: (01782) 745422. E-mail: admissions@staffs.ac.uk
(2) Staffordshire University, Beaconside Campus, Stafford, ST18 0AD.
Tel: (01782) 294000. Fax: (01782) 745422.

**DEBTS:** • Average debt: £1,800
• Access fund: £524,248 • Successful applications per year: 267

**EMPLOYMENT:** • Unemployed after 6 months: 7.2%
**Paid work:** Locally there's the usual kind of shop work and the University hires students for work such as mailing and decorating. Union Ents employs 100 students.

**TRAVEL:**
**National:** Trains: Stafford and Stoke are on the Merseyside and Manchester services to London (£19.45). The main Stoke site is right next to the station. Coaches: National Express services from both towns include London (£12) and more.
**Local:** The University runs a free minibus between sites 6 times a day but priority goes to staff and it's impossible to get to a 9am lecture. The 20-minute train journey might offer better odds. Local buses run by the bizarrely named PMT are also handy and cheap.

**ENTERTAINMENTS:** • Booze index: £1.53
**Town/city:** • Pint of beer: £1.80 • Glass of wine: £1.40
**University:** • Pint of beer: £1.20 • Glass of wine: £1.10

**ACCOMMODATION:**
**Living in:** • Self-catering: 15% • Cost: £27-56 (40 weeks)
**Living out:** • Ave rent: £36

# UNIVERSITY OF STIRLING
University of Stirling, Stirling, FK9 4LA.
Tel: (01786) 467046. Fax: (01786) 446800. E-mail: s-c-liason@stir.ac.uk

**DEBTS:** • Average debt: £1,450
• Access fund: £139,900 • Successful applications per year: 365
Twenty £1,000 bursaries are available for local and UK/EU students. Ten £2,000 academic bursaries for overseas students used against fees. Thirty sports scholarships.

**EMPLOYMENT:** • Unemployed after 6 months: 5.3%
**Paid work:** Usual stuff in Stirling, but limited. During vacations, try Glasgow or Edinburgh, a daily train journey away. Within the Students' Association, there's bar work and the University sometimes needs gaps filled in the library (by people rather than books).

**TRAVEL:**
**National:** Trains: Stirling Station, 2 miles from the campus, has direct services to London (£47.25) and Edinburgh (£3.15) which is a good place to change for most Scottish destinations. Coaches: National Express services to London (£16), Edinburgh (£5), Newcastle (£12.50) and all points beyond.
**Local:** A cheap bus service runs till midnight between the campus and the town centre, but the timetables appear to have been created by someone with a somewhat tenuous grasp on reality.

**ENTERTAINMENTS:** • Booze index: £1.43
**Town/city:** • Pint of beer: £1.70 • Glass of wine: £1.75
**University:** • Pint of beer: £1.50 • Glass of wine: £1.10

**ACCOMMODATION:**
**Living in:** • Self-catering: 70% • Cost: £46-62 (30-37 weeks)
**Living out:** • Ave rent: £45

# UNIVERSITY OF STRATHCLYDE
University of Strathclyde, McCance Building, 16 Richmond Street, Glasgow, G1 1XQ. Tel: (0141) 548 2426. Fax: (0141) 552 5860.

**DEBTS:** • Access fund: £800,000 • Successful applications per year: 1,000

**EMPLOYMENT:** • Unemployed after 6 months: 3%
**Paid work:** see University of Glasgow

**TRAVEL:**
**National:** see University of Glasgow
**Local:** Strathclyde University is 5 minutes walk from Queen Street Station and 10 minutes from Central Station.

**ENTERTAINMENTS:** • Booze index: £1.76
**Town/city:** • Pint of beer: £1.90 • Glass of wine: £1.60
**University:** • Pint of beer: £1.65 • Glass of wine: £1.95

**ACCOMMODATION:**
**Living in:** • Catered: 5% • Cost: £63 (35 weeks)
• Self-catering: 18% • Cost: £43-67 (37-50 weeks)
**Living out:** • Ave rent: £55

## UNIVERSITY OF SUNDERLAND

University of Sunderland, Student Recruitment, Edinburgh Building, Chester Road, Sunderland, SR1 25D. Tel: (0191) 515 3000. Fax: (0191) 515 3805.
E-mail: student-helpline@sunderland.ac.uk

**DEBTS:** • Access fund: £756,029 • Successful applications per year: 1,400
Student Services has debt counsellors and financial help-books. Some bursaries are available, hardship fund and loans.

**EMPLOYMENT:** • Unemployed after 6 months: 5%
**Paid work:** Students' Union runs a jobshop and also has about 150 casual posts to offer.

**TRAVEL:**
**National:** Trains: Sunderland station is 10 minutes walk from the Chester Road campus. There are direct trains to Newcastle, Middlesbrough (£3.95) and London (£47.50) and connections to the rest of the country. There's also the Metro Link in Newcastle. Coaches: Blueline and National Express services to many destinations including London (£25.50) and Manchester (£17.50).
**Local:** The buses are cheap (fares from 20p) and quite reliable. A free campus bus service runs between all key University buildings and halls of residence. Development of an underground system is imminent. There's also a shiny new bus/Metro station.

**ENTERTAINMENTS:** • Booze index: £1.54
**Town/city:** • Pint of beer: £1.85 • Glass of wine: £1.50
**University:** • Pint of beer: £1.35 • Glass of wine: £1.05

**ACCOMMODATION:**
**Living in:** • Catered: 3% • Cost: £49-58 (40 weeks)
• Self-catering: 25% • Cost: £36-53 (40-52 weeks)
**Living out:** • Ave rent: £35

## UNIVERSITY OF SURREY

University of Surrey, Guildford, Surrey, GU2 5XH. Tel: (01483)300800.
Fax: (01483) 300803.   E-mail: information@surrey.ac.uk

**DEBTS:** • Average debt: £800
• Access fund: £233,850 • Successful applications per year: 715
The access fund is largely used to help with accommodation problems. Up to £1,000 is available for undergrads and mature students in need. Sports bursaries and various scholarships are available.
**Banks on campus:** NatWest Bank with cashpoint.

**EMPLOYMENT:** • Unemployed after 6 months: 1.1%
Excellent drop-in centre and there's never a problem getting an appointment to see a careers advisor. The University boasts the lowest graduate unemployment rate in the country.
**Paid work:** The careers service helps out with work in the local area – mostly bar, shop and restaurant work.

**TRAVEL:**
**National:** Trains: From Guildford Station (half a mile from campus) mainline connections to London Waterloo (£7 – Including travelcard for Underground and buses). Trains every hour. Coaches: National Express from Guildford to London (£7.50) and elsewhere.
**Local:** Good bus service around town, including a minibus every 12 mins from campus to the centre (70p return). The Uni has recently joined up with a local bus company to offer a decent service throughout the area and a super lovely season ticket offer (£100).

**ENTERTAINMENTS:** • Booze index: £2.01
**Town/city:** • Pint of beer: £2.20   • Glass of wine: £2
**University:** • Pint of beer: £1.39   • Glass of wine: £2.50

**ACCOMMODATION:**
**Living in:** • Self-catering: 60%   • Cost: £35-67 (30/38 weeks)
**Living out:** • Ave rent: £62

## SURREY INSTITUTE OF ART & DESIGN
(1) Surrey Institute of Art and Design, Falkner Road, Farnham, Surrey, GU9 7DS.
Tel: (01252) 722441. Fax: (01252) 892616. E-mail: registry@surrart.ac.uk
(2) Surrey Institute of Art and Design, Epsom Campus, Ashley Road, Epsom,
Surrey, KT18 5BE. Tel: (01372) 728811. Fax: (01372) 726233.

**DEBTS:**     • Average debt: £1,450
            • Access fund: £98,000  • Successful applications per year: 299
£14,500 hardship fund for first years and a small (and we mean small)
SU welfare fund.

**EMPLOYMENT:** • Unemployed after 6 months: 18%
**Paid work:** The jobs notice board is updated regularly. The College employs
students as cleaners and security staff and the SU takes them on in the bar.

**TRAVEL:**
**National:** Trains: Farnham station is 3 / 4 of a mile from the College, on the line
to London (£7.15) and Guildford. Epsom station is 5 minutes walk from the
Institute site – a return trip to London costs a miserly £3.05. Coaches: Services
to London (£7.50), Birmingham (£20.75), Manchester (£27.50), among others.
**Local:** Local buses in Farnham are fairly regular, Epsom, being closer to London,
has more coordinated services.

**ENTERTAINMENTS:** • Booze index: £1.85
**Town/city:** • Pint of beer: £2.10   • Glass of wine: £1.80
**University:** • Pint of beer: £1.45   • GlaGlass of wine: £1.20

**ACCOMMODATION:**
**Living in:** • Self-catering: 16%   • Cost: £32-58 (38 weeks)
**Living out:** • Ave rent: £50

## UNIVERSITY OF SUSSEX
University of Sussex, Falmer, Brighton, BN1 9RH. Tel: (01273) 606755.
Fax: (01273) 678545. E-mail: ug.admissions@sussex.ac.uk

**DEBTS:**     • Average debt: £1,950
            • Access fund: £557,078  • Successful applications: 1,125
There's the hardship fund and students can also apply for a Vice-Chancellor's
Loan of £100 if their grants are late.

**EMPLOYMENT:** • Unemployed after 6 months: 3.4%
**Paid work:** The University has a Student Employment Office, providing part-time
and vacation work for students locally.

**TRAVEL:** See University of Brighton

**ENTERTAINMENTS:** • Booze index: £1.52
**Town/city:** • Pint of beer: £1.95   • Glass of wine: £1.45
**University:** • Pint of beer: £1.50   • Glass of wine: £1

**ACCOMMODATION:**
**Living in:** • Self-catering: 41%   • Cost: £48-63 (30/38 weeks)
**Living out:** • Ave rent: £45

**7**

## SWANSEA, UNIVERSITY OF WALES

University of Wales Swansea, Singleton Park, Swansea, SA2 8PP.
Tel: (01792) 205678. Fax: (01792) 295897. E-mail: admissions@swan.ac.uk

**DEBTS:** • Average debt: £1,000
• Access fund: £201,339 • Successful applications per year: 882
£700 per annum sports and cultural scholarships.
**Banks on campus:** NatWest cashpoint; Lloyds cashpoint and bank.

**EMPLOYMENT:** • Unemployed after 6 months: 3%
The careers service is very well-organised, friendly and pretty efficient. They
arrange job-link and work shadowing schemes.
**Paid work:** The careers centre runs a job surgery called 'Worklink'. Students
looking for work often end up in bars, but only sometimes working there. Engineers
and select scientists may find a little vocational vacation work in the local oil
industry, but otherwise it's tourism that brings in the loot.

**TRAVEL:**
**National:** Trains: Direct trains from Swansea station, 3 miles from the campus, to
Cardiff (£9.05), London (£23.70), Shrewsbury and beyond. Coaches: Services to
London (£22.75), Cardiff (£6.50), Manchester (£27.50).
**Local:** Regular buses between the student village and the town centre (£1.55) and
from the town to the railway station (55p).

**ENTERTAINMENTS:** • Booze index: £1.33
**Town/city:** • Pint of beer: £1.50    • Glass of wine: £1.20
**University:** • Pint of beer: £1.40    • Glass of wine: £1.10

**ACCOMMODATION:**
**Living in:** • Catered: 15%         • Cost: £58-72 (31 weeks)
             • Self-catering: 26%    • Cost: £40-62 (40-51 weeks)
**Living out:** • Ave rent: £40

## UNIVERSITY OF TEESSIDE

Formerly Teesside Polytechnic
University of Teesside, Middlesbrough, TS1 3BA. Tel: (01642) 218121.
Fax: (01642) 342067. E-mail: h.cummins@tees.ac.uk

**DEBTS:** • Average debt: £1,300
• Access fund: n/a • Successful applications per year: 815
There are short-term emergency loans.

**EMPLOYMENT:** • Unemployed after 6 months: 7.7%
**Paid work:** HSBC cash point.

**TRAVEL:**
**National:** Trains: Middlesbrough station offers direct links to Newcastle (£5.15),
Manchester (£18.15) and other major interchanges. For London (£42.25) change
at Darlington. Coaches: Coach services courtesy of Blue Line, City Link, Swiftline
and National Express to London (£21), Manchester (£11.75) and all over.
**Local:** Buses are cheap (50p max) and fairly regular but stop running after 11pm.
Trains run regularly all over the Teesside conurbation.

**ENTERTAINMENTS:** • Booze index: £1.95
**Town/city:** • Pint of beer: £2      • Glass of wine: £2
**University:** • Pint of beer: £1.55   • Glass of wine: £1.45

**ACCOMMODATION:**
**Living in:** • Self-catering: 11%    • Cost: £30-52 (37 weeks)
**Living out:** • Ave rent: £35

## THAMES VALLEY UNIVERSITY

(1) Thames Valley University, St Mary's Road, Ealing, London, W5 5RF.
Tel: (020) 8579 5000. Fax: (020) 8566 1353. E-mail: learning.advice@tvu.ac.uk
(2) Thames Valley University, Wellington Street, Slough, Berkshire, SL1 1YG.
Tel: (01753) 534585.

**DEBTS:** • Average debt: £1,150
• Access fund: £240,000 • Successful applications per year: 411
There are bursaries of up to £500 and some funding for overseas students.

**EMPLOYMENT:** • Unemployed after 6 months: 10%
Careers centres at both sites and careers tutors in each School.
**Paid work:** TVU Temps offers part-time and temp vacancies to students including
word-processing BBC scripts.

**TRAVEL:**
**National:** see University of London
**Local:** The nearest tube stations are Ealing Broadway (District and Central Lines)
and South Ealing (Piccadilly Line).

**ENTERTAINMENTS:** • Booze index: £2.35
**Town/city:** • Pint of beer: £2.20 • Glass of wine: £2.50
**University:** • Pint of beer: £1.50 • Glass of wine: £1

**ACCOMMODATION:**
**Living in:** • Cost: £70
**Living out:** • Ave rent: £75

## UNIVERSITY OF CENTRAL ENGLAND

University of Central England, Perry Barr, Birmingham, B42 2SU.
Tel: (0121) 331 5595. Fax: (0121) 331 6740. E-mail: recruitment@uce.ac.uk

**DEBTS:** • Average debt: £1,300
• Access fund: £778,045 • Successful applications per year: 2,174
UCE has decent support systems with its own non-Government Access Fund and
there are Chaplaincy and Hardship Funds and bursaries for students from low
income and disadvantaged backgrounds.
**Banks on campus:** NatWest Bank.

**EMPLOYMENT:** • Unemployed after 6 months: 6%

**TRAVEL:** See University of Birmingham

**ENTERTAINMENTS:** • Booze index: £1.61
**Town/city:** • Pint of beer: £1.90 • Glass of wine: £1.50
**University:** • Pint of beer: £1.45 • Glass of wine: £1.25

**ACCOMMODATION:**
**Living in:** • Catered: 2% • Cost: £60 (40 weeks)
• Self-catering: 24% • Cost: £45-66 (40-52 weeks)
**Living out:** • Ave rent: £42

## UNIVERSITY OF EAST ANGLIA

University of East Anglia, Norwich, NR4 7TJ. Tel: (01603) 593 967.
Fax: (01603) 458 596. E-mail: admissions@uea.ac.uk

**DEBTS:** • Average debt: £1,650
• Access fund: £306,755 • Successful applications per year: 405
There are five hardship funds, the VC's fund, a Nursery Fund and tuition fees
scholarships for undergrad and overseas students.
**Banks on campus:** Barclays and Lloyds with cashpoints.

**EMPLOYMENT:** • <u>Unemployed after 6 months: 5%</u>
**Paid work:** The jobshop is jointly run by the SU and the University. There's less unemployment in East Anglia than in most of the country and apart from the usual bar work, students can get better paid jobs in local government and other areas.

**TRAVEL:**
**National:** Trains: Nearest BR station is Norwich, 3 miles from the University campus. Direct services to London (2hrs, £19.95) and change there for most other destinations. Coaches: Services to, among other places, London (£15.25) and Glasgow (£42.50).
**Local:** Buses are reliable and wide ranging. Campus to town centre £1.70 return.

**ENTERTAINMENTS:** • <u>Booze index: £1.81</u>
| | | |
|---|---|---|
| **Town/city:** | • <u>Pint of beer: £2.10</u> | • <u>Glass of wine: £1.85</u> |
| **University:** | • <u>Pint of beer: £1.60</u> | • <u>Glass of wine: £1.40</u> |

**ACCOMMODATION:**
| | | |
|---|---|---|
| **Living in:** | • <u>Self-catering: 35%</u> | • <u>Cost: £40-58 (34-39 weeks)</u> |
| **Living out:** | • <u>Ave rent: £40</u> | |

# UNIVERSITY OF ULSTER
(1) The University of Ulster (Coleraine), Cromore Road, Coleraine, BT52 1SA.
Tel: (028) 7034 4141. Fax: (028) 7034 0947.
(2) The University of Ulster (Jordanstown), Shore Road, Newtownabbey, Co Antrim, BT37 0QB. Tel: (028) 9036 5131.
Students' Union, The University of Ulster (Jordanstown), Co Antrim, BT37 0QB.
Tel: (028) 90 365121. Fax: (028) 9036 2817.
(3) The University of Ulster (Belfast), York Street, Belfast, BT15 1ED.
Tel: (028) 9032 8515.
(4) The University of Ulster (Magee College), Northland Road, Londonderry, BT48 7JL. Tel: (028) 7137 1371. Fax: (028) 7137 5410.

**DEBTS:** • <u>Average debt: £1,000</u>
• <u>Access fund: £227,000</u> • <u>Successful applications per year: 1,709</u>
Financial help is also available from the Hardship Fund, Endowment Awards, Disabled Student Allowance and the Hardship Loan Fund.

**EMPLOYMENT:** • <u>Unemployed after 6 months: 9%</u>
The Jordanstown, Coleraine and Magee sites all have their own careers advisory services.
**Paid work:** The usual bar jobs and so on in Coleraine and the tourist trade brings summer opportunities with the National Trust among others. The Union employs 70 to 80 students on a casual basis.

**TRAVEL:**
**National:** Trains: Direct lines from Coleraine to Belfast and (London)Derry only on Northern Ireland Railways, frequent and frequently dirty trains. Trains from (London)Derry to Belfast and most other local destinations, and to Dublin from Belfast. Coaches: Goldline Express and Ulsterbus link Belfast, Coleraine and (London)Derry regularly.
**Local:** Comprehensive, but expensive local buses, but half-price fares for students around Coleraine. Ulsterbus offer an all-day £5 rambler ticket.

**ENTERTAINMENTS:** • <u>Booze index: £1.97</u>
| | | |
|---|---|---|
| **Town/city:** | • <u>Pint of beer: £1.80</u> | • <u>Glass of wine: £2.30</u> |
| **University:** | • <u>Pint of beer: £1.55</u> | • <u>Glass of wine: £1.23</u> |

**ACCOMMODATION:**
| | | |
|---|---|---|
| **Living in:** | • <u>Self-catering: 12%</u> | • <u>Cost: £33-36 (32-37 weeks)</u> |
| **Living out:** | • <u>Ave rent: £29</u> | |

## UMIST

University of Manchester Institute of Science & Technology, PO Box 88, Manchester, M60 1QD. Tel: (0161) 236 3311. Fax: (0161) 228 7040.
E-mail: ug.admissions@umist.ac.uk

**DEBTS:**   • Average debt: £1,450
       • Access fund: £250,000 • Successful applications per year: 500
The Students' Association-employed adviser points students in the right direction with financial, housing and welfare problems. Bursaries, scholarships and a hardship fund.

**EMPLOYMENT:** • Unemployed after 6 months: 3%
The careers service is one of the biggest in the country probably because its shared with Manchester University. A phenomenal proportion of UMIST students are sponsored by companies to study there.
**Paid work:** see University of Manchester

**TRAVEL:** see University of Manchester

**ENTERTAINMENTS:** • Booze index: £1.45
**Town/city:**  • Pint of beer: £1.50   • Glass of wine: £1.30
**University:**  • Pint of beer: £1.50   • Glass of wine: £1.50

**ACCOMMODATION:**
**Living in:**  • Catered: 12%       • Cost: £60-105 (31-51 weeks)
         • Self-catering: 38%  • Cost: £46-49 (31-52 weeks)
**Living out:**  • Ave rent: £38

## UNIVERSITY COLLEGE, LONDON

• The College is part of the University of London and students are entitled to use its facilities.
University College London, Gower Street, London, WC1E 6BT.
Tel: (020) 7 679 3000. Fax: (020) 7 679 3001. E-mail: degree-info@ucl.ac.uk

**DEBTS:**   • Average debt: £1,750
       • Access fund: £660,411 • Successful applications per year: 844
The SU has a hardship fund of £30,000 further bursaries are available through the college
**Banks on campus:** HSBC cashpoint.

**EMPLOYMENT:** • Unemployed after 6 months: 3%
UCL's careers service is separate from the University's, but students can use either.
**Paid work:** see University of London

**TRAVEL:** see University of London

**ENTERTAINMENTS:** • Booze index: £2.17
**Town/city:**  • Pint of beer: £2.20   • Glass of wine: £2.50
**University:**  • Pint of beer: £1.70   • Glass of wine: £1.85

**ACCOMMODATION:**
**Living in:**  • Catered: 12%       • Cost: £70-94 (30 weeks)
         • Self-catering: 20%  • Cost: £47-115 (37 weeks)
**Living out:**  • Ave rent: £75

**7**

Make calls and surf the net during
off-peak times only.

## UNIVERSITY OF WALES COLLEGE OF MEDICINE
University of Wales College of Medicine, Heath Park, Cardiff, CF4 4XN.
Tel: (029) 207 4170. Fax: (029) 2074 2914.

**DEBTS:** • Average debt: £1,450
• Access fund: £150,00 • Successful applications per year: 170
There's an emergency loan fund of £8,000. Selective scholarships.
**Banks on campus:** NatWest Bank.

**EMPLOYMENT:**
Unemployment is always rare for graduates from any medical school, but there is a careers service, operated by staff from the postgraduate departments. Nurses should bear in mind the fact that cash will be ludicrously tight.

**TRAVEL:**
**National:** see Cardiff, University of Wales
**Local:** Heath High Level and Heath Low Level stations are 3 / 4 mile away.
Reliable local buses (Nos 8 & 9) run from the city centre through the campus every 20 mins till around midnight. Taxis to or from the city centre cost about £4.

**ENTERTAINMENTS:** • Booze index: £1.62
**Town/city:** • Pint of beer: £1.90 • Glass of wine: £1.40
**University:** • Pint of beer: £1.30 • Glass of wine: £1.50

**ACCOMMODATION:**
**Living in:** • Self-catering: 11% • Cost: £38-43 (46 weeks)
**Living out:** • Ave rent: £46

## UNIVERSITY OF WARWICK
University of Warwick, Coventry, CV4 7AL. Tel: (02476) 523709.
Fax: (0870) 1269902. E-mail: ugadmissions@admin.warwick.ac.uk

**DEBTS:** • Average debt: £1,300
• Access fund: £400,000 • Successful applications per year: 300
There's also a hardship fund, as well as postgrad bursaries and music scholarships.

**EMPLOYMENT:** • Unemployed after 6 months: 3%
**Paid work:** At such a major conference venue there's plenty of vacation work. The Union runs a service publishing an opportunities list and linking students with jobs and vice versa both on and off campus. The Union itself employs over 300 students on a casual basis and the University runs a Temp Agency.

**TRAVEL:** see Coventry University

**ENTERTAINMENTS:** • Booze index: £1.55
**Town/city:** • Pint of beer: £1.70 • Glass of wine: £1.40
**University:** • Pint of beer: £1.60 • Glass of wine: £1.50

**ACCOMMODATION:**
**Living in:** • Catered: 4% • Cost: £68 (30 weeks)
• Self-catering: 36% • Cost: £43-56 (30-39 weeks)
**Living out:** • Ave rent: £35-40

Don't get stressed out over your finances.
You'll only make it worse. A calm approach
with good planning will see you alright.
You'll be in debt, but, hey, so's everyone.

## UNIVERSITY OF WESTMINSTER

University of Westminster, 309 Regent Street, London, W1B 2UW.
Tel: (020) 7911 5000. Fax: (020) 7911 5192. E-mail: Admissions@wmin.ac.uk

**DEBTS:**  • Average debt: £1,850
  • Access fund: £500,000  • Successful applications per year: 807
A booklet called 'Housing & Money Matters' is distributed free to students. There
are also short-term loans available.

**EMPLOYMENT:** • Unemployed after 6 months: 8%
**Paid work:** see University of London

**TRAVEL:**
**National:** see University of London
**Local:** All sites are on the Tube and bus. The Harrow site is the only one even
remotely difficult to get to.

**ENTERTAINMENTS:** • Booze index: £2.22
**Town/city:** • Pint of beer: £2.20  • Glass of wine: £2.50
**University:** • Pint of beer: £1.20  • Glass of wine: £1.50

**ACCOMMODATION:**
**Living in:** • Self-catering: 12%  • Cost: £63-75 (38-60 weeks)
**Living out:** • Ave rent: £75

## UNIVERSITY OF WOLVERHAMPTON

(1) University of Wolverhampton, Wulfruna Street, Wolverhampton, WV1 1SB.
Tel: (01902) 322222. Fax: (01902) 322680. E-mail: enquiries@wlv.ac.uk
(2) University of Wolverhampton, Telford Campus, Shifnal Road, Priorslee, Telford,
Shropshire, TF2 9NT. Tel: (01902) 323900.

**DEBTS:**  • Average debt: £700
  • Access fund: £330,500  • Successful applications per year: 1,529
Hardship Funds are appallingly advertised and therefore undersubscribed. Go get
that cash! Also bursaries and a fund for black South African students.

**EMPLOYMENT:** • Unemployed after 6 months: 5.3%

**TRAVEL:**
**National:** Trains: Wolverhampton Station is 5 minutes' walk from the main site and
operates services all over the country and into Brum (£3.80). Other destinations
include London (£18.50), Manchester (£12.85) and Edinburgh (£30.70). There are
also British Rail stations at Walsall and Telford. Coaches: National Express
services to London (£13.50), Manchester (£8.50), Edinburgh (£27.75) and
beyond.
**Local:** The many cheap buses are the best way of getting anywhere and connect
with Brum too, although there are the unreliable trains too. The supertram service
is called The Metro and links Wolverhampton with Birmingham (£2.60 return). The
University also provides a free, popular, but less than dependable, inter-site
shuttle bus for staff and students, between all the sites.

**ENTERTAINMENTS:** • Booze index: £1.64
**Town/city:** • Pint of beer: £1.80  • Glass of wine: £1.59
**University:** • Pint of beer: £1.40  • Glass of wine: £1.40

**ACCOMMODATION:**
**Living in:** • Self-catering: 18%  • Cost: £40-43 (38 weeks)
**Living out:** • Ave rent: £36-45

7

## UNIVERSITY OF YORK

University of York, Heslington, York, YO1 5DD. Tel: (01904) 433533.
Fax: (01904) 433538. E–mail: admissions@york.ac.uk

**DEBTS:** • Average debt: £1,400
• Access fund: £480,000 • Successful applications per year: 381
Overseas student scholarships, mature students bursaries, sponsorship and YUSU
hardship loans.
**Banks on campus:** Link cashpoint.

**EMPLOYMENT:** • Unemployed after 6 months: 6%
**Paid work:** Plenty of pubs and a few restaurants during term-time and the
conference trade brings opportunities during vacations. 'Unijobs' is a university run
one-stop job shop for students seeking work in the local area. The SU has a
vacancy board.

**TRAVEL:**
**National:** Trains: Mainline connections from York Station (2 miles from the
campus) to many destinations including London King's X (£29.70), Glasgow
(£27.05) and Birmingham (£16.85). Coaches: National Express to most
destinations, including London (£19), Newcastle and beyond.
**Local:** York is too small and compact for local trains except regionally to Leeds,
Hull and Bradford. Frequent bus services run everywhere (90p from campus to city
centre) but they don't run late at night.

**ENTERTAINMENTS:** • Booze index: £1.63
**Town/city:** • Pint of beer: £1.80 • Glass of wine: £2
**University:** • Pint of beer: £1.40 • Glass of wine: £1.40

**ACCOMMODATION:**
**Living in:** • Self-catering: 59% • Cost: £47-52 (30-38 weeks)
**Living out:** • Ave rent: £45

When sharing a house with boys, make sure
the phone bill is in their name. (Try
saying, 'But you're so much better at
numbers than I ever could be.') That way
when, inevitably, they don't do any
cleaning when you move out and you all
lose your deposits, you can just not pay
the last phone bill — or the proportion
of it you lost.

I Davies, University of York

Part 7: In the back
Chapter 17

# Useful Further
# contacts & info

## Push books and services

If you find this book helpful, try these...

- *The Push Guide to Which University 2002*, £14.99 – details of every aspect of student life at every university in the UK.

- *The Push Guide to Choosing a University 2002*, £7.99 – how to choose the right university for you and how student life should affect your choice.

- *Push Online* at www.push.co.uk – the online guide to choosing a university, with interactive search facilities to find the right university for you.

## General advice and information

Department for Education & Skills 020 7925 5000

*Financial Support for Higher Education Students in 2000/2001: A Guide*, also cited on www.dfes.gov.uk/studentsupport (or call 0800 731 9133 for your free copy)

Department for Education and Employment, Mowden Hall, Staindrop Road, Darlington, County Durham DL3 9BG.

*Investing in the Future: Supporting Students in Higher Education* is available from DfES by calling the above number or visiting www.open.gov.uk/dfes/dfeshome.htm

**For Scottish students:** *Scottish Higher Education for the 21st Century*, available from the Scottish Office on 0131 244 8075 or at www.scotland.gov.uk For specific advice, call 0131 244 5823

Student Awards Agency for Scotland (SAAS), Gyleview House, 3 Redheughs Rigg, Edinburgh, EH12 9HH. www.student-support-saas.gov.uk

7

**For students from Northern Ireland:** The Department of Higher and Further Education, Training and Employment (DHFETE, Adelaide House, 39-49 Adelaide Street, Belfast, BT2 8SD) publishes its own version of *Financial Support for Students in Higher Education 2001/2*. Call 02890 257 777 or visit www.dhfeteni.gov.uk

**For Welsh-speaking students:** Contact National Assembly for Wales, FHEI Division, 4th Floor, Cathays Park, Cardiff, CF10 3NQ. Tel: 02920 825 111. www.wfc.ac.uk/hefcw

Different arrangements for hardship funds and bursaries exist in Wales. Contact the Further and Higher Education Division of the National Assembly for Wales on 029 2082 6318.

The National Union of Students (NUS) produces a series of information sheets on student finance. Send an A4 stamped self-addressed envelope, with details of the subject about which you need info, to The Welfare Unit, NUS, 461 Holloway Road, London N7 6LJ. Tel: 020 7272 8900. www.nusonline.co.uk

**EU students (non-UK) should contact:** The European Team at the Department for Education and Employment (address as above). Call 01325 391199 during office hours or visit www.dfes.gov.uk/eustudents

**For sight-impaired students:** Braille and cassette editions are available from the Royal National Institute for the Blind (RNIB, PO Box 173, Peterborough PE2 6WS). Tel: 01234 023153.

UCAS Enquiries Line: 01242 227788. www.ucas.com

Department of Social Security (freephone helpline) 0800 666555

Educational Grants Advisory Service 020 7254 6251

Money Advice Association 020 7236 3566

National Association of Citizens Advice Bureaux 020 7833 2181

Credit Action 01223 324034

www.studentuk.com/money

Good advice on debt at www.virtualstudent.co.uk

www.lifelonglearning.co.uk

Local Government Agency: www.lga.gov.uk

www.namss.org.uk/finance.htm

# Bursaries, sponsorships and scholarships

Scholarship Search UK (SSUK, The Old House, Church Lane, Claxton, Norwich, Norfolk NR14 7HY) at www.scholarship-search.org.ukwas launched in April 2000 and is a free search facility for all undergraduate students. You can search by subject, awarding body or region. Tel: 01508 480 327.

www.freefund.com for info on all types of educational assistance. Check your own eligibility with the search facility.

The Windsor Fellowship (47 Hackney Road, London E2 7NX) runs undergraduate personal and professional development programmes (such as sponsorships, community work and summer placements) – this is primarily for gifted black and Asian students. Tel: 020 7613 0373.
Email info@windsor-fellow.demon.co.uk.

Education Grants Advisory Service: EGAS, 501-505 Kingsland Road, Dalston, London E8 4AU. Enclose a stamped addressed envelope with your enquiry letter. Tel: 020 7249 6636.

## Armed Forces

Army Officer Entry, Department 2763, Freepost 4335, Bristol BS1 3YX. Tel: 0345 300111.

Royal Air Force, Officer Careers, address as above. Tel: 0345 300100.

The Royal Navy and Royal Marines Careers Service, Dept BH94432, address as above. Tel: 0345 300123.

## NHS-funded studies

NHS courses in England and Wales. Tel: 0845 6060655
www.nhscareers.nhs.uk

The NHS Student Grants Unit, Room 212c Government Buildings, Norcross, Blackpool, FY5 3TA. Tel: 01253 332 627

NHS Bursaries in Wales: Student Awards Unit, NHS Human Resources Division, National Assembly for Wales, Cathays Park, Cardiff CF10 3NQ.
Tel: 029 2082 6893.

NHS bursaries in Scotland: The Student Awards Agency for Scotland, 3 Redheughs Rigg, South Gyle, Edinburgh EH12 9YT. Tel: 0131 244 4669.

NHS bursaries in Northern Ireland: The Department of Health, Social Services and Public Safety, Human Resources Directorate, Workforce Development Unit, Room 3B, Dundonald House, Upper Newtownards, Belfast BT4 3SF.

**7**

# Postgraduates: sources of funding

**The UK Research Councils:**

- Biotechnology and Biological Sciences Research Council (BBSRC), Polaris House, North Star Avenue, Swindon SN2 1UH. Tel: 01793 413200 www.bbsrc.ac.uk

- Economic and Social Research Council (ESRC), Polaris House, North Star Avenue, Swindon SN2 1UJ. Tel: 01793 413000  www.esrc.ac.uk

- Engineering and Physical Sciences Research (EPSRC), Polaris House, North Star Avenue, Swindon SN2 1ET. Tel: 01793 444000  www.epsrc.ac.uk

- Natural Environment Research Council (NERC), Polaris House, North Star Avenue, Swindon SN2 1EU. Tel: 01793 411500  www.nerc.ac.uk

- Particle Physics and Astronomy Research (PPARC), Polaris House, North Star Avenue, Swindon SN2 1SZ. Tel: 01793 442000  www.pparc.ac.uk

- Medical Research Council (MRC), 20 Park Crescent, London W1B 1AL. Tel: 020 7636 5422  www.mrc.ac.uk

**Arts and Humanities:** The Arts and Humanities Research Board (AHRB), (Postgraduate Awards Division,) 10 Carlton House Terrace, London SW1Y 5AH. Tel: 020 7969 5205

Council for the Central Laboratory of the Research Councils (CCLRC), Rutherford Appleton Laboratory, Chilton, Didcot, Oxfordshire OX11 0QX. Tel: 01235 821900  www.cclrc.ac.uk

**Further Postgraduate Sources:**

The Association of Graduate Careers Advisory Service (AGCAS), Armstrong House, Oxford Road, Manchester M1 7ED. Tel: 0161 277 5200. They publish a booklet called *Postgraduate Management Education*, which is available free from your careers service.

Royal Society Research Fellowships, Research Appointments Department, 6 Carlton House Terrace, London SW1Y 5AG. Tel: 020 7451 2547 www.royalsoc.ac.uk

**Charities:**

The Wellcome Trust, 183 Euston Road, London NW1 2BE. Tel: 020 7611 8438 www.wellcome.ac.uk

Association of Medical Research Charities (AMRC), 29-35 Farringdon Road, London EC1M 3JB. An organisation that represents almost 90 charities. Visit www.amrc.org.uk for further info. Tel: 020 7404 6454

# Students with disabilities

SKILL - National Bureau for Students with Disabilities, Chapter House, 18-20 Crucifix Lane, London SE1 3JW. www.skill.org.uk

For the DfES leaflet *Bridging the Gap*: A guide to the disabled students' allowances and information about the Disabled Students' Allowances, call the DfES information line on 0800 731 9133. See also the recommended book list (below) for the book *Higher Education and Disability*.

Action for Blind People, Grants Officer, 14-16 Verney Road, London SE16 3DZ. Tel: 020 7635 4821.

Association for Spina Bifida and Hydrocephalus, ASBAH House, 42 Park Road, Peterborough, PE1 2UQ. Maximum award £2,000.

The Dyslexia Institute Bursary Fund, 133 Gresham Road, Staines, Middlesex. TW18 2AJ. Tel: 01784 463851

Snowdon Award Scheme, 22 City Business Centre, 6 Brighton Road, Horsham, West Sussex RH13 5BB. Helps disabled students aged 17-25 in further, higher or adult education.

For disabled students looking for work: Workable has loads of jobs across all sectors and your university careers service or students' union will have their details. Alternatively, contact them direct: 67-71 Goswell Road, London EC1V 7EP. Tel: 020 7608 3161. Email: workableuk@aol.com.

# Paid work

Minimum wage: 0845 600 0678

www.tiger.gov.uk

Don't buy stuff just because it's marked down or on special offer. It's not enough that it's cheaper than usual. It's got to be cheaper than other things. A reduced price frozen pack of macaroni cheese is probably still three times the price of one you could make for yourself.

7

# Taking a year out

www.yearoutgroup.org/organisations.htm

www.gap–year.com is way cooler

Gap Year students: UCAS can provide a free booklet called *A Year Out* – also see the recommended books list below.

The Year in Industry scheme: National Director, University of Manchester, Simon Building, Oxford Road, Manchester M13 9PL. Tel/fax: 0161 275 4396. Email: enquiries@yini.org.uk or visit their website for an online application form: www.yini.org.uk

Visit www.yearoutgroup.org/organisations.htm for a full list, including:

- Academic Year in the USA and Europe: cultural exchange and study abroad in USA, France, Germany, Spain and Italy for three, four, five or nine months. Apply early. Tel: 020 8786 7711. Website www.aaiuk.org

- Africa and Asia Venture: four and five-month schemes offering great scope for cultural and interpersonal development in Kenya, Tanzania, Uganda, Malawi, Zimbabwe, India and Nepal. Mainly unpaid teaching work with extensive travel and safari opportunities. Tel: 01380 729009. www.aventure.co.uk

- BUNAC (British Universities North America Club) offers an extensive range of work/travel programmes worldwide, varying from a few months to a whole year, depending on destination and programme. Tel: 020 7251 3472 www.bunac.org

- Community Service Volunteers (CSV): full-time voluntary placements throughout the UK for people between 16 and 35. Allowance, accommodation and food provided. Freephone 0800 374 991 www.csv.org.uk

- Gap Activity Projects (GAP) Ltd: an independent educational charity founded in 1972, which organises voluntary work overseas in 30 different countries. Tel: 0118 959 4914 www.gap.org.uk

- Gap Challenge/World Challenge Expeditions: varied schemes for students 18-25, from voluntary conservation projects to paid hotel work in many different countries. Tel: 020 8537 7930 www.world-challenge.co.uk

- Health Projects Abroad: various schemes in rural Africa. Tel: 01629 640051. Email: info@hpauk.org www.hpauk.org

- Raleigh International: a charity-run scheme giving young people the opportunity to go on three-month expeditions all over the world for varied project work. Over 20,000 young people have taken part in a total of 168 expeditions in 35 countries since 1984. Tel: 020 7371 8585 www.raleigh.org.uk

- Students Partnership Worldwide: challenging and rewarding 4-9 month projects in developing countries. Tel: 020 7222 0138  www.spw.org

- Teaching & Projects Abroad: foreign travel and experience in teaching English, conservation work, medicine and journalism among others. Countries include China, Ghana, India, Thailand, Mexico and South Africa. Tel: 01903 859911  www.teaching-abroad.co.uk

- UKSA: according to them, they're 'the perfect marriage of gap year, radical watersports and awesome experience.' Windsurfing, kayaking, sailing, professional crew and skipper training. Tel: 01983 203013 www.uk-sail.org.uk/gapyear.html

- For teaching opportunities (no formal training needed to take up a temporary position), contact Gabbitas Educational Consultants, Carrington House, 126-130 Regent Street, London W1R 6EE. Tel: 020 7734 0161.

VSO runs special overseas youth programmes for under 25s.
Tel: 020 8780 7500 Email: enquiry@vso.org.uk  www.vso.org.uk:

- The World Youth Millennium Awards scheme (WYMA) for people between 17 and 25. Participants are paired with another young person from the exchange country and spend six months on a practical project (three months in the UK, three months in the exchange country).

- The Overseas Training Programme (OTP) is aimed at undergraduates under 25. It is a longer and more intensive scheme that requires support from your university.

- Youth Action (through the EU's European Voluntary Service – EVS) needs volunteers between 18 and 25 to work with disadvantaged communities in Russia and Romania.

- Youth to Youth (Y2Y) is aimed primarily at young people from disadvantaged backgrounds, teaming up with overseas participants to work on a range of community-based projects

## Summer work abroad

AIESEC: International Exchange Programme. Many types of placements for students and recent graduates. Some universities have a branch on campus. If not, contact them at: AIESEC UK, 29-31 Cowper Street, London EC2A 4AT. Tel: 020 7549 1800.

Camp America: Dept YO, 37a Queens Gate, London SW7 5HR. Tel: 020 7581 7373.

If you fancy working on a kibbutz, contact: Kibbutz Representatives, 1a Accommodation Road, London NW11 8ED. Tel: 020 8458 9235. Also try Project 67, based in London, on 020 7831 7626 Email: project67@aol.com

Other organisations include Summer Camp USA and KAMP. Both involve working with children on summer camps – the former requires some previous experience. Also try the Work America Programme or read one of the recommended books listed below. For example, the *Vacation Work* series (website www.vacationwork.co.uk).

The website www.get.hobsons.com has a section on placements and vacation work opportunities.

Association for Sandwich Education and Training: ASET Directory of Sandwich Courses, ASET Secretary, 3 Westbrook Court, Sharrow Vale Road, Sheffield S11 8YZ. Tel: 0114 266 9999  Email aset@aset.demon.co.uk

**For international students or UK students studying overseas:**
www.britishcouncil.org/education/index.htm has info about UK courses and qualifications available and also those in the home country of international students.

Erasmus Student Network: www.esn.org

Student Travel: www.studentflights.co.uk

www.deltatravel.co.uk/student (Manchester, Liverpool and Birmingham)

# Insurance

For more information about Endsleigh's student policies and the location of your nearest branch, contact Endsleigh Insurance Services Ltd on 01242 223300 or visit www.endsleigh.co.uk/protection/student.cover.html  A number of universities have branches on campus.

www.insuranceforstudents.co.uk

# Career development loans

DfES's Career Development Loan Helpline: 0800 585505

**Banks' Career Development Loan helplines:**

- Barclays Bank 0845 609 0060

- Co-operative Bank 0345 212212

- Royal Bank of Scotland 0800 121127

- Clydesdale Bank 01228 401444

For a free booklet on Career Development Loans call freephone 0800 585 505

# Student loans

For information about student loans: Student Loans Company, 100 Bothwell Street, Glasgow G2 7JD. Help Line 0800 40 50 10.
General Enquiries 0870 60 60 704  www.slc.co.uk

**Birth Certificates for Student Loans:** To get hold of copies of Birth or Adoption Certificates, which you need for Student Loan Applications, contact:

- For England and Wales: Birth Certificates: The Public Search Room, The Family Records Centre, 1 Myddleton Street, London, EC1R 1UW.
  Tel: 020 8392 5300. www.open.gov.uk/pro/prohome.htm
  Adoption Certificates: The Registrar General, The Office of Population Censuses and Surveys, The General Register Office, Adoptions Section, Smedley Hydro, Trafalgar Road, Birkdale, Southport PR8 2HH.
  Tel: 0151 471 4200

- For Scotland: The Registrar General, New Register House, Edinburgh, EH1 3YT. Tel: 0131 334 0380

- For Northern Ireland: The Registrar General, Oxford House, 49/55 Chichester Street, Belfast BT1 4HL. Tel: 01232 250000

- For the Republic of Ireland: The Registrar General, Joyce House, 8/11 Lombard Street East, Dublin 2. Tel: 03531 6711863

# Recommended books

*The Push Guide to Which University 2002*, £14.99 (The Stationery Office) – details of every aspect of student life at every university in the UK.

*The Push Guide to Choosing a University 2002*, £7.99 (The Stationery Office) – how to choose the right university for you and how student life should affect your choice.

*A Guide to Scholarships and Awards* by Brian Heap (Trotman). Scholarships etc plus information for overseas students and a list of charitable and other awards. Each university is broken down with a list of awards they offer.

*The Sponsorship and Funding Directory 2001* (Hobsons), available in most schools, colleges and public libraries. As above, also lists charities that offer educational sponsorships.

*Awards: A Directory of Scholarship and Bursary Awards* (ISCO)

*Engineering Opportunities for Students and Graduates* (Institution of Mechanical Engineers). If you are studying any kind of engineering course, this book lists several sponsors and universities with sponsored courses. Call 020 7222 3337 or email education@imeche.org.uk

**7**

*Higher Education and Disability: Into Higher Education 2001* (SKILL), £2 for students (otherwise £6) from Chapter House (020 7450 0620). Information line: 0800 328 5050

*Student Life – A Survival Guide* (Lifetime Careers 2001). Call Orca Bookservices Ltd on 01202 665432

*The Educational Grants Directory* by Sarah Harland (Directory of Social Change). Lists all sources of non-statutory help for students in financial need. As it states: 'The £50 million available from sources in this guide is becoming increasingly important to higher education students who may find themselves getting deeper into debt as state support for them drops still further.' Updated annually.

*Everything you need to know about going to University* by Sally Longson*

*Summer Jobs Abroad 2001* and *Summer Jobs USA* and *Summer Jobs Britain 2001*, three titles from a selection of useful books geared primarily at students and young people, published by Vacation Work, Oxford (tel. 01865 241978). They also publish a comprehensive and authoritative guide called *Working Your Way Around the World* and, for students interested in the voluntary sector, two titles: *The International Directory of Voluntary Work* and *The Directory of Work & Study in Developing Countries*.

*The Gap Year Guidebook* (Peridot Press). www.peridot.co.uk has lots of useful links; also www.gap-year.com

*Planning your Gap Year* by M Hempshell (How to Books)

*Taking a Year Off* by Val Butcher (Trotman)

*Opportunities in the Gap Year* (ISCO)

*A Year Off... A Year On?* (Lifetime Careers Publishing)

*Working Holidays* (Central Bureau of Educational Visits and Exchanges). If you can't find a copy in your local library contact the Bureau on 020 7389 4004

*Studying for a Degree: How to Succeed as a Mature Student* by Stephen Wade (How to Books)

*Making the most of being a student* by Judy Bastyra and Charles Bradley (Kogan Page, in association with Student Pages)

*Know Your Rights: Students* by Shirley Meredeen (How to Books)

*Students' Money Matters* by Gwenda Thomas (Trotman)

*Balancing Your Books 2001/2*:ECCTIS/CRAC guide to student finance

*The Independent Complete Parents' Guide to Higher Education* (Trotman)

# Other useful websites

The Liberal Democrats petition regarding fees: www.scraptuitionfees.com

The Times Higher Education Supplement is 'the UK's most authoritative source of information about higher education'. It isn't, but see for yourself at www.thes.co.uk

www.redmole.com/student_mole

www.studentuk.com – a general guide plus money section.

www.times-money.co.uk/student

www.studentmoneynet.co.uk - this website offers a very good budget planner (Excel spreadsheet) as well as some sound advice and general financing info.

If you're looking for a job, check out www.studentjobs.org.uk

Also: www.ncwe.com or the student section of www.loot.com, both of which offer details of companies who offer student placements. There is also a site called www.hotrecruit.co.uk and this has student-specific jobs nationwide.

www.jobpilot.co.uk/content/channel/student is another one to try, and don't forget that *The Guardian* newspaper has student and graduate opportunities advertised regularly (especially in Saturday editions), or try www.guardian.co.uk/jobs

www.dti.gov.uk/er/pay.htm tells you about the national minimum wage and hours of employment and also has a 'young worker' section.

www.cujo.co.uk provides an online 'student supastore', help and advice for students from special offers, classifieds, house shares… including extensive student property search engine.

www.hotbeast.com is designed to help students and graduates build networks.

www.student123.com – to help with all areas of student life.

www.studentsgetoff.com – providing discounts on books, booze, clubs, haircuts, mobiles, movies, travel… all a student could need. Except for winning lottery numbers, unfortunately.

www.studentswapshop.co.uk – speaks for itself.

www.books4beer.com – as above: cash in your old textbooks for a weekend of ethanolic fun.

www.uniservity.net – academic, social and financial web resources.

www.uniserveuk.com – offering lots of sound advice to students, with a great money section.

Other useful student websites: www.yoonee.co.uk and www.uni4me.com

# Index

**7**

**7**

344